God's Word is Our Joy

Volume Three

Seasons of Advent and Christmas

Seasons of Lent and Easter

Cycl

God's Word is Our Joy

Lucien Deiss, C.S.Sp.

Readings	Advent and Christmas
Prayers	Lent and Easter
Homilies	Cycle B

WORLD LIBRARY PUBLICATIONS, a division of J. S. Paluch Co., Inc.
3815 N. Willow Road, Schiller Park, Illinois, 60176

Originally published as *Homélies Bibliques.*

Scripture references within the homilies are the author's.

Printed in the United States of America.

Contents

Foreword

This collection presents biblical homilies for the Sundays and the feasts of the liturgical year. Each Sunday or feast includes:

I. The **lectionary scriptures** for each Sunday or feast: three readings plus the responsorial psalm. It is obvious that one cannot speak each Sunday or feast about all three readings and the psalm. What is necessary—and sufficient—is to speak to satisfy the community. In the early tradition (cf. 1 Tm 4, 13), the homily is called *paraklèsis*, consolation. The homily should not cause indigestion from too many biblical texts but consolation by the word of God.

In a book, however, one can offer more, so that the one who preaches can make proper choices for the benefit of the community.

Where I found it necessary or useful, I have presented some exegetical explanations that should clarify the principal biblical difficulties. The notes at the end of each chapter have been reduced to the essentials. They either justify a position or invite the reader to examine certain points more thoroughly.

II. An **introductory prayer** for the celebration. This is generally composed of a blessing (in the genre of biblical blessings) and a prayer of petition.

III. The **homily**, which represents the principal part of this work.

I have stated in another publication what a homily was in Jewish and Christian tradition.[1] In this book I wanted to follow the golden rule of the homily that Jesus formulated in these terms: "Today in your hearing, this Scripture has been fulfilled."

IV. A **concluding prayer**. This prayer responds to the word that has been actualized in the homily. It has a freer structure than the general intercessions but can be used as a source for them.

This new edition of *God's Word Is Our Joy* provides an enlarged edition of some homilies published formerly by North American Liturgy Resources. Several explanations about responsorial psalms that seemed important liturgically have been added.

I hope to present here some help not only for the deacon or priest preparing the homily but also for all communities celebrating without the presence of their priest and for all the faithful who want to improve their knowledge and love of Jesus Christ, the living Word of God.

Introduction

Strictly speaking, this work does not present homilies but homily texts. There is a difference between the homily and its text, like the one that exists between the living word spoken to the assembly and the same "dead" word lying in the shroud of the pages of a book. It is the difference that also exists between a song that one sings in the assembly and the same song that one looks at in a book; an organ piece of J. S. Bach that one plays and the piece that one admires in a collection of printed music. This is to say that not one of these homilies was ever spoken as it is printed here. No homily should ever be spoken as it is printed.

If there is a fundamental difference between the homily and its printed text, between the spoken word and the written word, there is also, one must add immediately, a fundamental resemblance between the spoken homily and the printed homily.

I hope that the printed text, delivered here without life and without defense, will know how to become living and find the reader's heart.

I hesitated a long time before deciding to publish these texts. All publication leads to communication. All communication in the religious domain is formidable. The author confides in the reader. He opens his mind, filled with personal memories, his intelligence, with his own vision of the world, and also his heart. Here, communication bears upon the most precious thing that the author and the reader have in common: God.

In his *Apology of Origen,* [3] Pamphile (+c. 310) speaks in this way about his teacher:

> In his research, Origen proceeded with great humility and fear of God… He recommended to the reader to verify his statements. His opinions, he knew well, were not equally probable or certain, for there are too many mysteries in the Scriptures.

I consider the ideas presented here to be simple suggestions or propositions. It is up to the readers to compare them with what they carry in their hearts to see if these ideas are true and suit them. Many paths toward the actualization of the word are possible. Before the mystery of God, all paths require our humility.

May I also add this: Each time I must speak as a priest, I begin to tremble. It is not speaking that makes me tremble; it is speaking about God, in the name of God, which is formidable. On the Last Day, may the Lord recognize as his own each of the words that are found in this book.

While writing, I thought often about Saint Augustine. In his *Confessions*, which give proof of a fascinating theological depth and which are at the same time adorned with an incomparable literary quality, he is not afraid to talk about personal ideas. He relates, for example, how his mother Monica, when she was still a young girl, "swigged" some wine in a cave and was betrayed by a servant as *meribibula*, a little drunk;[4] or how he himself, at the age of sixteen, through pure mischievousness, robbed a neighbor's pear tree to throw fruit to the pigs.[5] In that spirit, I did not want these homilies, which I delivered in simplicity, to appear solemn and excessively severe. In spite of our fears, speaking about God must remain a feast; to listen to someone speak about God must remain a joy.

An ancient proverb, born in the biblical milieu, affirms:

> The best preacher
> is your heart.
> The best book
> is the world.
> The best teacher
> is time.
> And the best friend: you do not have any friend who loves you
> as much as God loves you.

These homilies do not want in any way to take the place of the "best teacher." They simply and earnestly desire to lead you to him.

Lucien Deiss, C.S.Sp.

NOTES TO THE INTRODUCTION:

1. *God's Word and God's People* (Collegeville, MN: The Liturgical Press, 1976): 123–136 and 284–309. *Celebration of the Word* (The Liturgical Press, 1993): 54–81.
2. Luke 4, 21.
3. *Apology of Origen*, PG 17, 543.
4. *Confessions*, IX, VIII. 18. Cf. Oeuvres de Saint Augustine, vol. 14 (Paris: Desclée de Brouwer, 1962): 106. "Meribibula" means literally small drinker *(bibula)* of pure wine *(merum)*.
5. *Confessions*, II, IV, 9. Cf. op. cit., vol. 13 (1962): 344–346.

Seasons of Advent and Christmas

FIRST SUNDAY OF ADVENT

Reading I — Is 63, 16-17, 19; 64, 2-7

A reading from the book of the prophet Isaiah

You, Lord, are our Father,
our redeemer you are named forever.
Why do you let us wander, O Lord, from your ways,
and harden our hearts so that we fear you not?
Return for the sake of your servants,
the tribes of your heritage.
Oh, that you would rend the heavens and come down,
with the mountains quaking before you,
While you wrought awesome deeds we could not hope for,
such as they had not heard from of old.
No ear has ever heard, no eye ever seen,
any God but you
doing such deeds for those who wait for him.
Would that you might meet us doing right,
that we are mindful of you in our ways!
Behold, you are angry, and we are sinful;
all of us have become like unclean men,
all our good deeds are like polluted rags;
We have all withered like leaves,
and our guilt carries us away like the wind.
There is none who calls upon your name,
who rouses himself to cling to you;
For you have hidden your face from us
and have delivered us up to our guilt.
Yet, O Lord, you are our father;
we are the clay and you are the potter:
we are all the work of your hands.

The Word of the Lord.

Responsorial Psalm — Ps 80, 2-3. 15-16. 18-19

R/.(4) Lord, make us turn to you,
let us see your face and we shall be saved.

O shepherd of Israel, hearken,
from your throne upon the cherubim, shine forth.
Rouse your power,
and come to save us.

R/. Lord, make us turn to you,
let us see your face and we shall be saved.

Once again, O Lord of hosts,
look down from heaven, and see;
Take care of this vine,
and protect what your right hand has planted
[the son of man whom you yourself made strong.]

R/. Lord, make us turn to you,
let us see your face and we shall be saved.

May your help be with the man of your right hand,
with the son of man whom you yourself made strong.
Then we will no more withdraw from you;
give us new life, and we will call upon your name.

R/. Lord, make us turn to you,
let us see your face and we shall be saved.

Reading II — 1 Cor 1, 3-9

A reading from the first letter of Paul to the Corinthians

Grace and peace from God our Father and the Lord Jesus Christ.

I continually thank my God for you because of the favor he has bestowed on you in Christ Jesus, in whom you have been richly endowed with every gift of speech and knowledge. Likewise, the witness I bore to Christ has been so confirmed among you that you lack no spiritual gift as you wait for the revelation of our Lord Jesus [Christ]. He will strengthen you to the end, so that you will be blameless on the day of our Lord Jesus Christ. God is faithful, and it was he who called you to fellowship with his Son, Jesus Christ our Lord.

The Word of the Lord.

Gospel **Mk 13, 33-37**

A reading from the holy gospel according to Mark.

Jesus said to his disciples: "Be constantly on the watch! Stay awake! You do not know when the appointed time will come. It is like a man traveling abroad. He leaves home and places his servants in charge, each with his own task; and he orders the man at the gate to watch with a sharp eye. Look around you! You do not know when the master of the house is coming, whether at dusk, at midnight, when the cock crows, or at early dawn. Do not let him come suddenly and catch you asleep. What I say to you, I say to all: Be on guard!"

The gospel of the Lord.

INTRODUCTORY PRAYER

We bless you, God our Father, at all times,
especially at this time of Advent
which you gave us
to prepare for the coming of your Son, Jesus.

We pray for those who have not hope,
who do not know there is a Savior to hope for.
Reveal to them that you await them
as a Father waits for his children,
and that you have reserved a place for them
in the house of your eternal joy.

We pray for those who doubt and are afraid.
Show them that your Son, Jesus, accompanies them
on the paths of their distress,
that he is light in their night of anguish.

We pray also for your Church, a people of hope.
Strengthen our hearts in holiness, without reproach.
And, on the day of your love,
gather us together in your Kingdom,
with your Son, Jesus,
in the joy of the Holy Spirit,
forever and ever. Amen.

HOMILY

1. Return, Lord, for the Sake of Your Servants

The first reading is an excerpt from a long psalmic prayer[1] in the third part of the Book of Isaiah (called "Trito-Isaiah"). It seems to date from the period that follows the return from Babylonian captivity after the promulgation of the Edict of Cyrus in 538.

This prayer expresses well the disillusion of the Zionists: They were dreaming of returning to a land where, according to tradition, milk and honey flowed; in reality, they found a ruined and devastated country. This prayer also sings about their hopes: that God would come back into the midst of his people, that he would rebuild Zion and restore the Temple to its former glory.

The liturgy has retained an excerpt from this psalm, presenting it as a prayer for the season of Advent.

"Like Dirty Rags"

The resurrection of Jesus has made us come back from the captivity of our sins and has opened for us the doors to the true Promised Land, the paradise of Christ. And yet in this walk to heaven we labor, sometimes dancing in the midst of our hopes, sometimes floundering in the midst of our disillusions.

The time of Advent is a time of waiting, during which we ask again the fundamental questions of our existence, those questions which form the dignity of human life: "Who are you, Lord, that you invite us in this way into the Kingdom of your holiness and of your joy?" "Who are we before you?" "What is the mere moment of our life worth before your eternal majesty?" The Book of Isaiah answers us today:

> We are all unclean people
> and all our good deeds are like dirty rags.
> We have all fallen like leaves
> and our sins carry us away like the wind. Is 64, 6

Like dirty rags... yes, before God, our righteousness is dirty, our beauty is ugly, our sin carries us away like dead leaves that whirl in the late autumn wind.

And yet there is no room to despair in sadness at the memory of dirty rags. For the Word of God also teaches us to say:

Yet, O Lord, you are our Father.
We are the clay; you are the potter;
we are all the work of your hands. Is 64, 7

What advantage is there in being a vase in the hand of a potter? None! Unless the hand of the potter is the hand of God: "yes, like clay in the hand of a potter, thus are you in my hand, O house of Israel."[2] Unless the hand of the potter is the hand of God: "Lord, you are our Father." For then the vase is no longer clay in the hand of the potter but a child in the hand of the Father. Thus are we in the hand of God!

Of little importance are the dirty rags of our life, of little importance are our sins, dead leaves carried away by the mercy of the wind. For this Father is a God of forgiveness and mercy. Paul has sublime words on the subject of this divine pottery. First he calls to mind the sovereign liberty of God in the work of creation: The potter is the master who fashions with clay the vase that pleases him. How could a work enter into discussion with the one who made it? But our divinely given freedom is not caprice or whim. It is the sovereign initiative of mercy. God manifests in this way "the riches of his glory in vessels of mercy."[3] That is what we are: pottery in the hand of God, but filled with mercy!

Thus, all our existence is clay in the hand of God. Our intelligence as well as our love, our soul as well as our body. In a word, all our being is molded by God. We are entirely in his hand. Moreover, our intelligence as well as our love, our soul as well as our body, all our existence is a receptacle of God's grace.

Advent is the time when we resume consciousness of our misery—what we are before God: the dirty rags of our life, the dead leaves carried away by the wind, and of what God is for us: the tenderness of a Father who keeps us in his hands and fills us with his mercy.

If You Would Rend the Heavens and Come Down

I like this prayer very much. It is unique in the Old Testament:

Oh, if you would rend the heavens
and come down,
with the mountains quaking before you! Is 63, 19

Does this prayer truly express the desire of my heart? Am I ready to make it mine? Am I straining toward that rending of the heavens when the Lord will come with his angels and all his saints? Am I ready to leap to this encounter? To put it more simply: Am I ready to die to meet my Lord? This statement is not at all extravagant. It is normal in our lives which are threatened by death at each moment. It expresses well the healthiness of a faith which implores with the psalm:

> Lord of the universe, make us come back,
> let your face shine and we will be saved. Ps 80, 4

God tore open the heavens at Sinai; he came down to his people. Then, according to tradition, the mountains melted like wax before the fire of his presence.

God rent the heavens again at the Jordan during Jesus' baptism. Mark writes (he is the only one to repeat the verb used by Isaiah):

> Jesus, coming out of the water,
> saw the heavens rent
> and the Spirit descending upon him like a dove. Mk 1, 10

In Jesus the mercy of the Father descended upon earth and lives forever among us. Advent is not a solitary walk toward God. It is with the Christ that we return—through the rending of heaven—to the Father.

2. Awaiting the Revelation of Jesus Christ

According to his habit, Paul begins his letter with a prayer of thanksgiving. "I give thanks at each moment," *eucharisto:* I make eucharist, I give thanks.

The object of this eucharist is the riches of grace: "In Jesus Christ, you have been filled with all riches." Sometimes we regard it as absolutely normal to have received the gift of faith and to know the love of Christ Jesus. Paul reminds us that faith is a gift of God and that we never should cease to give thanks for those riches.

These riches place us before God, "in the awaiting of the revelation (literally: of the apocalypse) of our Lord Jesus Christ."[4] A Christian is a person of hope. When Paul speaks about the pagans, he calls them "the others who have no hope."[5] This waiting in hope gives unity to our life. Without it, our actions would no longer have any unity. They would be scattered like the pearls of a precious necklace whose string breaks. With hope, on the contrary, our days—even the most humble and the most insignificant—take meaning and sing the joy of meeting the Lord.

Blameless on the Day of Jesus

How can we prepare for the "revelation of our Lord Jesus Christ?" Paul explains:

> (Jesus) will strengthen you
> so that you may be blameless
> on the Day of our Lord Jesus Christ. 1 Cor 1, 8

That was a traditional teaching in the Pauline churches:[6] No one can appear in the presence of Jesus if he or she is not blameless. The adjective blameless (*a-negkletos*) designates one who cannot be called into judgment. It is tied to the idea of holiness without blemish. The time of Advent is a time of purification, of sanctification. We must each see what must be purified in our lives in order to draw nearer to Christ Jesus.

How Ahmad Prepared Himself to Meet God

Ahmad was an old blind man who, while awaiting paradise, spent his days at the hospice of Isfiya, on Mount Carmel.

What he lacked most in his life was not the light of the sun of Allah but the tenderness of a look which would have rested upon him, the gentleness of a love that would have covered his stooped shoulders like a cloak of joy. Ahmad is in deficit of love. He has not had his share of joy and smiles in his life. Surely, there had to have been an error in accounting of his case.

Sister Caritas—she bears her name, charity, well—seeks to re-establish the equilibrium in the present balance of his life. She does her best. She loves him like a mother, and old Ahmad allows himself to be pampered like a little boy.

We only hope that this life in deficit does not end in bankruptcy; for Ahmad has nothing, truly nothing, to attract affection. Nature, who distributes her gifts in a capricious manner, has been unkind to him. It is lucky for him that he never saw himself in a mirror. He was spared the sight of an immense nose, screwed on like a bulb in the middle of his face, a slobbering mouth that drooped on one side, a furrowed brow and cheeks hollowed out like the slopes of the desert of Judah.

In order to give him value in his own eyes, to show him that he too is useful to the community, that his work and even his existence are appreciated,

Caritas entrusts to Ahmad a particularly important post: Ahmad is made a dishwasher. More exactly, he washes the cups. In this world of sick, crippled and lame, this is almost a priesthood. The badge of his order is the dishcloth.

At the end of the meal, while others flop uselessly into chaise lounges, Ahmad advances slowly toward the sink, where the dishpan is found. He is like a priest going up to the altar, like a judge advancing toward the tribunal, like a king taking possession of his throne. The dishcloth, according to the technique put into practice, serves as a drainer. Ahmad begins by wiping his brow, sometimes even his hands on the dishcloth—who can see him?—then he spreads it out on the right of the dishpan. Now comes the work. Not just anyone can fulfill this ministry: finesse, intelligence, and lucidity are needed. Bending over the sink a bit, he grabs a cup, with his hand detects its degree of dirtiness, adjusts there the pressure of his finger, rinses it noisily, and finally deposits the cup on the dishcloth, where it drains itself.

All the cups are thus inspected, washed, rinsed, and drained. All except one: the cup of Handey, his personal enemy. She is a blind woman as old as Ahmad and as ugly as he. What happened between the two of them? No one knows. Perhaps they had "words." Each day, Ahmad savors his vengeance. His gnarled fingers recognize Handey's cup from among a thousand. It is the only one that has the audacity to have a little handle. As soon as he locates it, this unfortunate cup, he simply passes it under the water. Then leaning to the right, he deposits it, but beyond the dishcloth, with a large "huh" of spite. Let it drain as best it can, without the help of a dishcloth!

Caritas has been seeking for a long time to make an opening in the heart of Ahmad through which forgiveness of his enemies could enter. "It is Ramadan, the time of prayer, of fasting, of forgiveness. Allah loves you, Ahmad, not if you fast, but if you forgive." But each time it is the "huh" of spite that deposits Handey's cup beyond the space of the dishcloth. Sometimes Caritas gives Ahmad a second chance; she takes the enemy's cup, already washed, then replaces it, unknown to him, in the dish pan, but in vain. This only serves to augment the spite of the reproachful "huh."

Finally it was the last day of Ramadan. For several days Caritas had not said anything. We must respect the freedom of the most humble, know how to wait for the delays of progress of grace. When Ahmad felt the handle of the cup, his hand shook a little, his lip trembled, his furrowed brow wrinkled even more. He heaved a long sigh, like a sigh of fatigue after a long combat. Then, slowly, his gray-haired hand placed the cup with the handle on the dishcloth, with the others.

On that day, the angels in heaven must have danced with joy to celebrate the forgiveness of Ahmad, the old blind man of Isfiya, toward Handey, the old blind woman.

Ahmad died three weeks later. Allah, "the merciful, the compassionate," welcomed him into his arms. Caritas washed his wrinkled face, dressed him in a white shirt, undoubtedly the first one of his life. The little old men and women surrounded him to say goodbye before he was buried. When they saw his all-peaceful face, his mouth which had become straight, his eyes closed as though he were sleeping, and the white shirt, an old man cried out: "Ahmad is beautiful!"

Yes, he was beautiful! Beautiful for having forgiven.

3. Watch in the Awaiting of Christ

The gospel this Sunday presents the end of the eschatological discourse according to Mark. This discourse deals with the coming of the Son of Man at the end of time "with much power and glory."[7]

The ending of this discourse is introduced by the affirmation that no one except the Father—not even the Son nor the angels—knows the day or the hour of this parousia.[8] This total ignorance commands the fundamental attitude of the Christian:

> Watch, for you do not know
> when the Lord is coming! Mk 13, 35

This theme of vigilance is developed beginning with the parable of the porter. It is presented in two strophes or stanzas, one could say, each stanza being introduced and concluded by the recommendation to watch:

> Take care, remain watchful,
> for you do not know when the moment will be...
> To the porter, the master commanded to watch.
> Watch then, for you do not know
> when the Lord of the house is coming...
> What I say to you,
> I say to all of you: Watch! Mk 13, 33-37

The Parable of the Porter

The master of a house leaves on a journey. He asks the porter to watch, for he may return unexpectedly, in the middle of the night. This is the nucleus of the parable.

In its most ancient form, this parable seems to have been addressed first to the scribes and to specialists in the law. They possessed "the key of knowledge;" they could open or close the kingdom of heaven.[9] Notice that with Jesus had come the time of judgment. Did they use their knowledge to open for the crowds the understanding of the message of Jesus? Or, on the contrary, were they neglectful about their privileges by closing the doors of the kingdom to the poor whom Jesus was evangelizing?

To the scribe-porters were added in succession other servants, those to whom the master "gave power, to each one according to his task."[10] Actually, these servants do not have anything to do since, to welcome the master who returns from the journey, the porter would have sufficed. But these servants enlarge the teaching of the parable. Clearly, the time of the scribes was followed by the time of the Church. Between those times the man who had left on a journey became "the Lord of the house." The recommendation to watch, addressed first to the porter and then to the servants having authority, is now extended to all the faithful: "What I say to you, I say to all: Watch!"[11]

Mark is undoubtedly thinking about those who had been established like porters in the Church of his time—bishops, presbyters, deacons, all those who had ministries—who had grown drowsy in the prestige of their roles. He is also thinking about the whole Christian community, which could fall asleep in the assurance of being saved. To all, Mark says: "Watch! Jesus can come back in the midst of the night!"

The Watchful Christian

Watch? But to do what? The night watch—quite like insomnia—is only a long boredom, and Mark does not tell us here either the why or the how of the Christian watch.

But he specifies it a few verses later, in the account of the agony in the Garden of Olives. Those who knew Mark's gospel well also knew how the recommendation to watch continued:

> Watch and pray
> in order not to enter into temptation. Mk 14, 38

The Passion of Jesus had marked the beginning of the great temptation, the hour of the assault of the powers of evil, first against Jesus, then later against the Church. The eschatological waiting is a watch in prayer in order to be able to face the temptations of Satan.

The master can come back "in the evening, in the middle of the night, at the crowing of the rooster, or even in the morning." You will say: There is a very imprudent traveler! He leaves for a long journey; therefore, he can organize his return as he thinks proper, and he is deciding to come back during the night. But in the country of Jesus, no one travels at night! Jesus himself recommends, "Walk while you have the light, lest darkness stop you. The one who walks in the dark does not know where he is going."[12] And that is not to mention encounters with highway robbers! Therefore, no one travels at night except the one whom Mark calls "the Lord of the house."

Tradition, as attested in the *Targum*, knew the "poem of the four nights." In it, one celebrated the four nights that marked the history of the world. It is about that night at the end of time which it has been said: "It is the fourth night when the world will arrive at its end to be dissolved; the yokes of iron will be broken and the perverse generations will be annihilated… and the Messiah King will come from on high."[13]

Here is one last remark: the Greeks and the Romans divided the night into four watches: evening, middle of the night, cock-crow and morning. These are the watches that Mark gives. The Babylonians and the Israelites counted only three watches.[14] Therefore, we can think that Mark, transforming the Palestinian night into a Greek or Roman night, adapted the gospel for his readers. This adaptation, in the present case, is minimal. But the principle from which it proceeds is of extreme importance: It is suitable to adapt the gospel—within sound limits—so that one can understand it better and, consequently, put it into practice better. We must all adapt to our own particular lives the admonition of Jesus: "Watch and pray!"

The Advent of the Priestly People

As priestly people, the Church celebrates, especially during the time of Advent, the joy of all the hopes of the world. We also share the pain of all deceived expectations.

Thank you, Lord, for all the awaitings where you are present, mysteriously, at the heart of our desires.

Thank you for the awaiting of a mother who carries a baby, for whomever receives one of these little ones receives you.

Thank you for the awaiting of the husband and wife who see each other again after a long separation, for where two are gathered in your name you are present in their midst.

Thank you for the awaiting of the aged who receive the visitor that they were watching for from their window. "I was sick and you visited me."[15]

Thank you for the awaiting of those who are dying, for it is you whom their hand is seeking, and while their eyes are closing, it is you whom their gaze meets.

Thank you, Lord, especially for the awaiting of sinners who are hoping for forgiveness. For it is you who placed in their hearts the assurance that you take pleasure in forgiving.

Mercy for strangers who live in our midst and who wait for a look of love. "I was a stranger and you welcomed me."[16]

Mercy for the sick who are imprisoned in their suffering. Mercy for those who are bound by chains of sin, for you alone are their deliverance.

It is the awaiting of the whole world that we gather in our hands when we extend them toward you, Lord.

The Always-open Door

A prodigal leaves the paternal home. At the table each day his place is set; his seat remains empty. After long years, broken by the disillusions of life, the prodigal returns home. "Father," he asks, "how is it that the door was open in the middle of the night?" "It was to welcome you. Since you left, the door has always been open."

This is merely an old Irish legend. God did more. Not only was the door always open and the place always set, but he also sent Jesus to look for us and take us by the hand. He is at the same time the path of return, the door always open, the table always prepared. He is the Savior. To him be glory and our love. Amen.

CONCLUDING PRAYER

We are clay in your hands,
but you, Lord, are the Potter.
Make us receptacles of your mercy.
You are our Father; come to save us
in your Son, Jesus.

Awaken your power,
Lord, come to save us!

We are scattered like abandoned sheep,
but you, Lord, are our Shepherd.
Gather us into your sheepfold.
You are our Father; come to save us
in your Son Jesus.

Awaken your power,
Lord, come to save us!

We are the devastated vine
invaded by brambles and thorns,
but you, Lord, are the Vinedresser.
Make us bear ruddy fruit.
You are our Father; come to save us
in your Son, Jesus.

Awaken your power,
Lord, come to save us!

Our good works are like dirty rags.
We are falling like dead leaves
carried away by the autumn wind,
but you, Lord, are dazzling holiness.
Help us to live in a blameless way
until the Day of Christ Jesus.
You are our Father; come to save us
in your Son, Jesus.

Awaken your power,
Lord, come to save us!

We wander like abandoned children.
But you, Lord, are the God of love.
Never more will we go far from you.
You are our Father; come to save us
in your Son, Jesus.

Awaken your power;
Lord, come to save us!

Once again, God our Father,
Rend the heavens and come to live among us
in your Son, Jesus our Lord. Amen.

NOTES TO FIRST SUNDAY OF ADVENT

1. Is 63, 7 to 64, 11. For the date, see P. E. Bonnard, *Le second Isaïe,* Coll. "Etudes Bibliques" (Paris: Ed. Gabalda et Cie, 1972): 445.
2. Jer 18, 6.
3. Rom 9, 20–21 citing Is 29, 16 and Rom 9, 23.
4. 1 Cor 1, 7.
5. 1 Thes 4, 13.
6. Col 1, 22. Eph 1, 4.
7. Mk 13, 26.
8. Mk 13, 32.
9. Mt 23, 13 and Lk 11, 52.
10. Mk 13, 34.
11. Mk 13, 37.
12. Jn 12, 35.
13. Trans. R. Le Déaut. SC 256 (1979), pp. 96, 98.
14. Strack–Billerbeck, *Kommentar zum Neuen Testament aus Talmud und Midrasch,* vol. 1 (Munich: C. H. Beck, 1961), pp. 688–691.
15. Mt 25, 36.
16. Mt 25, 35.

SECOND SUNDAY OF ADVENT

READING I   Is 40, 1-5. 9-11

A reading from the book of the prophet Isaiah

Comfort, give comfort to my people,
  says your God.
Speak tenderly to Jerusalem, and proclaim to her
  that her service is at an end,
  her guilt is expiated;
Indeed, she has received from the hand of the Lord
  double for all her sins.
A voice cries out:
In the desert prepare the way of the Lord!
  Make straight in the wasteland a highway for our God!
Every valley shall be filled in,
  every mountain and hill shall be made low;
The rugged land shall be made a plain,
  the rough country, a broad valley.
Then the glory of the Lord shall be revealed,
  and all mankind shall see it together;
  for the mouth of the Lord has spoken.

Go up onto a high mountain,
  Zion, herald of glad tidings;
Cry out at the top of your voice,
  Jerusalem, herald of good news!
Fear not to cry out
  and say to the cities of Judah:
  Here is your God!
Here comes with power
  the Lord God,
  who rules by his strong arm;
Here is his reward with him,
  his recompense before him.
Like a shepherd he feeds his flock;
  in his arms he gathers the lambs,
Carrying them in his bosom,
  and leading the ewes with care.

The Word of the Lord.

Responsorial Psalm — Ps 85, 9-10. 11-12. 13-14

R/. (8) Lord, let us see your kindness,
and grant us your salvation.

I will hear what God proclaims;
the Lord—for he proclaims peace to his people.
Near indeed is his salvation to those who fear him,
glory dwelling in our land.

R/. Lord, let us see your kindness,
and grant us your salvation.

Kindness and truth shall meet;
justice and peace shall kiss.
Truth shall spring out of the earth,
and justice shall look down from heaven.

R/. Lord, let us see your kindness,
and grant us your salvation.

The Lord himself will give his benefits;
our land shall yield its increase.
Justice shall walk before him,
and salvation, along the way of his steps.

R/. Lord, let us see your kindness,
and grant us your salvation.

Reading II — 2 Pt 3, 8-14

A reading from the second letter of Peter

This point must not be overlooked, dear friends. In the Lord's eyes, one day is as a thousand years and a thousand years are as a day. The Lord does not delay in keeping his promise—though some consider it "delay." Rather, he shows you generous patience, since he wants none to perish but all to come to repentance. The day of the Lord will come like a thief, and on that day the heavens will vanish with a roar; the elements will be destroyed by fire, and the earth and all its deeds will be made manifest.

Since everything is to be destroyed in this way, what sort of men must you not be! How holy in your conduct and devotion, looking for the coming of the day of God and trying to hasten it! Because of it, the heavens will be destroyed in flames and the elements will melt away in a blaze. What we await are new heavens and a new earth where, according to his promise, the justice of God will reside. So, beloved, while waiting for this, make every effort to be found without stain or defilement, and at peace in his sight.

The Word of the Lord.

Gospel **Mk 1, 1-8**

The beginning of the holy gospel according to Mark

Here begins the gospel of Jesus Christ, the Son of God. In Isaiah the prophet, it is written:

"I send my messenger before you
to prepare your way:
a herald's voice in the desert, crying,
'Make ready the way of the Lord,
clear him a straight path.'"

Thus it was that John the Baptizer appeared in the desert proclaiming a baptism of repentance which led to the forgiveness of sins. All the Judean countryside and the people of Jerusalem went out to him in great numbers. They were being baptized by him in the Jordan River as they confessed their sins. John was clothed in camel's hair, and wore a leather belt around his waist. His food was grasshoppers and wild honey. The theme of his preaching was: "One more powerful than I is to come after me. I am not fit to stoop and untie his sandal straps. I have baptized you in water; he will baptize you in the Holy Spirit."

The gospel of the Lord.

INTRODUCTORY PRAYER

Lord Jesus, we pray to you:
Prepare in the desert of our hearts
the path of your return.
Lower the hills of our pride
by the example of your humility.
Fill the valleys of our despair
through our hope in you.
Straighten the twisted paths of our lies
by your truth.

And let the flowers of your joy
bloom in our hearts.
Then we will be able to see your glory
and worship your presence, which we will see
in the face of each of our brothers and sisters. Amen.

HOMILY

1. Comfort, Comfort My People...

The exile of the chosen people in Babylon lasted from the year 587, the date of the taking of Jerusalem, to 538, the date of the Edict of Cyrus, which allowed the return of the exiles. These forty-nine years of exile (seven times seven years), could be considered a perfect duration according to God's plan, both to make reparation for past sins and to inaugurate the new era of return to Jerusalem. During the years 550 to 539, an anonymous prophet, a disciple of Isaiah, arose in the midst of the exiles. For convenience, we call him Deutero-Isaiah, that is, Second Isaiah. His oracles were grouped into the second part of the Book of Isaiah (Is. 40 to 55), which is called the "Book of the consolation of Israel." It begins with these words: "Comfort, comfort my people."

The poems of Deutero-Isaiah exercised a considerable influence on the New Testament. After the psalms, they are the most cited texts in the New Testament. One could say that Deutero-Isaiah was "the favorite book of Jesus and his disciples."[1]

The first reading this Sunday presents the beginning of the first poem of Deutero-Isaiah.

The New Exodus

The Exodus holds a similar place in the conscience of Israel as the life of Jesus holds in the Christian conscience. The liberation from Egypt, the gift of the Law at Sinai, and the celebration of the Covenant constitute the events that founded this people of kings, priests and prophets. In the remainder of their history, all subsequent liberation was considered a renewal of the Exodus. Moreover, Deutero-Isaiah will see the liberation from the Babylonian captivity as an extraordinary overstepping of the ancient marvels of the Exodus.

How are the prophecies of Deutero-Isaiah fulfilled? Rather modestly. One had dreamed:

> Those whom Yahweh has freed return.
> They arrive at Zion with cries of joy.
> Eternal happiness shines upon their faces,
> gladness and joy accompany them. Is 51, 11

But the texts reveal that the time of return was a difficult time, without religious enthusiasm, and without national grandeur. Those who had sown in tears, instead of harvesting while singing, continued to weep.

Actually, the prophecies of the Old Testament are fulfilled in their plenitude not in the history of Israel but in the history of Jesus. As Paul says, Jesus is the "yes" through which the Father fulfills all his promises.[2] Then he entrusts to his Church the mission of continuing to fulfill them.

Therefore, three eras can be distinguished in the fulfillment of these prophecies;

- The era of Deutero-Isaiah and the partial fulfillment of the prophecies;
- The era of Jesus, the time of the plenitude of the fulfillment.
- The era of the Church, the time in which the liturgy makes us relive and actualize these prophecies.

The Comforts of Israel

When deported to Babylon, Jerusalem, the Holy City, resembled a princess reduced to drudgery. She groaned: "No one comforts me."[3]

The return to the Holy Land begins the time of comfort and forgiveness.

> Comfort, comfort my people, says your God.
> Speak to the heart of Jerusalem; proclaim to her
> that her hard service is ended,
> that her sin is expiated. Is 40, 1-2

God realized his promise completely in messianic time. Jesus is the Messiah whom tradition calls precisely "the Consolation of Israel." He creates the messianic people about whom it is said: "Blessed are those who mourn, for they will be consoled."[4] God makes consolers out of the consoled. Paul sums up admirably this vocation of consoler in the era of the Church:

> Blessed be the God and Father of our Lord Jesus Christ, the Father of compassion and the God of all comfort. He comforts us in all our tribulations so that we may be able to comfort others in whatever tribulation they may have through the comfort that we receive from God. 2 Cor 1, 3-4

The psalmist sings this very beautiful prayer:

> You, Lord, have counted my wandering steps
> Collect my tears in your flask. Ps 56, 9

One could say that each time God sees a poor person weep, an angel is sent to collect the tears in a flask so that not one of them is lost—for God wants to comfort everyone. We can think that this angel, in charge of the flasks of tears, still has much to do today. And so the prophecy of Deutero-Isaiah has become our prayer: Look, Lord, at our brothers and sisters who mourn. Do not forget to fulfill your promise and console them. Make us consolers as well.

Prepare the Path of the Lord

The return to the Holy Land is presented as the triumphal march of Yahweh at the head of his people. Even today, when a king or a president visits a city or province, we rush to do necessary road work; we repair old roads or pave new ones to facilitate the travel of the guest and also to impress him. When Yahweh leads his people from Babylon to Jerusalem, he must pave the whole desert of Syria:

> A voice proclaims:
> In the desert, prepare the way of the Lord.
> Make straight in the wasteland
> a highway for our God.
> Let every valley be filled,
> let every mountain and every hill be made low,
> let every rugged ground become a plain
> and the high places, wide valleys.
> Then the glory of the Lord will be revealed. Is 40, 3-5

This prophecy was familiar to the early community.[5] The four gospels cite it at the beginning of the ministry of the public life of Jesus. Mark places it at the very beginning of his gospel. Indeed, it was easy to apply it to the preaching of John in the desert. The Hebrew text stated: "A voice cries out:

In the desert prepare the way of Yahweh." But the Greek translation said: "A voice cries out in the desert: Prepare the way of the Lord." It is obviously this reading that the gospels retained.

Another change slipped into the text. Instead of saying, "Make straight the highways of Yahweh," one said: "Make straight his paths," that is, the paths of Jesus. Jesus was, therefore, presented as the Lord who guided his people across the desert to the Promised Land.

How can we, in the era of the Church, realize this prophecy in our life?

There is always a desert to cross—whether it be the desert of Sinai or the desert of Syria—in order to enter into the Promised Land. There is always the desert of our life to cross and spiritual roadwork to accomplish in order to enter into Paradise. It is in our life that the voice resounds: "Prepare the way of the Lord!" To the degree that we move forward in this "exodus," God moves forward in our hearts on the road that we have prepared for him.

"Make straight his paths." Straighten what is twisted in us, Lord. Correct the meandering of our lies.

"Let every hill be made low!" Smooth with a carpenter's plane the swelling of our pride, Lord. Fill the gulfs of our weaknesses.

"Then the glory of the Lord will be revealed." The "glory of God" guided the people of the Exodus across the desert of Sinai. It had sojourned in the Temple of Solomon. It then left the Temple and accompanied the deported to the riverbanks of Babylon. It was finally revealed in Jesus, as John's gospel affirms: "We have seen his glory, the glory of the only Son, full of grace and truth."[6] Have the eyes of our hearts contemplated the glory of Jesus? Is this glory, seen on the face of Jesus, reflected on our own faces, and does its splendor radiate out to the faces of our brothers and sisters who walk with us toward God?[7]

What questions the time of Advent poses for us! It is in our hands that God deposits the realization of the prophecies of Deutero-Isaiah.

The Shepherds of the New Exodus

God walks at the head of his people. The herald precedes him, announcing the "Good News" of his coming (*euagglizomenos*: one who proclaims the Gospel).

> Lift up your voice with force,
> you who carry the Good News to Jerusalem...

Here is your God;
here is the Lord God!
He comes with power;
his arm is victorious.
Like a shepherd who tends his flock,
his arm gathers the flock.
He carries the lambs on his heart;
he takes care of the mother sheep. Is 40, 9-11

The oracle resembles a page of the gospel. We know with what power the Good Shepherd came among us: the power of his love; giving his life for his sheep.

Once again: how is this prophecy realized in us? We say sometimes that each day brings us closer to eternity. Some say closer to our grave. Others say closer to nothingness. Deutero-Isaiah affirms that each day brings us closer to God. "Here is the Lord! He comes with power!" This power is not the power of death, which no one can resist, but the power of the Shepherd, who carries the weakest lambs on his bosom and who also takes care of the mother sheep. Who would have dared to create these images and to think that God carries us in this way, with our weaknesses, on his bosom? Advent is the time of the tenderness of God, who comes before each one of us, who leads us into the New Jerusalem which his love built for us—heaven.

Such is the hope for which we live. Such is the hope that Deutero-Isaiah charges us to share with our brothers and sisters who travel with us.

2. Show Us, O Lord, Your Love

For a responsorial psalm, the liturgy has chosen Psalm 85, one of the traditional psalms for Advent.

The first part of this psalm celebrates the return of the exiles into the Holy Land. It ends with the prayer:

Show us, O Lord, your love,
and grant us your salvation. Ps 85, 8

It is to this prayer that the second part of the psalm responds. It is presented as a prophetic oracle, an oracle that the prophet utters in the name of God:

I am listening: What does the Lord God say?
What he says is peace for his people. Ps 85, 9

Four characters enter into the scene: They are Love, Truth, Justice, Peace.

> Love and Truth meet;
> Justice and Peace kiss.
> Truth shall spring forth from the earth,
> and Justice shall lean down from heaven. Ps 85, 11-12

In Jesus, Love and Truth met; Justice and Peace kissed. He is the Truth that sprang forth from the virginal womb of Mary; he is the Justice that leaned down over the earth from heaven. Saint Ephrem (+373) sang the mystery of Christ in this way:

> Mary is the field that never knew the plow.
> From this field arose the sheaf of benediction.
> Without seed, she gave Fruit to the world.
> Come to me, sages and prophets!
> In your revelations, you have seen truth,
> laborers who have sown,
> then slept, full of hope.
> Arise and clap your hands,
> seeing the fruits of the Harvest:
> Here in my arms is the Cluster
> which gives living bread.
> With me, rejoice:
> for I bear the Sheaf of joy![8]

Who today will present the Sheaf of joy if not those who are satisfied with living bread? And when our brother or sister prays: "Show us, O Lord, your love, and give us your salvation," who will be able to reveal to them that their prayer was heard if not those in whom, as in Jesus, Love and Truth have met, Justice and Peace have kissed?

3. The New Heavens and the New Earth

Antiquity rather easily used the literary device called the pseudonym: In order to give more credit to a teaching, one attributed it to an author whose authority was universally known. It is in this way that, near the end of the first century or the beginning of the second, an anonymous Christian of Jewish origin but of good Hellenist education wrote a booklet that he presented as the Second Letter of Peter. (Today we would call this a forgery.) He affirmed at the same time that he was placing himself under the authority of Peter. After all, he had acted for a good cause by defending the faith. The true forgers, he affirmed, were the false teachers who falsified the Christian faith. It is in this way that we have the Second Letter of Peter which, although not from Peter, the Church recognizes as being divinely inspired.

The Delays of the Parousia

The first Christian generation lived awaiting the imminent parousia. Christ had affirmed, ''This generation will not pass away before all these things [which had been proclaimed in the eschatological discourse] happened."[9] The ruin of Jerusalem in the year 70 had shown that the time of judgment was near. One could then estimate that the end of the world and the coming of Jesus in glory was likewise near.

But around the years 100-110, some people were asking themselves if the delays of the parousia had not been changed into slowness. Those who refused to believe the words of Jesus mocked them. The author declares: "At the time of the last days, mockers will come with their mockings..." They will say: "Where is the promise of his parousia?"[10] He answers them: "The Lord is not slow, keeping his promise, as some understand slowness."[11] But then how can one interpret such a long delay? Here is his explanation; it is sublime:

> The Lord is patient with us
> not wanting anyone to perish
> but that everyone have the time to repent. 2 Pt 3, 9

Thus the delay of God is the delay of his patience, and his patience is the patience of his forgiveness, which grants time for repentance.

This principle was valid at the time when the Second Letter of Peter was written. Nineteen centuries have elapsed since then, but the principle is valid for all the ages. Each day of our lives, the patience of God comes to meet us and offer us the time of repentance.

The New Heavens and the New Earth

To describe the Day of the Lord, the author uses traditional images from Jewish apocalypses:

> The heavens will disappear with a roar;
> the burning elements will be dissolved;
> the earth with all its works will be consumed. 2 Pt 3, 12

There is no room to founder in agony before the blaze of these images. This description of the final conflagration simply signifies that the old world will disappear. A day will come when the angel will shout, "The old world is gone!" Then God will declare: "Look, I am making a new universe!"[12] From the ashes of the old world will surge a new world filled with justice!

> We are waiting according to his promise
> for the new heavens and a new earth
> where justice will dwell. 2 Pt 3, 12

The essence of "the parousia of the day of God" is therefore the parousia of his justice.[13] We prepare ourselves for that parousia "in the holiness of life," in order to appear before God "without spot and without blemish."[14] The time of Advent is a time of holiness and purification. This is the way we create the new heavens and the new earth—first in our hearts.

4. The Beginning of the Gospel According to Mark

The beginning of the gospel according to Mark chimes like the overture of a symphony of joy:

> The beginning of the Gospel of Jesus Christ,
> the Son of God. Mk 1, 1

This translates: The beginning of the gospel, that is, of the Good News. The Good News that Deutero-Isaiah was proclaiming when he announced, "Look, the Lord God is coming!" The Good News of Jesus, of the one whose name means Savior; Christ, of the one who is the Anointed of God, his Envoy, his Messiah, Son of God. The ministry of Jesus, especially his Passion, will reveal his holiness. The centurion will say, "Truly, this man was the son of God."[15] The Resurrection will reveal what plenitude of meaning must be given to the title Son of God.

Two Themes

Two themes answer each other in the overture of this symphony of God's joy. The first is the theme of the coming of God:

> See that I sent my messenger before you
> to prepare your way.
> A voice of one who cries in the desert:
> "Prepare the way of the Lord; make straight his paths." Mk 1, 2-3

We have recognized the themes of Deutero-Isaiah. The Good News of Jesus is that the people, under his leadership, were going to start walking toward the joy of the Promised Land. Mark notes with a certain emphasis: "The whole country of Judah and all those of Jerusalem came out to him."[16] All "came out," as if it were a matter of coming out of Babylon and coming "to him," to John who, it is said, was found in the desert. And John will lead the people to Jesus; the first disciples of Jesus will be the disciples of John.

This text of Mark resembles the "Rule of the Community" of Qumran. It is said in the Rule that the members of the community "will separate themselves from the dwelling of perverse men in order to go into the desert to prepare there the way of That One, as it is written: 'In the desert, prepare a way… Make straight in the wasteland a road for our God.'"[17]

The second theme is the one of the return of humankind back to God. God comes to humanity; humanity comes back to God. We go back to him through repentance. John proclaims a baptism of repentance. The external rite is baptism; the internal grace is repentance. It is a matter of turning oneself toward God, of coming back to him.

> Come back to me,
> declares the Lord Almighty,
> and I will come back to you. Mal 3, 7

The New Elijah

Jewish tradition thought that Elijah was going to come back to prepare the coming of the Messiah. "The scribes said that Elijah must come first."[18] They even thought that it was Elijah who would give the messianic anointing to the Messiah.[19] In the face of the unbelief of the scribes, it was a good tactic to affirm that John preceded Jesus "with the spirit and power of Elijah."[20]

Mark does it his own way. First he cites the prophecy of Malachi: "See that I am sending my messenger before you." Now in Malachi's text, this messenger was identified with Elijah.[21] Then he shows John "dressed in camel's hair [that is, in a garment woven out of camel's hair] and with a loincloth around his loins." This is not a matter of folkloric garb but rather a theological garment: It is the very garment of the prophet Elijah.[22] Therefore, Mark's readers know from the beginning of his gospel that John is really the new Elijah.

As for Elijah himself, he would come back in person at the time of the Transfiguration. At that time he accomplished the essential work of his prophetic vocation in the New Testament: to lead the Christian community to the contemplation of the transfigured Christ.

Each of us can be an Elijah today for our brothers and sisters if we lead them to the transfigured Christ, if we contemplate with them the glory of the risen Jesus. Each one of us can also be a new John if we prepare the ways of the Lord, first in our hearts, then in the hearts of our brothers and sisters.

CONCLUDING PRAYER

Let the Day come, O Lord,
when our misery
will meet your mercy.

Show us, O Lord, your love.
Give us your salvation.

Let the Day come, O Lord,
when our sin
will meet your forgiveness.

Show us, O Lord, your love.
Give us your salvation.

Let the Day come, O Lord,
when our poverty
will meet your riches.

Show us, O Lord, your love.
Give us your salvation.

Let the Day come, O Lord,
when our road
will meet your house.

Show us, O Lord, your love.
Give us your salvation.

Let the Day come, O Lord,
when our tears
will meet your smile.

Show us, O Lord, your love.
Give us your salvation.

Let the Day come, O Lord,
when our joy
will meet your heaven.

Show us, O Lord, your love.
Give us your salvation.

Blessed be you for that Day
when our eyes will finally meet yours!
Throughout the path of our life,
you never cease to come before us
through your Son Jesus,
our Savior and our brother. Amen.

NOTES TO SECOND SUNDAY OF ADVENT

1. P. E. Bonnard, *Le Second Isaïe*, p. 81.
2. 2 Cor 1, 20.
3. Lam 1, 21.
4. Mt 5, 5.
5. This prophecy was a part of the *Testimonia*, that is, of the collection of the messianic prophecies from which the early community announced the mystery of Jesus. See C.H. Dodd, *Conformement aux Ecritures* (Paris: Ed. du Seuil, 1968): 28–30, 42–44.
6. Ex 24, 17–18. Kgs 8, 11. E 1, 28. Jn 1, 14.
7. 2 Cor 4, 6.
8. Lamy, *Sancti Ephrem, Syri Hymni et Sermones*, 1902, II, p. 526. Cited in L. Jacquet, *Les Psaumes*, vol. II (Duculot, 1977): 643.
9. Mk 13, 30.
10. 2 Pt 3, 4.
11. 2 Pt 3, 9.
12. Rv 21, 4–5. The way in which God will transform the old world into a new world remains hidden from us.
13. 2 Pt 3, 12.
14. 2 Pt 3, 11. 14.
15. Mk 15, 39.
16. Mk 1, 4–5.
17. Règle de la Communaute, VIll, 13–14. *Les textes de Qumran*, vol. I (Paris: Letouzey et Ané 1961): 58.
18. Mk 9, 12.
19. Justin (+around 165), *Dialogue avec Triphon*, VIII, 3.
20. Lk 1, 17.
21. Mal 3, 1 and 3, 23. – It is for the purpose of simplification that Mark attributes the whole of the biblical citation to the "prophet Isaiah," whereas it is composed in reality of Mal 3, 1 and of Is 40, 3.
22. Mk 1, 6 and 2 Kgs 1, 8.

THIRD SUNDAY OF ADVENT

Reading I — Is 61, 1-2. 10-11

A reading from the book of the prophet Isaiah

The spirit of the Lord God is upon me,
because the Lord has anointed me;
He has sent me to bring glad tidings to the lowly,
to heal the brokenhearted,
To proclaim liberty to the captives
and release to the prisoners,
To announce a year of favor from the Lord
and a day of vindication by our God.
I rejoice heartily in the Lord,
in my God is the joy of my soul;
For he has clothed me with a robe of salvation,
and wrapped me in a mantle of justice,
Like a bridegroom adorned with a diadem,
like a bride bedecked with her jewels.
As the earth brings forth its plants,
and a garden makes its growth spring up,
So will the Lord God make justice and praise
spring up before all the nations.

The Word of the Lord.

Responsorial Psalm — Lk 1, 46-48. 49-50. 53-54

R/. (Is 61, 10) My soul rejoices in my God.

My being proclaims the greatness of the Lord,
my spirit finds joy in God my savior,
For he has looked upon his servant in her lowliness;
all ages to come shall call me blessed.

R/. My soul rejoices in my God.

God who is mighty has done great things for me,
holy is his name;
His mercy is from age to age
on those who fear him.

R/. My soul rejoices in my God.

The hungry he has given every good thing,
   while the rich he has sent empty away.
He has upheld Israel his servant,
   ever mindful of his mercy.

R/. My soul rejoices in my God.

Reading II 1 Thes 5, 16-24

A reading from the first letter of Paul to the Thessalonians

Rejoice always, never cease praying, render constant thanks; such is God's will for you in Christ Jesus.

Do not stifle the spirit. Do not despise prophecies. Test everything; retain what is good. Avoid any semblance of evil.

May the God of peace make you perfect in holiness. May you be preserved whole and entire, spirit, soul, and body, irreproachable at the coming of the Lord Jesus Christ. He who calls us is trustworthy, therefore he will do it.

The Word of the Lord.

Gospel Jn 1, 6-8. 19-28

A reading from the holy gospel according to John

There was a man named John sent by God, who came as a witness to testify to the light, so that through him all men might believe—but only to testify to the light, for he himself was not the light.

The testimony John gave when the Jews sent priests and Levites from Jerusalem to ask "Who are you?" was the absolute statement, "I am not the Messiah." They questioned him further, "Who, then? Elijah?" "I am not Elijah," he answered. "Are you the prophet?" "No," he replied.

Finally they said to him: "Tell us who you are, so that we can give some answer to those who sent us. What do you have to say for yourself?" He said, quoting the prophet Isaiah, "I am

   'a voice in the desert crying out:
   Make straight the way of the Lord!'"

Those whom the Pharisees had sent proceeded to question him further: "If you are not the Messiah, nor Elijah, nor the prophet, why do you baptize?" John answered them: "I baptize with water. There is one among you whom you do not recognize—the one who is to come after me—the strap of whose sandal I am not worthy to unfasten." This happened in Bethany, across the Jordan, where John was baptizing.

The gospel of the Lord.

INTRODUCTORY PRAYER

God our Father,
source of all joy and fountain of happiness,
we give you thanks at all times,
but especially at this time of Advent,
for the marvels that you have accomplished
in your humble servant, the Virgin Mary.

In her, your mercy extends from age to age
upon those who worship you.
Through her, you bring down the powerful
from their thrones
and you lift up the humble.
Through her, you remember your mercy
as you promised to our fathers.

We pray to you:
Give us a soul of praise
that knows how to acclaim your marvels.
And with Mary, we will bless you
through your Son, Jesus, in the Holy Spirit,
forever and ever. Amen.

HOMILY

1. The Good News Proclaimed to the Poor

The exiles in Babylon had returned to their country, enraptured by the hopes with which the prophets had intoxicated them. They had been promised:

> They will arrive in Zion, shouting with joy,
> eternal happiness will transfigure their faces,
> gladness and joy will accompany them,
> sorrow and mourning will have ended. Is 35, 10

But the prophecies were delayed in being fulfilled. The Zionists found themselves exposed to the hostility not only of the neighboring nations, but even of the Jews who had remained in the country.[1] An anonymous prophet rose up to console them:

The Spirit of the Lord God is upon me,
for the Lord has anointed me.
He has sent me to bring the Good News to the poor,
to heal the brokenhearted,
to proclaim freedom to the captives,
and release to the prisoners,
to proclaim a year of favor from the Lord. Is 61, 1-2

Jesus, the Messiah of the Poor

We know this prophecy from the Book of Isaiah well. It is the dawn that gives light to the ministry of Jesus. After his baptism by John, Jesus went back to Nazareth. It was the day of the sabbath, Luke relates. Jesus went to the synagogue. After the reading of the Law, that is, of a section of the Pentateuch,[2] he arose to read the Prophets. He was given the scroll of Isaiah. He unrolled it and "found" the text which reads: "The Spirit of the Lord God is upon me..." He read it, then gave the scroll back to the sacristan. And while the eyes of everyone in the synagogue were fixed upon him, he said: "Today this Scripture is fulfilled in your hearing."[3]

Thus, according to Lucan tradition, the first words of Jesus in his first preaching is the affirmation that he is really the prophet invested by the Spirit of God to proclaim to the poor the Good News of their deliverance.

This tradition of Luke is confirmed by Matthew's tradition. Jesus begins the first of his great discourses, the Sermon on the Mount, with the beatitude of the poor:

Blessed are the poor in spirit,
for theirs is the Kingdom of heaven. Mt 5, 3

Jesus fulfilled the prophecy of the Book of Isaiah, but he surpassed it at the same time by realizing what the most foolish would not have even dared to dream. The prophet proclaimed "a year of grace from the Lord," a sabbatical year during which the slaves would find their freedom, during which the poor would find their goods.[4] But Jesus opens not a year; he opens an eternity of grace. Furthermore, he gives the kingdom to the poor.

We also note that when Luke cites Isaiah's text, he stops the prophecy just before the announcement of the "day of vengeance from God." He signifies in this way that the Good News of Jesus is not vengeance but grace offered to all. He saves the oppressed but also proposes the gospel to the oppressors. He frees the prisoners but does not imprison the jailers. He dries the tears of those who weep but does not make others cry. He is truly the joy of God on earth, the salvation offered to the whole world.

"Fulfilled in Your Hearing"

Now that the risen Lord has returned to his Father, who is going to fulfill the prophecy of the Book of Isaiah? Who is going to see to it that the word of Jesus remains true throughout the ages: "Today this scripture is fulfilled in your hearing?"

The fulfillment of the prophecy rests on each one of us. Vatican II teaches that "the holy people of God share in prophetic function of Christ."[5] Everyone who is baptized receives the Spirit of Jesus; everyone is sent to carry the Good News to the poor. And this question rises to the surface of our heart: Does my life proclaim the gospel to the poor? Is it Good News for those who find themselves in that extreme destitution brought on by not knowing that the love of God is upon them?

The Spirit has sent me to heal the brokenhearted. Is my presence serving those who are broken—broken simply because life has not shown itself to be sweet, because misfortune or wickedness has pursued them like the plague—healing presence for their heart?

The Spirit has sent me to proclaim freedom to captives, release to prisoners. There are many captives around me, prisoners who are locked in a distress worse than a dungeon, bound in prejudices worse than chains. Does the freedom that Christ gave me proclaim to them their deliverance? Does the Church appear to them as a land of freedom?

We must be the Good News of Christ for our brothers and sisters. But on the other hand we are also awaiting the full revelation of his gospel. Which one of us can claim that we do not need to be evangelized? We might phrase the question in this way: Jesus brings the Good News to the poor: Am I poor enough to be counted among those whom he evangelizes?

Jesus heals the brokenhearted: Has suffering broken my heart? Or rather: Has suffering opened my heart to the gospel? For it is not because we have a broken heart that we enter into the Kingdom but because suffering has opened our heart and has rendered it capable of welcoming God.

Jesus proclaims freedom to the captives: Am I persuaded that without Christ I remain in my chains, which are the limits of my mediocrity or the bonds of my sin?

The prophecy of Isaiah has now become our prayer: Count us, Lord, among your poor; send us your Son, Jesus, to heal the wound of our hearts. Also send your Holy Spirit so that our lives may be Good News for all those who walk with us toward your coming.

2. The Canticle of Mary (the Magnificat)

To the proclamation of the Good News that the prophet brings, the community responds:

> I delight with joy in the Lord,
> my soul exults in my God. Is 61, 10

This is the beginning of the Magnificat, the canticle of Mary. This canticle serves as the responsorial psalm this Sunday.

The Song of the Chosen People

We know the context of the Magnificat. After the Annunciation, Mary pays a visit to her relative Elizabeth, who is six months pregnant. As soon as Elizabeth hears Mary's greeting, she is filled with the Holy Spirit; the child she is carrying leaps in her womb, and she cries out:

> Blessed are you among women
> and blessed is the fruit of your womb! Lk 1, 42

The familiarity between the two women and also the elementary rules of propriety required that Mary congratulate Elizabeth, her elder and her kinswoman. Now, Mary does not have one word of congratulation to address to Elizabeth. She seems to be totally unaware of the grace that has befallen her. And she begins to sing her own canticle. This is a situation that raises a question:

I think, on my part, that Mary was a perfectly well-mannered and polite girl and that she surely congratulated Elizabeth. However, Luke did not transmit these congratulations to us. He wants to lead us, through the Magnificat, toward a larger horizon than that of the joy of two mothers.

People have sometimes made the poetic genius of Mary stand out. Her canticle is splendid poetry, revealing an intensely lyrical soul. But Rev. Lagrange makes an observation on this subject: "One does not find in the canticle any refined thought and, let us say it openly, no original image... Why attribute to Mary a profane superiority which her Son did not make a case for either?"[6]

The splendor of the Magnificat lies somewhere else. Mary really belongs to those biblical people whose minds, enriched by prayer, are capable of creativity. She composed a new canticle from formulas borrowed from the Old Testament. Her canticle is a bouquet of biblical texts: In ten verses are gathered together about twenty biblical citations[7] coming from the Pentateuch (Genesis and Deuteronomy), from the historical books (Samuel and Chronicles), from the prophetic books (Isaiah, Ezekiel, Micah, Zephaniah, Habakkuk) and from the wisdom books (Job and Sirach). The Magnificat is the most marvelous prayer that the Old Testament could have offered to the New. For in Mary, the Daughter of Zion it is, so to speak, the whole Old Testament that magnifies the Lord and welcomes its Savior. This Savior is Jesus, whom Mary carries within her.

Actually, there is a very nice play on words in the canticle, a play which was evident in the Hebrew and Aramaic texts and which, of course, disappeared in the Greek translation. "Jesus" means "Savior." In Aramaic, Mary says this:

> My soul exalts the Lord;
> my spirit exults in God, my Jesus.

That is, in this Savior that she is carrying in her womb. (What a grace it would be if all mothers could thus tremble with joy in God for the little child that they carry within them!) Thus, it is the whole Old Testament, with its joys and its pains, with its hopes and its deceptions, with its holiness and also with its sin, which emerges here and sings to its Savior.

The Song of the Earth

There is more, however. Israel is the first fruits of the nations,[8] but the first fruits are inseparable from the entire harvest. Israel is a "kingdom of priests, the treasured possession of God among all the peoples."[9] But people-priests are inseparable from the nations for whom they exercise their priesthood. In the song of Israel, therefore, it is all of humanity that acclaims Jesus, even if it does not know that the Savior of Israel is also its Savior.

Fulfilling the Prophecy

Filled with the Spirit, Mary prophesies:

From now on all generations
will call me blessed! Lk 1, 48

Each time we celebrate the praise of Mary, we fulfill the prophecy, we conform ourselves to God's will. "The concealment of Mary"[10]—as if it were necessary to hide the fact that Jesus was born from the womb of a woman!—and the omission of praise—as if it were unsuitable for a Church dominated by men to celebrate a woman—are all errors against scripture and therefore against God's will. Praise of Mary must have its place as much in our personal prayer as in the prayer of the Church.

What better way to fulfill the prophecy of Mary than to repeat her canticle of praise to God? Thus, we loan Mary our heart and our lips so that, through our heart and lips, she might continue to bless the God who does wonders for her.

Every evening, the Church ends its prayer by repeating the Canticle of Mary. Having become—through the Resurrection of Jesus—a "kingdom of priests for his God and Father,"[11] the Church expresses not only its own praise for the day that has just passed but also places once again the praise of all humanity at the feet of its Savior-God.

3. The Parousia of Our Lord Jesus Christ

A Time of Holiness

On the First Sunday of Advent, Paul told us that Christ himself would strengthen us so that we might be without blame on the day of the coming of the Lord. Last Sunday the author of the Second Letter of Peter invited us to live in such a way that Christ would find us without stain or blemish on the day of the new heavens and the new earth.[12] Today Paul comes back again to this theme in the First Letter to the Thessalonians:

May the God of all peace himself sanctify you completely.
May your whole being—spirit, soul, and body—
be kept blameless for the parousia
of our Lord Jesus Christ. 1 Thes 5, 23

The First Letter to the Thessalonians dates from near the year 50; it is among the first writings of the New Testament. The second writing, called the Second Letter of Peter, dates from the years 100-110; it is the among the last writings of the New Testament. Therefore, the theme that links holiness and the parousia of Christ marked the whole epoch of the first Christian generations. Holiness and purification are the paths that lead to the encounter with Christ.

A Time of Continual and Joyous Prayer

The time that precedes the parousia—the time in which we are living—is a time of continual and joyous prayer. Paul enjoins the Thessalonians:

> Be joyful always.
> Pray without ceasing.
> Give thanks at all times.
> That is God's will for you in Christ. 1 Thes 5, 15

Paul does not want to say that it is necessary to recite prayers at all times. We would soon be exhausted. The prayer according to the will of the Father is the continual joy of living in his presence.

It is in this way that Saint Francis de Sales (+1622) taught his dear friend Saint Jeanne de Chantal to pray:

> She used to pray freely, always ready to leave her orations as soon as one needed her; and she made up for these incomplete prayers, without scruples, by continual "returns to God" in imitation of Monsignor... The servants said among themselves: Madame's first guide (that is, spiritual director) only made her pray three times a day and we were all bored with it, but Monsignor of Geneva (that is, Francis de Sales) makes her pray at all hours and that does not disturb anyone.[13]

A Life of Prayer

Here is an old story. It is said that Peter took it from Isidore, who took it from Anselm, who took it from tradition...

At that time, there was a poor cowherd who kept cows high in the mountains. The higher he went up in the pastures, the more his blue eyes reflected heaven, for his heart always dwelled with God.

Sunday morning, when the jubilant ringing of the bells rose from the valley, he would kneel in the midst of his animals. And while his dog watched him, he prayed in this way: "Lord, my brothers in the valley are very lucky. Together they praise and bless you; they sing to you with organ and zither; they magnify you with candles and incense. And I, poor cowherd, have only the warbling of the swallows to offer you as music, only the scent of the edelweiss as incense, and the rustling of the wind in the pines as a zither. And for a homily, I hear only the silence of my heart. Then, Lord, listen to my prayer: If you have a cow to keep, entrust it to me. For you, I would watch it for free, the best that I can, because I love you. Amen."

A Roman theologian of great renown who, by chance, was passing by there—it was the time of his vacation—heard the prayer of the cowherd with blue eyes and a heart of gold. He said to him: "Dear friend, of course it is good to pray, but the prayer must conform to holy theology. For God, Creator of heaven and earth, who is pure Spirit, does not have any cows to keep." Then he taught him to pray theologically. He also showed him how to make an oration in three parts (thesis, antithesis, and synthesis). Finally, he advised him to learn by heart the songs of the *Gradual Simplex* that the gloriously reigning pope had asked all Christians to know by heart. Then he continued his excursion.

He had not arrived at the turn of the path when the cowherd with the heart of gold had forgotten everything. For a week, he no longer dared to pray. He thought: "Lord, the prayer that I knew was not good. And the one that is good I do not know!" And large tears flowed from his blue eyes. His dog, seeing him cry, licked his hands.

Sunday morning, when the chime of jubilant bells rose from the valley to celebrate the Day of the Lord, he knelt in the middle of the animals and murmured very low (so that no theologian might hear him): "Lord, if I dared to pray to you, I would say that if you had a cow to keep—or even several cows—for you I would keep them for free, simply because I love you. Amen."

Scripture says that "the prayer of the humble pierces the clouds."[14] The prayer of the poor cowherd went straight up before the throne of God. And God called his angels: "This Sunday morning, it is the prayer of the cowherd that I like the most. For others pray with words or canticles. He prays with his life." Today, there are still many cowherds who pray with their lives. There are also theologians who pray with their lives. The ideal is for prayer to express our lives, for our whole lives are prayers.

4. Christ In Our Midst

"John the Baptist appeared in the desert proclaiming a baptism of repentance for the remission of sins."[15] What did this baptism signify? Was it similar, for example, to the daily ritual ablutions that the members of the sect at Qumran practiced? "From Jerusalem, the Jews—" more precisely, some officials of Judaism—"sent priests and Levites to John the Baptist"[16] to open an inquiry. This inquiry about baptism immediately became focused on the person of John; then, it rebounded to the person of Jesus. From this inquiry came the questions: Who is John? Who is Jesus? What is the relationship between the two of them?[17]

Who is John?

The decisive question was: Would John not be the Messiah? The answer sprang forth clear as the dawn:

> John confessed, and he did not deny.
> he confessed: "No, I am not the messiah." Jn 1, 20

Two other hypotheses that were circulating among the people were likewise eliminated: No, John is not Elijah, whose coming, it was believed, must precede the coming of the Messiah. Neither is he the great prophet who, after long centuries of silence, has to make the voice of God heard again, and about whom Moses has said: "Yahweh your God will raise up for you in your midst, from among your brothers, a prophet like me to whom you will listen."[18]

The Lamp Which Burns and Shines

How then can we define the mission of the Baptist? He is the one who bears witness to the light:

> He came to bear witness,
> to bear witness to the light,
> so that all might believe through him.
> He was not the light,
> but he had to bear witness to the light. Jn 1, 7-8

In the psalm God had proclaimed: "I have prepared a lamp for my Christ." John is that "lamp which burns and shines" before the Messiah.[19]

The Voice Crying in the Desert

John is also a voice:

> I am the voice of one who cries in the desert:
> Prepare the way of the Lord. Jn 1, 23

We know this prophecy well. It accompanies us throughout Advent. It proclaims the return of the deported from Babylon. It is this new spiritual Exodus that the baptism of John prepares.

Who is Jesus?

The ministry of John explains the ministry of Jesus. If John is the lamp which burns and shines, Jesus is the Light of the World. If John is the voice which prepares the way of return, Jesus is the one who accomplishes it.

But at the heart of John's answer is the affirmation:

> Among you stands
> one whom you do not know. Jn 1, 26

This mysterious word on the hidden and unknown Messiah could be understood on different levels. On the one hand, John the Baptist could have been alluding to the popular belief that was circulating in the Jewish milieu that the Messiah, at the beginning of his life, would remain hidden for a certain time in the midst of his people.[20] Then he would reveal himself in his glory. Only then would people recognize him. In John's gospel, this was really the case of Jesus: He had remained hidden for thirty years, then manifested himself at the wedding in Cana, "He manifested his glory and his disciples believed in him."[21] But on the other hand, the word of John could also have a more profound significance, valid for the Christians of all ages. As long as this world lasts, the mystery of Jesus remains veiled. Only when he appears in the glory of the parousia, on the last day, will his mystery be fully manifested. While awaiting this day, he stands in our midst and we can affirm his mystery only in faith.

The word of John the Baptist on the hidden and unknown Messiah inspires our prayer today.

Jesus stands hidden in our midst under the features of the poor. When we share the bread of friendship with the poor, it is Christ whom we satisfy.

He stands in our midst amid the poverty of the least of our brothers and sisters. When we make them an offering of love, it is Christ whom we love.

Wherever there is someone to love, there is the unknown and hidden Christ to discover.

An *agraphon* (a word Jesus could have uttered, but which the gospels have not retained) says:

Wherever there are two,
they are not without God.
And where someone is alone, I say:
I am next to him.
Lift up a rock, and you will find me there.
Split a log, and I am there.[22]

Perhaps we sometimes seek Christ far away, unto the ends of the earth, when he is present in the silence of our heart.

Yes, Lord, you stand in the heart of life, which is so banal and at the same time so sublime. May we be able to recognize you!

In the heart of our joys and in the exasperation of our suffering, you stand, Lord. May we be able to welcome you!

In the heart of our weakness and our mistakes, you stand, Lord, like a call of forgiveness. May we be able to come back to you after each defeat!

In the very heart of our agonies, when we say: "Into your hands I commend my spirit," you stand, Lord, to welcome us. May we be able to offer ourselves to you!

In this way, Paul sums up the grace of the gospel that he proclaims to the nations: "Christ among us! The hope of glory."[23] May that day come when there will no longer be any hope of glory, but simply Christ among us! Amen.

CONCLUDING PRAYER

You stand, Lord, in our midst.
Help us recognize your presence,
and come to save us.

You are present, Lord, in your messengers
who proclaim the Good News to the poor.
You are also present, Lord, in the desire
of those who live in darkness
and who stretch out their hands to you in the night.

Come, Lord Jesus Christ!

You are present, Lord, in your messengers
who console those who mourn
and heal the brokenhearted.
You are also present, Lord, in the tears
of those who weep.

Come, Lord Jesus Christ!

You are present, Lord, in your messengers
who proclaim freedom to captives.
You are also present, Lord, in the chains
of those who are imprisoned for you.

Come, Lord Jesus Christ!

You are present, Lord, in the holiness
of those who prepare for your coming.
You are also present, Lord, in the prayer
of the sinner who implores your forgiveness.

Come, Lord Jesus Christ!

You are present, Lord, in the heart of the Virgin
when she sings your marvels.
You are also present, Lord, in our hearts
when we unite in her praise.

Come, Lord Jesus Christ!

You are in our midst, Lord,
and we are called by your name.
Do not forsake us.
Give us your Son, Jesus, our Savior, Amen.

NOTES TO THIRD SUNDAY OF ADVENT

1. See, for example, Neh 5.
2. Concerning the readings in the synagogal service, see L. Deiss, *God's Word and God's People* (Collegeville, MN: The Liturgical Press, 1976): 97–113.
3. Lk 4, 16–21. Gospel of the Third Sunday, Cycle C.
4. Sabbatical Year: Lv 25, 1–7 Jubilee Year: Lv 25, 10–17.
5. Constitution *Lumen Gentium*, 12.
6. M. J. Lagrange, *Evangile selon Saint Luc*, Coll. "Etudes Bibliques," 1927, p. 54.
7. R. E. Brown, *The Birth of the Messiah* (New York: Doubleday & Company, 1977): 358–360 gives 24 references (counting the apocrypha and the texts of Qumran). –R Laurentin, *Court Traité sur la Vierge Marie*, 5th ed. (Paris: Lethielleux, 1967): 199 gives 21 biblical references. I have analyzed the Magnificat myself in *Mary, Daughter of Sion* (Collegeville, MN:The Liturgical Press, 1972): 101–126. As for the origin of the Magnificat, people have also thought of a "very archaic Judeo–Christian canticle" to which Luke would have added v. 48. See P. Grelot, *Introduction à la Bible, Le Nouveau Testament*, 6 (Paris: Desclée de Brouwer, 1986): 194.
8. Rom 11, 16.
9. Ex 19, 5–6.
10. The expression comes from R. Laurentin, *Marie, Mère du Seigneur* (Paris: Desclée de Brouwer, 1986), p. 194.
11. Rv 1, 6
12. 1 Cor 1, 8. 2 Pt 3, 14.
13. M. Henry–Couannier, Saint Francois de Sales et ses amitiés (Paris: Monastère de la Visitation, 1979): 174.
14. Sir 35, 17 (Note: I regret that I cannot specify the origin of the story of "the cow to keep for God" and that I cannot place it in its true tradition.)
15. Mk 1, 4.
16. Jn 1, 19.
17. Conflicts had broken out in the past between the Johannites and the disciples of Jesus (Jn 3, 25–30.) Unknowns about the mystery of Jesus existed for a long time after the Resurrection (Acts 19, 1–7). Note: The gospel includes two sections: Jn 1, 6–8 and Jn 1, 19–28. It is generally thought that Jn 1, 6–7, which is actually read in the Prologue, was originally linked to Jn 1, 19. The arrangement of the Lectionary has borne this hypothesis in mind.
18. Dt 18, 18. This prophecy belonged to the Testimonia. See C. H. Dodd, *Conformément aux Ecritures*, pp. 55–57.
19. Ps 132, 17. Jn 5, 35.
20. Justin (+about 165), *Dialogue avec Tryphon*, 110.
21. Jn 2, 11.
22. Cited in J. Jeremias, *Les Parôles inconnues de Jésus*, Coll. "Lectio Divina," 62 (1970): 104. (See the remarks on the origin of the agraphon, pp. 105–109.)
23. Col 1, 27.

FOURTH SUNDAY OF ADVENT

Reading I 2 Sm 7, 1-5. 8-11. 16

A reading from the second book of Samuel

When King David was settled in his palace, and the Lord had given him rest from his enemies on every side, he said to Nathan the prophet, "Here I am living in a house of cedar, while the ark of God dwells in a tent!" Nathan answered the king, "Go, do whatever you have in mind, for the Lord is with you." But that night the Lord spoke to Nathan and said: "Go, tell my servant David, 'Thus says the Lord: Should you build me a house to dwell in?'

"'It was I who took you from the pasture and from the care of the flock to be commander of my people Israel. I have been with you wherever you went, and I have destroyed all your enemies before you. And I will make you famous like the great ones of the earth. I will fix a place for my people Israel; I will plant them so that they may dwell in their place without further disturbance. Neither shall the wicked continue to afflict them as they did of old, since the time I first appointed judges over my people Israel. I will give you rest from all your enemies. The Lord also reveals to you that he will establish a house for you. Your house and your kingdom shall endure forever before me; your throne shall stand firm forever.'"

The Word of the Lord.

Responsorial Psalm Ps 89, 2-3. 4-5. 27. 29

R/. (2) For ever I will sing the goodness of the Lord.

The favors of the Lord I will sing forever;
  through all generations my mouth shall proclaim your faithfulness.
For you have said, "My kindness is established forever";
  in heaven you have confirmed your faithfulness.

R/. For ever I will sing the goodness of the Lord.

"I have made a covenant with my chosen one,
  I have sworn to David my servant:
Forever will I confirm your posterity
  and establish your throne for all generations."

R/. For ever I will sing the goodness of the Lord.

He shall say to me, 'You are my father,
  my God, the Rock, my savior.'
Forever I will maintain my kindness toward him,
  and my covenant with him stands firm."

R/. For ever I will sing the goodness of the Lord.

READING II — ROM 16, 25-27

A reading from the letter of Paul to the Romans

To him who is able to strengthen you in the gospel which I proclaim when I preach Jesus Christ, the gospel which reveals the mystery hidden for many ages but now manifested through the writings of the prophets, and, at the command of the eternal God, made known to all the Gentiles that they may believe and obey—to him, the God who alone is wise, may glory be given through Jesus Christ unto endless ages. Amen.
The Word of the Lord.

GOSPEL — LK 1, 26-38

A reading from the holy gospel according to Luke

The angel Gabriel was sent from God to a town of Galilee named Nazareth, to a virgin betrothed to a man named Joseph, of the house of David. The virgin's name was Mary. Upon arriving, the angel said to her: "Rejoice, O highly favored daughter! The Lord is with you. Blessed are you among women." She was deeply troubled by his words, and wondered what his greeting meant. The angel went on to say to her: "Do not fear, Mary. You have found favor with God. You shall conceive and bear a son and give him the name Jesus. Great will be his dignity and he will be called the Son of the Most High. The Lord God will give him the throne of David his father. He will rule over the house of Jacob forever and his reign will be without end."

Mary said to the angel, "How can this be since I do not know man?" The angel answered her: "The Holy Spirit will come upon you and the power of the Most High will overshadow you; hence, the holy offspring to be born will be called Son of God. Know that Elizabeth your kinswoman has conceived a son in her old age; she who was thought to be sterile is now in her sixth month, for nothing is impossible with God."

Mary said: "I am the maidservant of the Lord. Let it be done to me as you say." With that the angel left her.

The gospel of the Lord.

INTRODUCTORY PRAYER

Blessed among women be the Virgin Mary!
Let all generations proclaim her blessed.
Amen.

Blessed be Jesus, the fruit of her love!
In him, God remembered his mercy
as he has promised to our fathers.
Amen.

Blessed be God our Father!
He makes us his adoptive children
in Jesus Christ, his only Son.

May all our lives endlessly bless his love.
To him be glory in the Church and Christ Jesus
for all generations and forever and ever.
Amen.

HOMILY A

1. The Founding Charter of the House of David

Sometimes through crafty covenants, sometimes through victorious wars, David had definitively triumphed over the arrogance of the Philistines, pushing them as far as their ancient districts on the coastal plain. Then he left Hebron—the capital of the state of Judah but too remote from the North—and chose Jerusalem as his capital. The old Jebusite city at that time was only a little town without importance; it had no past and therefore was not committed either to the "southerners" or the "northerners." David conquered it craftily with a handful of mercenaries and made it the "city of David." In order to confer more dignity upon it, he brought the Ark, formerly residing in the Canaanite city of Qiryat-Yearim, and installed it there in great honor. From then on, he governed from Jerusalem all the country situated between the "Great Sea" and the Euphrates, between the Entrance of Hamath and the Torrent of Egypt.

The time of the Exodus and endless wanderings was definitively closed at that time. Forgotten also was the anarchical period of the Judges when, according to the "off-hand comment" of the chronicler, "everyone did what seemed right to him in Israel."[1] Finally, Israel had entered into modern times. "The people set apart, who was not ranked among the nations,"[2] now possessed its monarchy in imitation of neighboring peoples. The new royal city was lacking only the religious center which would be the heart of the nation: The Temple.

The Construction of the Temple

Excavations in the Middle East have revealed a number of inscriptions on which kings boast of having built temples for their divinities. Ur-Bawa, prince of Lagas from 2155 to 2142, displays his piety in this way:

> I, Ur-Bawa, for Nin-Girsu, my master (he was the principal god of Lagas), have excavated the city of the temple... I packed together its earth like precious stones; I refined it in fire like precious metal... I made the ground of the foundation... I built for him [the temple of] E-ninnu.[3]

Ur-Bawa had, moreover, ecumenical piety. His devotion extended to a number of divinities of the Sumerian pantheon. He left us a litany of temples that he had built: For Nin-hursaga, the mother of the gods, the temple of Nin-Gursu; for Bawa, the gracious goddess of Lagas, the temple of the holy city; for Innana, the noble queen of heaven, the temple of Urub; for Enki, the god of wisdom and of magic, always well-disposed with regard to men, the temple of Girsu; for Nin-dara, the powerful god, a temple; for Nin-a-gala, his personal patron goddess, a temple; for Nin-kimara, the gracious goddess, the temple of his heart...[4]

Once the temple was built, it was enough for the king to place his own statue in it facing the divinity: It would present the royal prayers to the god, the god would hear him and the Kingdom would prosper:

> To (the goddess) Bawa, the gracious woman... the queen of the holy city... May the little statue, to which my mistress lends an ear, tell her my prayers![5]

Therefore, David's desire to construct a Temple for Yahweh is part of a long tradition. It is an honorable desire, even if political motives are involved. Once consulted, Nathan the court prophet, answers: "Go, do everything that you have in your heart, for Yahweh is with you."[6]

But that same night, the word of God was addressed to Nathan: "Go say to my servant David: Thus speaks Yahweh..." And everything is called into question. It is not David but Solomon who will build the Temple. And instead of David's project for God, Nathan reveals God's project for David.

This prophecy is considered the founding charter of the Davidic dynasty. The essential part of the prophecy rests on a play on words: It is not David who will build a House (i.e., the Temple) for Yahweh; it is Yahweh who will build a House (i.e., a dynasty) for David. With sovereign power the transcendent freedom of God is affirmed, to whom no one can assign a dwelling—as the pagan nations do with a vulgar Baal—but who chooses from the pasture, from "among the sheep," whom he wants, who accompanies him in all his ways, who keeps him in all dangers, who gives him victory in all battles, who builds himself the house that he wants with whom he loves, who fills it with his eternal favor, who affirms his throne "for eternity."[7]

Fulfillment of the Prophecy

Rare are the prophecies that are affirmed with such power and with such splendor. And yet the hope of humanity is one thing and its realization by God is another. From the death of Solomon in 933, the two sisters Oholah and Oholibah (the capitals of the Kingdom of the North and the Kingdom of the South[8]) separate and prostitute themselves, sometimes with Egypt and sometimes with Assyria and Babylon. Oholah, Samaria, the capital of the North, will fall under the assaults of Sargon II in 721. Oholibah, Jerusalem, the capital of the South, will succumb in 587. As for the Temple, it will no longer remain. As a reminder of it, we now have only the Wailing Wall, whose origin is uncertain and before which we see the Jewish community weep.

And yet, God does not forget his promise. He renews it about a thousand years later to a young Galilean in Nazareth. In fact, one could say that the angel Gabriel will repeat, word for word, the message of Nathan to David:

Nathan to David, 2 Sm 7	Gabriel to Mary, Lk 1
The Lord is with you (3).	The Lord is with you (28)
He will be for me a son (14).	He will be called Son of the Most High (32)
His house and his kingdom will endure forever. His throne will be established forever (16)	He will reign forever. and His kingdom will have no end (33)

"Remember David," begged the psalm.[9] God remembered him in Mary, the daughter of David. Or rather, the prophecy is not simply "fulfilled;" it is surpassed infinitely—as much as Jesus surpassed David while being the son of David, as much as heaven surpasses earth while keeping it within bounds, as much as eternity surpasses time while including it, so much does the fulfillment surpass the promise.

The kingdom of David was to be stable "forever." In 587, it would fall forever. Its "eternity" would last four centuries. And the dynastic house that God had promised to build would soon, according to the words of the prophet Amos, be no more than a fallen tent.[10] But the Kingdom of Jesus is built for eternity.

The Temple built with such splendor, where the children of Israel used to gather together to praise Yahweh, would go down in flames at the same time as Jerusalem. But the new Temple built by Jesus is eternal; it is his risen body indwelt by the glory of heaven. All people are invited to live in it and to celebrate the Father in it.

David is called "son of God;" he shares the paternal love of God with all the righteous of the Old Testament. Jesus is the only Son; upon him rests the totality of God's love, and he allows his brothers and sisters to share in that plenitude. "From his plenitude we have all received grace upon grace."[11]

David is the "savior" of his people. Jesus is the Savior of the whole world. His salvation is eternal life.

The Prophecy of Nathan Today

What does Nathan's prophecy mean today? In order to go to God, why make the detour through David when we have direct access through Jesus, the Son of God? To state it more simply: What is to be done with the prophecy of Nathan in a homily?

By his incarnation as the Son of David, Jesus placed his divinity in the midst of humanity, a people who had become his brothers and sisters.

Without Christ, the Son of David, each time a child is conceived and given life as a "child of man," it is also called to die one day. Now, each time a child is conceived, it is a child of God, called to eternity by Jesus, who became our brother.

Without Christ, the Son of David, each time a person, through weakness or through malice, commits a sin, he or she is lost before God. Now a Savior stands next to them, a brother who takes them by the hand and pulls them up from their fall.

Without Christ, the Son of David, each time people build a temple to God, they remember at the same time that "the Most High does not live in dwellings made by human hands."[12] Now in Christ Jesus we have a Temple which has become our own dwelling, occupied for eternity by the glory of God.

Nathan's prophecy has now become our prayer. With the two blind men of Jericho, we implore: "Jesus, Son of David, have mercy on us![13] Touch the eyes of our heart. Let us see you! With the Canaanite woman who prayed to you for her daughter, we beg: "Have mercy on us![14] Drive the evil away from the hearts of our children!" With the children who acclaimed you in the Temple, we sing to you: "Hosanna to the Son of David![15] Let your reign come among us!" You say of yourself: "I am the Root and the Son of David, the radiant Morning Star!"[16] Make your dawn rise in the heaven of the Church!

What is Mary's place in the mystery of the Church? She is to the people of the New Covenant what she is to Christ: their mother.

2. The Mystery of God Revealed in Jesus Christ

The second reading contains the doxology which ends Paul's Letter to the Romans. It is a solemn and majestic text whose interlaced and tumultuous sentences follow each other like waves of the sea emptying onto the shores of God's glory.

Paul's letters were read in liturgical assemblies. Therefore it was natural, according to Jewish tradition, to end them with a doxology to which the community would assent through its "Amen." Paul could have borrowed some elements from the Jewish doxological tradition, enriching them with personal elements. Here is the literal translation of this doxology, with its own additional richness:

To the One who has the power to establish you,
according to my Gospel and the message of Jesus Christ;

according to the revelation of the mystery
enveloped in silence in times eternal,
but manifested now
through prophetic writings;

according to the command of the eternal God,
made known to all the nations
to lead them to the obedience of faith;

to the only wise God, through Jesus Christ,
to him be glory forever. Amen. Rom 16, 25-27

Jesus revealed the mystery that inhabited the silence of eternal times. The nations are invited now to offer to God the obedience of their faith. The time has now come to praise God, to glorify his wisdom. By having us read this doxology on Christmas Eve, while "we await the new heavens and the new earth where justice will dwell,"[17] the Church reminds us that the time of our Advent, the time of our life which precedes eternity, is a time of praise and blessing of God.

The Quality of our Waiting

The quality of our waiting is the quality of our praise to God.

About thirty of us were at the train station waiting for the train to Paris-St. Lazare.

There are those who wait for the train, but who do not wait for anything else in their life. In the morning, they wait for the evening; in the evening, they wait for the morning. Their life is like the wheel in a squirrel cage. The squirrel turns the wheel unceasingly, but it never moves towards freedom.

There are those who simply wait for their pleasure. But can pleasure fill a human life? And what deceptions! Jesus speaks about the heart which "is weighed down in debauchery, in drunkenness, and the cares of life," while the Day of the Lord comes upon them "like a trap."[18]

There are those who think they have everything and, therefore, do not wait for anything more. There were two lovers on the train platform. Whether the train came or did not come, whether it arrived on platform A or B or on another platform, late or on time, it was all the same to them since they were together.

I thought about the immense crowd of my brothers and sisters who, since the origins of humanity, have been on a pilgrimage to God. Some, their eyes riveted on earth, no longer see the brightness of heaven. Their ears, surfeited with the music of the world, no longer hear the call of God. May the mercy of the Lord be revealed to them at the end of the journey! May it welcome them to the eternal feast!

For Christians, there is no dead time, no empty day. Each moment of our life is filled with praise to God in the joy of waiting, in the vigilance of love. We are so close to seeing God! We are so close to finally discovering the splendor of his face. We beseech:

> Who will make us see goodness?
> Let the light of your face shine upon us. Ps 4, 7

That is why our waiting is filled with praise to God. Amen.

NOTES TO FOURTH SUNDAY OF ADVENT - HOMILY A

1. Jgs 21, 25.
2. Nm 23, 9.
3. Inscriptions royales sumériennes et akkadiennes, Coll. *"Littératures anciennes du Proche Orient,"* 3 (Paris: Editions du Cerf, 1971), p. 115.
4. Inscriptions royales, pp. 115–116.
5. Inscription of Nam–mahami (2113, 2111), son–in–law of Ur–Bawa. *Inscriptions royales*, p. 120.
6. 2 Sm 7, 3.
7. 2 Sm 7, 8–17.
8. Ez 23.
9. Ps 132, 1.
10. Am 9, 11.
11. Jn 1, 16.
12. Acts 7, 48.
13. Mt 20, 30–31.
14. Mt 15, 21–22.
15. Mk 11, 9–10. Mt 21, 9, 15.
16. Rv 22, 16.
17. 2 Pt 3, 13.
18. Lk 21, 34–35.

HOMILY B

The Annunciation

Luke 1, 26-38

The account of the Annunciation is among the most popular in Luke's gospel. And yet, in spite of twenty centuries of meditation and exegetical examination, it is always maintains a certain mystery. Of course, there is first the mystery of Mary's heart. Who can claim to understand its richness? There is also the very text of Luke and its biblical deep-rootedness. In reality, when Matthew cites Scripture, he emphatically underlines it through phrases such as "All this took place to fulfill the word the Lord uttered through the prophet."[1] In Matthew, therefore, one is clearly warned. But when Luke cites Scripture, he does it in an allusive manner. Whoever knows the Bible well, especially in its Greek translation, recognizes the quotation. Whoever does not know it, passes it by. One reads and understands the text, but not as Luke wrote it and understood it.

This allusive method lays the foundation of the richness of the Lucan text. It also creates a certain ambiguity: One can discover in this biblical milieu many or few allusions.

In order to understand the text, we do not have a choice. We must take Luke's path. May the Spirit of Jesus, who was with the Virgin at the Annunciation, guide us on the road; may we be introduced to the wondrousness of the mystery of Jesus and of his mother.

Introduction

Where does this account come from? Obviously from Mary. She alone could have spoken about this experience so strictly personal to her.

We can reasonably think that she shared it with Joseph. When? We do not know. We cannot imagine such a perfect couple—perfect because they were chosen by God!—concealing from each other the mystery that constituted the heart of their love. But Joseph does not say a single word in the Gospels. He is simply, in a sublime way, the Righteous, the Obedient, the Silent One.

From whom does Luke get this account? We do not know that either. He simply says to us that he made his personal inquiry into the sources.[2] A pre-

Lucan text could have existed. We know that Mary participated in the birth of the Church of Pentecost and that she had an excellent memory, since she kept all her memories in her heart.[3] That is all that we can assert.

Here is a naive question: In what language did Gabriel speak to Mary? In Aramaic, of course, with, I imagine, a touch of the Galilean accent that was recognized so well in Jerusalem.[4] But Luke wrote in Greek. And it is precisely in Greek that Gabriel shows great mastery. From the first two words of his message, he makes a superb alliteration: *"Chaire, Kecharitômènè,"* "Rejoice, Full of grace." This alliteration could not exist in Aramaic. Besides, Luke knows perfectly well that the Palestinian "good day" is not the Greek "Rejoice" but the Hebrew "Peace," "Shalom."[5] What can we conclude? Luke works from an Aramaic source but he makes it his own with his literary and, undoubtedly, theological stamp.[6]

Therefore, we do not have a mechanical reproduction of dialogues. We have something better: a gospel. And this gospel had to correspond to that image which the early community who had known Mary had kept of her.

As in every good story, Luke begins by situating the characters:

> The angel Gabriel was sent by God into a village of Galilee by the name of Nazareth, to a virgin betrothed to a man by the name of Joseph, of the house of David. And the name of the virgin was Mary. Lk 1, 26-27

The Angel Gabriel

The word angel is the transliteration of the Greek *aggelos,* which means messenger. Angels are the ordinary messengers of divine revelations. They manifest the transcendence and mystery of God at the same time.

In the announcement to Zechariah, Gabriel presents himself in this way: "I am Gabriel; I stand before God. I have been sent to speak to you and to tell you this Good News." Formerly, Gabriel had already known how to explain to Daniel the meaning of his difficult visions.[7] The Jewish tradition thought that his special mission was to guard the entrance of Paradise and to pray for humanity.

When Luke writes that Gabriel "entered" to Mary, no visual representation of the scene is possible; Luke simply means that Gabriel brings Mary the divine message.

Mary

Mary is presented as betrothed to Joseph. In the Jewish milieu, betrothal signified that the marriage was definitively concluded but that the girl had not yet been introduced into the house of her husband. She was, however, considered married. The breaking of the engagement would have involved divorce and, in the case of the death of her fiancée, she would have been considered a widow.

How old could Mary have been at the time of the Annunciation? In Palestinian tradition at the time of Christ, girls were ordinarily engaged between twelve and twelve and a half years of age. The fiancée was led into the house of her husband about one year later. Therefore, God had decided to place the future of the salvation of the world into the hands of a girl approximately thirteen years old!

Joseph

Joseph is presented here as being of the house of David. His marriage to Mary will assure, before the law, the Davidic ancestry of Jesus.

Joseph's humility is extreme. He does not intervene in any way in Luke's account. He is simply the husband who loves with a perfect love the one woman on earth most loved by God.

What age could Joseph have been when he took Mary into his home? Some traditions liked to consider Joseph as very old. He has been portrayed as a patriarch bent under the weight of years, an old man to whom the Virgin was entrusted like a child. The tradition called "Arabic History" made Joseph the Carpenter as much as ninety years old! That allowed an easy explanation of the perpetual virginity of Mary! In reality, according to the law, the marriageable age of boys was thirteen years and one day. It was said that God, from his throne on high, watched men to see when they took a wife. If someone was not married at twenty, God said: "Let his bones be scattered!"[9] We can legitimately suppose that in the case of the marriage of Joseph and Mary—a marriage arranged by God!—the husband and wife were well-suited to each other.

Nazareth

At the time of the Gospels, Nazareth was a locality without a biblical past, without political prestige. People asked: "Can anything good come out of Nazareth?"[10]

2. The Daughter of Zion

Joy To You, Full of Grace

Gabriel said to Mary:

> Joy to you, Full of grace!
> The Lord is with you. Lk 1, 28

At the root of the message of the Annunciation is the prophecy of Zephaniah. We have here one of the summits of those allusive citations so peculiar to Luke. Here are the parallels:

Zephaniah 3, 14-18	Luke 1, 28-33
Rejoice, Daughter of Zion, The Lord, the king of Israel, is in you.	Rejoice, Full of Grace, The Lord is with you.
Do not fear, O Zion	Do not fear, Mary.
The Lord is in your womb, the king of Israel, a valiant Savior.	You will conceive in your womb… He will reign. You will give him the name of Jesus (=Savior).

In the symbolism of the Old Testament, the Daughter of Zion represents the community of the Covenant, the fiancée of Yahweh.[11] In the New Testament, the mystery of the Daughter of Zion is continued in the Church, "pure virgin betrothed to Christ."[12] What was said formerly in a general way of the Daughter of Zion is now said in a personal way of Mary. In the moment of the Annunciation, she is the purest and the deepest realization of the mystery of the Church. And what was said of old to the Daughter of Zion and then to Mary, is said today to the entire Church, the heiress of the promises made to the Daughter of Zion and realized in Mary.

Rejoice! The first word is an invitation to messianic joy. The first effect of the coming of Christ is the joy of God on earth. Let us note that the angels in Luke's Gospel are especially joyful; the first words spoken to the shepherds of Bethlehem will likewise be a message of joy: "I announce to you a great joy!"[13]

Full of grace. Before people, the name of the Virgin was Mary, Miriam in Hebrew, Maria in Greek. Before God, her name was *Kecharitôménè*, that is "favored with (divine) grace." The word *Kecharitôménè* is the perfect passive participle of the verb *charitoun*, which means "to fill with grace," *charis*. The word *charis* means favor, benevolence, but also beauty (as one says that a girl is gracious); it sometimes also means joy. The passive perfect indicates a permanent state. How can all that be translated with one word? Gabriel explains: "You have grace with God." Mary comments: "He has cast his eyes on the humility of his servant,"[14] as if she were saying that God had regarded her, the little Galilean, with eyes of love, of beauty, and of joy. We can keep the traditional "full of grace" by remembering that Mary shares in the plenitude of grace which belongs to the only Word, "full of grace and truth."[15]

"The Lord is with you." The formula is familiar in the Old Testament, especially in the accounts of vocation. It signifies that God helps the one whom he calls with work to be done. Thus, God is with Isaac when he renews the Covenant at Beersheba; he is with Jacob at Bethel, next to the heavenly ladder; he is with Moses so that he might lead the people of the Exodus; he is with Gideon when he calls him to deliver his people from the oppression of the Philistines; he is with Jeremiah when he says, as he does to Mary, "Do not be afraid. I am with you."[16]

We understand at the same time with what plenitude of presence God is with Mary and to what point this grace is personal to her. Indeed, what can happen that is more personal to a young woman than to be pregnant? In this way God is with Mary, that he lives truly "in the womb" of the Daughter of Zion.

Upon reading the account of the Annunciation, we read the account of our own vocation. Each dawn that rises on us is a word of God which says to us: "Rejoice! Let your life be praise of the glory of the grace that I give to you in Christ!"[17] Each event, including each suffering, is a message: "Do not be afraid! I am with you as I was with Mary, all the days, until the end of the world!"[18] Even each persecution is an invitation to receive the Spirit: "The Spirit of glory, the Spirit of God, rests upon you!"[19] Each day is an annunciation.

3. The Virginal Conception

Mary's Question

Mary is quite overwhelmed at the words of the angel and asks what that salutation means. Gabriel then announces to her that she will conceive a son:

> You will call him by the name of Jesus.
> He will be great and will be called the son of the Most High.
> The Lord God will give him the throne of his father David.
> He will reign over the house of Jacob forever,
> and his kingdom will be without end. Lk 1, 31-33

Gabriel's message recaptures the essential part of Nathan's prophecy. We talked about it earlier.

Mary asks Gabriel:

> How will this be
> since I do not know a man? Lk 1, 34

In biblical vocabulary, "to know" is a euphemism for having had sexual relations. Actually, Mary had been given to Joseph in marriage. Thus, she could "know" him. Therefore, did her question have a meaning? What meaning?

This has often been interpreted in the sense, if not of a vow, at least of a commitment to virginity. She would have said: "I do not know a man" to affirm the state in which she decided to remain (as one says for example, "I do not smoke"). Mary—and Joseph—could have taken a commitment to virginity as the Essenes did at that time.

An immense and sometimes very beautiful body of literature exists around this question. Who would not want to glorify the mother of Jesus as they did in past centuries? But the true beauty of a text is its truth. What is the meaning of Mary's question, situated at the heart of her maternity?

A comparison with the celibacy of the Qumranians does not seem enlightening. In reality, that celibacy "did not have an ascetic goal of spirituality but a goal of ritual purity pushed to its extreme limit by generalizing the sexual prohibitions that the Law imposed on the priests before the fulfillment of their sacrificial functions."[20] The virginal conception of Jesus has nothing to do with the fear of any kind of ritual impurity. Such a fear is totally outside the horizon of Luke's gospel.

On the other hand, a commitment to virginity on behalf of Mary would manifest an autonomy that the girls of her time did not have. In Israel, a girl did not do whatever she wanted. She was always under the power of a man, either her father if she were not yet married or her husband if she were. In any case, it was her father who decided her marriage, who gave her to a man as a wife. Scriptures advised: "Give your daughter in marriage and you will have accomplished a great work."[21] If Mary's father gave her to Joseph as a wife, it was not in the hope that she would remain a virgin but that she would assure him descendants. That at least is what one can reasonably deduce from Luke's text.

It has sometimes also been thought that Mary, having decided to remain a virgin, would oppose her commitment to virginity to the grace of the maternity that is offered to her. That allowed the ascetic milieu to say: "Look at Mary: she prefers to remain a virgin rather than to become the mother of Jesus, if she had to lose her virginity in that way." But how could we suppose for one instant that Mary, so humble and so submissive, would have opposed her personal will to God's will?

Mary's question: "How will this be?" actually places us at the heart of her dialogue with God. And the heart of that dialogue is revealed to us by her answer, which terminates the scene of the Annunciation: "I am the servant (literally: the slave) of the Lord!" Mary is completely at the disposal of God's will for her. She understands very well that the angel has told her that she is going to conceive her child at that very moment. Therefore, she asks how this can be done since she does not presently know a man. The form of the verb, *ou gignosko*, "I do not know," is in the present tense. How can she reconcile the maternity offered to her now with her actual condition of being a wife, though still a virgin and with her situation of being a fiancée not yet living with her husband?

A simple and luminous explanation was proposed in the Middle Ages by Cajetan (1480-1547). It is being used at the present time by excellent authors.[22] It respects the text perfectly and gives it a perfectly normal meaning. It also reveals that the essential point for Mary is not to live in marriage nor to remain a virgin but to fulfill God's will: She is his servant. More than virginity, more than marriage, even more than maternity, what constitutes the summit of her religion is this total obedience to God's will.

It is precisely in this obedience that she became the mother of Jesus and the wife of Joseph while remaining what tradition will call love to call the *Aeiparthenos,* the Always-Virgin.[23]

The Holy Spirit Will Come Upon You

The angel answers Mary:

> The Holy Spirit will come upon you
> and power of the Most High will overshadow you.
> And this is why the holy child which will be born of you
> will be called the Son of God. Lk 1, 35

Luke liked to associate the words spirit and power. Thus, he says of John that he will precede the Lord with "the spirit and power of Elijah." He also affirms that Jesus "had been anointed with the Holy Spirit and power."[24] In the text of the Annunciation, the words spirit and power designated first the breath and strength of God coming upon Mary. After the Resurrection of Jesus and the gift of the Holy Spirit at Pentecost, the Christian community could see in it the coming of the Holy Spirit upon Mary at the Annunciation.

The power of the Most High overshadows Mary. Luke seems to evoke the coming of the glory of the Lord over the Ark of the Covenant:

Exodus 40, 35	Luke 1, 35
The cloud overshadows *(episkiazein)* the tabernacle. The glory of the Lord fills the dwelling.	The power of the Most High will overshadow *(episkiasei)* you. What will be born from you will be called Holy, the Son of God

Mary appears here as the New Testament's Ark of the Covenant. Just as the Ark was filled with the divine glory, Mary is filled with the presence of the Holy One, the Son of God.

The child is called "son of God," which is well-suited to the son of David according to the prophecy of Nathan. But after the Resurrection, the Christian community gave the title "Son of God" a new plenitude, the plenitude that Paul gives it when he affirms that Jesus "was established Son of God with power, according to the Spirit of holiness, through his resurrection from the dead."[25]

Daughter of Abraham

In biblical mentality, a child is the fruit of the blessing of God's love which rests upon the union of a man and a woman. That is the reason that the story of the people born from Abraham, a people innumerable as the grains of sand on the seashore and the stars in the sky, begins with the sterility of Sarah, Abraham's wife; the sterility of Rebecca, Isaac's wife; and the sterility of Rachel, Jacob's wife. One could not signify in a better way that a child is a gift from heaven.

When Sarah, old and barren, receives the announcement of the birth of Isaac and asks, "Can I really give birth while I am old?" God answers her that nothing is impossible for him. This is the word that Gabriel repeats to Mary. Here is the parallel between the two texts:

Genesis 18, 14 (Septuagint)	Luke 1, 37
It is not impossible for God a word.	Will not be impossible for God any word.

The fruitfulness of Mary the virgin is situated in a straight line from the fruitfulness of Sarah the sterile. The two children, Isaac and Jesus, are gifts from God, the Master of the impossible. Isaac is the marvelous child, born of Abraham and of the old age of Sarah; Jesus is the divine child, born of the Holy Spirit and of the virginity of Mary. In Mary, God remembers Abraham. She sings:

> The Almighty has done marvels for me. Lk 1, 49

And this power is the power of the mercy of God who, in Mary as in Abraham, triumphs over the impossible:

> He remembers his mercy
> as he had promised to our fathers,
> in favor of Abraham and his race, forever. Lk 1, 54-55

The Present Faith in the Virginal Conception

One ascertains in the Christian community, especially since the year 1960, a certain erosion of faith in the virginal conception.[26] I hesitate to speak about it, but one does not resolve a problem by hiding it in the dungeons of piety; neither does one stop an erosion by ignoring it. Our faith allows us to envision all difficulties with serenity.

Several factors have accelerated this erosion.

At the root, there was a somewhat superficial presentation of the mystery, as if the virginal conception was only a gynecological marvel proposed for our admiration, or further, as if it were more suitable, for reasons of aesthetic, that Jesus be born of a virgin.

There was also a lively and rapid devaluation of the estate of virginity in general. Virginity still had, if not the halo of a certain moral value, at least a value on the matrimonial market (which is still the case in some civilizations). In our society marked by the exaltation of sexuality and youthful cohabitation, virginity is no longer generally perceived as a value.

There is also a better regard for conjugal love and sexual relations. Those who make love cannot be reduced to the role of "begetters." Sexual relations can express beauty, even the purity of spiritual love. Why not between Joseph and Mary?

Finally, the effort of a certain theology sought to render the mystery more accessible. The virginal conception would only be a *théologoumenon*, a theological idea expressed under the form of an account. The idea to be expressed is that this child is the Son of God. The account that expresses this is the following: The conception of this Child was virginal. The idea would have created the account, but the account does not rest on any historical or biological fact.

I personally see no difficulty in admitting that if Jesus could have been born of a woman, the Virgin Mary, by the power of the Holy Spirit, he could have likewise been born of the love of a man and a woman, from Joseph and Mary, by the power of that same Holy Spirit. It is neither easier nor more difficult for the eternal Word to be incarnated in a non-fertilized human egg than in a fertilized human egg. But that is not the point. The only point is: What does Scripture say?

Neither Mark, who wrote the oldest Gospel, nor Paul, who exalts the lordship of the risen Christ so much, speaks to us about the virginal conception. Mark's readers simply learn that the mother of Jesus was called Mary, that his brothers were called James, Joses, and Simon and that he also had sisters whose names are not given to us.[27] If, in Mark's eyes, the virginal birth had been an important element of his Christology, and if he had known it, would he have omitted speaking about it? The question remains open.

We cannot conclude anything from Paul's silence either. Perhaps he knew about the virginal conception, but those of his writings which have come down to us never speak about it. He simply says that Jesus is "born of a woman, born under the Law,"[28] which places Mary on the side of the Jewish Law.

In Luke's gospel, even if one admits that the center of the account is not the virginity of Mary but the conception of Jesus, his incarnation into our humanity, the virginity of Mary seems to me a fact which is certain and cannot be overlooked. According to Luke, Jesus is born, as it is said in Greek, "by the Holy Spirit, of the Virgin Mary." He does not have a father according to the flesh. Joseph is simply his father, "according to what people believed," as it is said in the genealogy of Jesus.[29]

This fact is confirmed by the witness of Matthew who writes:

> Here is what was the generation of Jesus: his
> mother Mary, having been betrothed to Joseph,
> found herself with child by the Holy Spirit before
> they had lived together. Mt 1, 18

The sources of the Infancy Accounts of Jesus used by Matthew did not overlap the sources used by Luke. The least that we can affirm for certain is this: In the early community there was a firm tradition concerning the virginal conception of Jesus.

Spiritual Meaning of the Virginal Conception

Like all the mysteries of Christ, the virginal conception has multiple meanings. I will take up the following:

In biblical tradition, no child is conceived "naturally." A child is always the gift of God's love to human love, his blessing. This gift was signified in a sublime way when it blessed the virginity of Mary. How could a woman, all alone, give birth to a child of eternity? How could human weakness conceive the Son of David, whose Kingdom is eternal? How could a "slave" give birth to the Son of God? This child is truly going to be the sign of the Almightiness of God operating in the nothingness of humanity, the sign of the extreme humility of the little Galilean who welcomes the mercy of God.

Forget the thousand and one representations of the scene of the Annunciation—though some of these tableaux are pure masterpieces—where we see Mary adorned like a princess, draped in a robe studded with stars of gold, crowned with a halo of glory, and Gabriel with wings glowing in a whirlwind of light. Think not about a royal dwelling of stone but about a Galilean house made out of mud, one of those houses about which Jesus said that one could pierce the walls.[30] Imagine a simple and poor interior. Mary and Joseph count themselves among the poor; at the time of the Presentation of Jesus at the Temple, they offer the sacrifice of the poor.[31] It is in this decor that the story of Jesus, the Savior of the world, the King of the ages, the Lord of eternities, begins; it is in these surroundings that God engages in a dialogue with a girl of twelve to thirteen years of age! What a reversal of a situation in a society dominated by men, where one said, even in Christian assemblies: "As in all the churches of the saints, let the women be quiet in the assemblies."[32] They had to be quiet in the assemblies, but they dialogued with God on the subject of the salvation of the world! One did not find them a place in the "assemblies of the saints" except when being submissive to men, wearing a veil as a sign of submission "because of the angels,"[33](!) while here the angel Gabriel says to Mary that she is full of grace, filled with the love and the beauty of God. What an exaltation of the humble, what a fall of the powerful and of their thrones in a religion dominated by experts of the Law, the doctors of the Law, and the priests! They thought that they knew everything about God and the world; they uttered thoughts so deep that the people could not understand them, and here God takes the advice of a girl. He asks her to accept an invitation to work with him! What humility also on the part of God! In the Te Deum we pray "Non horruisti Virginis uterum" (You did not abhor the womb of a Virgin). Not only did he not abhor it, but he made it of the Temple of his glory. And the little Galilean, with a babushka on her head and dusty feet in her sandals, became the mother of the Eternal One!

The mystery which was realized once in the obscurity of Nazareth on the day of the Annunciation has become the law of Incarnation for all ages. Each day can become an Annunciation for us, when God comes to us in his Word and in the events of life. Each day he invites us in this way to welcome the Word in the cradle of our heart, to make it grow until the day of eternity. It is really about this daily annunciation that this prayer from the Letter of Ephesians speaks:

> May the Father, according to the riches of His
> glory, strengthen you with power according to
> His Spirit so that Christ may live in your hearts
> through faith. Eph 3, 16-17

May we, like Mary, be able to welcome the power of God in our weakness and his Holy Spirit in our heart of sin, to offer to God the humility of our obedience, to always worship his holy will, and to allow the Virgin of the Annunciation to repeat in us:

Here is the servant of the Lord.
May it be done to me according to your word.

Then Christ will be born in our hearts for eternity. Amen.

CONCLUDING PRAYER

From now on all generations
will call me blessed.

Rejoice, Virgin Mary!
The Lord is with you forever.
Truly the Lord has done marvels for you.
You are blessed among all women,
and blessed is Jesus,
the fruit of your love.

Pray for us, Mother of the Lord.

Rejoice, Full of grace!
The Lord has looked upon you with eyes of love.
You are blessed among all women,
and blessed is Jesus,
the fruit of your love.

Pray for us, Mother of the Lord.

Rejoice, Daughter of Zion!
You will conceive and give birth to a son.
You will give him the name Jesus,
for he will save his brothers and sisters from death.
You are blessed among all women,
and blessed is Jesus,
the fruit of your love.

Pray for us, Mother of the Lord.

Rejoice, Daughter of David!
God will give to your child the throne of David,
and the reign of his love will have no end.
You are blessed among all women,
and blessed is Jesus,
the fruit of your love.

Pray for us, Mother of the Lord.

Rejoice, Temple of God's glory!
The Holy Spirit will come upon you,
and the splendor of his light will fill your heart.
You are blessed among all women,
and blessed is Jesus,
the fruit of your love.

Pray for us, Mother of the Lord.

Rejoice, Mother of God!
The holy Child which will be born from you
will be called Son of God.
You are blessed among all women,
and blessed is Jesus,
the fruit of your love.

Pray for us, Mother of the Lord.

Rejoice, Daughter of Abraham!
For nothing is impossible for the love of God.
You are blessed among all women,
and blessed is Jesus,
the fruit of your love.

Pray for us, Mother of the Lord.

Rejoice, Servant of the Lord!
You became the mother of Jesus,
our Savior and our brother.
You are blessed among all women,
and blessed is Jesus,
the fruit of your love.

Pray for us, Mother of the Lord.

Lord Jesus, Son of the Virgin Mary,
you wanted all generations
to proclaim your mother blessed.
We also want to fulfill the prophecy
and sing the glories of your mother.
Accept our life as praise
offered in the service of our brothers and sisters,
through love for you, Jesus,
Son of Mary, our Savior and our brother. Amen.

NOTES TO FOURTH SUNDAY OF ADVENT - HOMILY B

1. Mt 1, 22–23 citing Is 7, 14.
2. Lk 1, 3.
3. Lk 2, 19. 51. Acts 1, 14.
4. Mt 26, 73.
5. Lk 10, 5; 24, 36.
6. Lk 1, 19.
7. Dn 8, 15–16; 9, 20–27.
8. H. Schurmann, *Das Lukas Evangelium*, Coll. "Herders theologischer Kommentar zum Neuen Testament," III, 1, 1969, pp. 42–43.
9. Strack–Billerbeck, *Kommentar*, vol. 2, pp. 146 and 374.
10. Jn 1, 46.
11. The literature on the Annunciation is immense. I would point out R. Laurentin, *Les Evangiles de l'Enfance du Christ*, (Paris: Desclé at Desclée de Brouwer, 1982). *Mary in the New Testament* (Philadelphia: Fortess Press; New York; Paulist Press. Toronto: Ramsey, 1978). I myself have analyzed the Annunciation in *Mary, Daughter of Zion*, pp. 54–126.
12. 2 Cor 11, 2.
13. Lk 2, 10.
14. Lk 1, 30. 48.
15. Jn 1, 14.
16. Gn 26, 24; 28, 13–16. Ex 3, 12. Jgs 6, 16. Jer 1, 6–8.
17. Eph 1, 6.
18. Mt 28, 20.
19. 1 Pt 4, 14.
20. P. Grelot, *Introduction à la Bible, Le Nouveau Testament*, 6 (Paris: Desclée, 1986): 219. The study on the account of the Annunciation (pp. 187–224) is remarkable.
21. Sir 7, 25.
22. P. Grelot, Introduction, p. 218.
23. The title appears for the first time at the beginning of the fourth century in the writings of Pierre d'Alexandrie (+311), PG 18, 517. B.
24. Lk 1, 17 and Acts 10, 38.
25. Rom 1, 4–5.
26. See the excellent expose of R. Laurentin in the Bulletin de la Société Francaise d'Etudes Mariales (Paris: 222 Faubourg St. Honore, 1981): 36–66.
27. Mk 6, 3.
28. Gal 4, 4. It has been proposed to see in Jn 1, 13 an allusion to the virginal birth by reading: "He (=Jesus) who was born…" (instead of; "Those who are born." See R. Laurentin, *Les Evangiles de l'Enfance*, pp. 480–482. But this reading does not assert itself in a certain manner.
29. Lk 3, 23. Twice in Lk 1, 27 Mary is spoken about as a virgin. Perhaps Luke is remembering the Virgin who gives birth according to the Greek text of Is 7, 14? But the word *parthenos*, "virgin," can signify more simply the situation of Mary who had not yet been introduced into the house of Joseph. In the vocabulary of the Septuagint, *parthenos*, "virgin," keeps a certain ambiguity. Thus Dinah is called a virgin even though she had been violated by Shechem, Gn 34, 11–12.

30. Mt 6, 19.
31. Lk 2, 24 and Lv 5, 7
32. 1 Cor 14, 33–34. This text is presently considered as an interpolation. But the spirit of the text still remains present in the Church. See the remarks of J. M. Aubert, *Dichotomie sexuelle, antiféminisme et structures d'Eglise*, in Le Supplément, 161 (1987): 53–62.
33. 1 Cor 11, 10.

CHRISTMAS

MASS AT MIDNIGHT

Reading I — Is 9, 1-6

A reading from the book of the prophet Isaiah

The people who walked in darkness
  have seen a great light;
Upon those who dwelt in the land of gloom
  a light has shone.
You have brought them abundant joy
  and great rejoicing,
As they rejoice before you as at the harvest,
  as men make merry when dividing spoils.
For the yoke that burdened them,
  the pole on their shoulder,
And the rod of their taskmaster
  you have smashed, as on the day of Midian.
For every boot that tramped in battle,
  every cloak rolled in blood,
  will be burned as fuel for flames.

For a child is born to us, a son is given us;
  upon his shoulder dominion rests.
They name him Wonder-Counselor, God-Hero,
  Father-Forever, Prince of Peace.
His dominion is vast
  and forever peaceful,
From David's throne, and over his kingdom,
  which he confirms and sustains
By judgment and justice,
  both now and forever.
The zeal of the Lord of hosts will do this!

The Word of the Lord.

Responsorial Psalm — Ps 96, 1-2. 2-3. 11-12. 13

R/. (Luke 2, 11) Today is born our Savior, Christ the Lord.

Sing to the Lord a new song;
  sing to the Lord, all you lands.
Sing to the Lord; bless his name.

R/. Today is born our Savior, Christ the Lord.

Announce his salvation, day after day.
  Tell his glory among the nations;
Among all peoples, his wondrous deeds.

R/. Today is born our Savior, Christ the Lord.

Let the heavens be glad and the earth rejoice;
  let the sea and what fills it resound;
  let the plains be joyful and all that is in them!
Then shall all the trees of the forest exult.

R/. Today is born our Savior, Christ the Lord.

They shall exult before the Lord, for he comes;
  for he comes to rule the earth.
He shall rule the world with justice
  and the peoples with his constancy.

R/. Today is born our Savior, Christ the Lord.

Reading II — Ti 2, 11-14

A reading from the letter of Paul to Titus

The grace of God has appeared, offering salvation to all men. It trains us to reject godless ways and worldly desires, and live temperately, justly, and devoutly in this age as we await our blessed hope, the appearing of the glory of the great God and of our Savior Christ Jesus. It was he who sacrificed himself for us, to redeem us from all unrighteousness and to cleanse for himself a people of his own, eager to do what is right.

The Word of the Lord.

Gospel **Lk 2, 1-14**

A reading from the holy gospel according to Luke

In those days Caesar Augustus published a decree ordering a census of the whole world. This first census took place while Quirinius was governor of Syria. Everyone went to register, each to his own town. And so Joseph went from the town of Nazareth in Galilee to Judea, to David's town of Bethlehem—because he was of the house and lineage of David—to register with Mary, his espoused wife, who was with child.

While they were there the days of her confinement were completed. She gave birth to her first-born son and wrapped him in swaddling clothes and laid him in a manger, because there was no room for them in the place where travelers lodged.

There were shepherds in the locality, living in the fields and keeping night watch by turns over their flocks. The angel of the Lord appeared to them, as the glory of the Lord shone around them, and they were very much afraid. The angel said to them: "You have nothing to fear! I come to proclaim good news to you—tidings of great joy to be shared by the whole people. This day in David's city a savior has been born to you, the Messiah and Lord. Let this be a sign to you: in a manger you will find an infant wrapped in swaddling clothes." Suddenly, there was with the angel a multitude of the heavenly host, praising God and saying,

"Glory to God in high heaven,
peace on earth to those on whom his favor rests."

The gospel of the Lord.

INTRODUCTORY PRAYER

Glory to God in the highest of heavens;
peace on earth to all of us
on this Feast of Christmas!

God, our Father in heaven, loves us.
He manifests to us his goodness and his tenderness this day
by giving us his Son Jesus
to be our Savior and brother.
He instills in the hearts of those who seek him
the love and joy of the Holy Spirit.

Yes, glory to our Father in heaven
for his Son Jesus born among us, a child in time,
in the love of the Holy Spirit
forever and ever. Amen.

HOMILY

For those who believe, as well as for those who do not, Christmas is the most popular, the most loved, and the most awaited feast. A whole folklore accompanies it: the Christmas tree, the lights, the gifts. For Catholics there is also this Mass at the heart of this night, the entrance into the warm church radiant with light, the discovery of the crèche, the ox, the donkey, the sheep, the shepherds, Mary and Joseph, and we see the child Jesus placed in the crèche under the gaze of the star.

Christmas is a rest stop of joy in our fastidious ascension toward the summit of a mountain. It is an oasis of peace in the desert of our life.

Since God gives us this joy, we welcome it very simply—even with its folklore—as a sign of his tenderness. We receive it as a child accepts a gift, without asking questions. We will always have the time to confront real problems, to ask ourselves what mountains we are climbing, to look at what desert we are crossing. These are problems that only this child, born for us on this holy night, can resolve.

1. The Epiphany of Love

Mary and the newborn babe, the crèche, the shepherds and the angels; this is Christmas according to the Gospel of Luke. Now Luke lived with Paul; he was his companion on the missionary journeys.[1] Together they experienced fatiguing apostolic walks from one Christian community to another, through thousands of dangers—"dangers from rivers, dangers from bandits, dangers in the city, dangers in the desert," recalls Paul.[2] Together they patiently endured interminable hours on sailboats which advanced at the mercy of the wind, sailing into port at cities whose names we hardly know (such as Assos, Mitylene and Chios).[3] It seems unimaginable that during those long hours of familiarity, Luke would never have spoken to Paul about the birth of Jesus, about Mary his mother, about Joseph the carpenter. It seems likewise unimaginable that Paul would never have had the curiosity to ask questions about what had become the heart of his life. Paul does not speak anywhere about the birth of Jesus. When he presents the mystery of Christmas, he strips it down in order to show only the essential part of this mystery, which is also its most sublime point: Christmas is the epiphany of God's love on earth. In the Letter to Titus, which has the honor of being the second reading for Mass at Midnight and Mass at Dawn, it is said:

> Appeared (*épéphanè*) the grace of God
> for the salvation of all people. Ti 2, 11
>
> Appeared (*épéphanè*) the goodness of God our Savior
> and his love for all people. Ti 3, 4

How prodigious, Lord Jesus, is your incarnation on earth! How marvelous your unbelievable entrance into human history! How radiant is your entry into the life of all those men and women who, for hundreds of centuries, have prepared your body, your heart, your mind, your spirit and your soul!

Such a long time was needed for the first rose to be born from the heart of the soil and to open its astonishing petals at the light of the first morning! Such a long time was needed for the first doe to leap with her fawn through the savannah in bloom! Such a long time was needed for the first human body to rise from the dust of the earth!

In 1974, the American Donald Johanson discovered in Ethiopia the skeleton of a young woman who had lived about three and one-half million years ago.[4] She was about one meter tall and weighed about thirty kilos. He called her Lucy. Lucy belongs to our ancestors.

Let us take her as a symbol of our prehistory. A path of three and one-half million years was needed to come from Lucy to Jesus, to come from that little woman to the epiphany of God's love in the child of Bethlehem!

Every time a man, at the dawn of humanity, smiled at his Lucy, it was your smile, Lord Jesus, that he was preparing in our midst.

Every time a man, three or four million years ago, shared the fruits of his hunt or his gathering with his Lucy and his children, it was your love, Lord Jesus, that he was proclaiming at the beginning of all love, your love which is resplendent today with the light of heaven.

Every time a man embraced the body of his Lucy with arms of tenderness, every time he caressed his children, it was your tenderness, Lord Jesus, that he was prophesying, you who loved to caress the little children and bless them in the arms of their mothers.

Every time he joined together with his Lucy in the joy of love, it was your body, Lord Jesus, that he was preparing, you who became like us in all things except sin. How many gestures of love between a man and a woman were needed to finally give birth to your body, the sublime sign of God's love among us? In you, the love of men and women knew its divine fruit.

Qoheleth, in his bitter and disenchanted refrain, claimed: "There is nothing new under the sun!" This day, Qoheleth is found to be a liar. Today, there is an unheard proclamation of newness: Eternity has entered into time; the Creator is joined to his creation; Lucy, the daughter of our earth, after three or four million years, has given birth, through the Virgin Mary, to a child of heaven. The hands of this child, with fingers more fragile than twigs, will be the hands which will imprison the stars. His eyes, now closed in slumber, will shine on the day of judgement like blazing fire; his face will shine more brightly than the sun;[5] his mouth, a rosebud which now rests on the bosom of Mary, will be the mouth which will pronounce the eternal judgement of life or death over the nations. God has come among us.

And this God, Paul tells us, is a God of love.

The Divinization of Humanity

Tradition has repeated around the crèche of Jesus this refrain, with a thousand variations: God was made man so that man might become God, or "God is in man, and man is in God."[6] Saint Athanasius (295-373) explains:

> When the humanity of Jesus is born of Mary, the mother of God, it is our birth that Jesus takes in himself. Therefore, we are no longer simply of the earth who must return to the earth; we are united to the Word of heaven who must lead us to heaven...
>
> The Word took a body; he became human. Thus we, taken by the flesh of the Word, are deified through him; we become heirs of eternal life.[7]

Gregory of Nazianzen (about 329-390) explains very nicely:

> Jesus wanted to sleep to bless our sleep; he wanted to be tired to consecrate our tiredness; he wanted to weep to give merit to our tears.[8]

Therefore, by being born of us, Lord Jesus, you deified everything. Your crèche became the center of the divinization of the earth and of all humanity.

In you, Lord Jesus, our gaze upon the universe and its beauty, on heaven and its splendors, became the gaze of the Son of David admiring his own creation.

In you, admiration for everything beautiful and marvelous in the heart of human beings—did you not admire the faith of the centurion and the persevering prayer of the Canaanite woman?—became the admiration of the Word of God for his own gifts.

In you the love of a man and a woman—and its triumphant fructification in a child—gave birth to the only Son, full of grace and truth.

Moral of Divinization

People speak about a moral of the Covenant, a moral founded on the truths of the Covenant. We can likewise speak about a moral of divinization. This is the moral of Christmas. If Jesus deified everything, he therefore also deified our actions. If we have become adoptive children through the only Son, we must act as children of God. Jesus sums up the moral of the children of God in this way:

> Love your enemies, do good…
> And you will be children of the Most High. Lk 6, 35

Paul, in the second reading, presents this moral founded on the epiphany of God's grace in this way:

> The grace of God has appeared. It teaches us
> to renounce godlessness and earthly desires
> in order to live with moderation, righteousness
> and piety in the present world. Ti 2, 12

2. The Feast of Creation

Today is the feast of creation.

A French carol sings:

> He is born, the divine Child.
> Play, oboes; resound, bagpipes!

When I was a child, I was fascinated by this play of the oboes, by this resounding of the bagpipes. I imagined that they had to be fabulous instruments since they were invited to play before the crèche of Jesus.

Since then, the Bible has taught me that it was necessary to enlarge the orchestra to universal dimensions that welcome the coming of Jesus. In fact, the two responsorial psalms of Christmas (96 and 98), which belong to what are called the "psalms of the kingdom" invite all of creation to acclaim the coming of Jesus: Heaven celebrates, the earth jubilates, the sea and all that is in it roars with gladness, the fields and everything in them are overcome with pleasure, the rivers clap their hands, the trees of the forest dance with joy, the mountains are intoxicated with happiness "before the Lord, for he comes."[9] What a wonderful dance around the crèche!

The Praise of Past Centuries

The praise of material creation is presented to God through the praise of the people who live in it.

These psalms of the kingdom pose an insurmountable question for us: Where is the praise of the people of past centuries? When we place human history into the history of the universe, we are first stupefied, then bewildered. We say to ourselves that there is surely something that is not in place in God's plan... In reality, the holy history of the people of God, from Abraham to our day, spans nearly four thousand years. But the history of humanity covers three to four million years. That gives us a portion of approximately four thousand to four million years (even if we were off by a million years, that would not be a great matter), a ratio of one to one thousand. This is to say that in the existence of humanity, God has been praised one year per thousand; or there has not been any praise of God in nine hundred ninety-nine years per thousand. What became of all the people of prehistory? How does God apply the riches of salvation to those who do not know how to praise him, the God who "wants all people to be saved and come to the knowledge of truth?"[10]

The Praise of our Time

Prehistory keeps its mystery; our present situation is hardly better. The population of the world today is about five billion people. All are loved by the Lord. All are called to be saved by blessing Jesus.

Worshiping the little child in the stable are about one billion people: six to seven hundred million Catholics, four hundred million Protestants, and seventy million Orthodox. We are happy when the cries of our disputes are no longer heard outside.

In front of the cave are those who venerate the God of Abraham: twenty million Jews and eight hundred million Moslems, disciples of Mohammed (d. 632 CE).

Far from us, but always close to the heart of God, are five hundred million servants who are adherents of Hinduism, a cluster of religions whose most distant origins in the valley of the Indus date back to the seventh millennium.[11]

There are 250 million disciples of Buddha, who preached in the valley of the Ganges about 525 years before the Christian Era.

At the same time, Confucius (551-479) was preaching his ethics to his Chinese followers. There are almost 200 million followers of Confucianism, which is actually more of a philosophy than a religion.

Let us not forget the 40 million Shintoists, the 25 million Taoists, the 200 million animists...then all the unknown that must be counted to arrive at 5 billion. Each one is known, loved and called by the child of Bethlehem.

What an overwhelming spectacle are these billions of hands extended toward you in the night, Lord! With Peter, who ran after you when the new dawn rose over Capernaum, we say to you: "Everyone is looking for you!"[12] On this day of your holy birth, listen to the prayers of those who stammer your name without really knowing it. Enlighten the eyes that seek you in the night. Since your gifts and your call know no bounds, cast your eyes upon Israel. Is not Israel the people you created for your praise?[13] Dry its tears; heal its anguish. Receive also the submission of the faith and the love of our Moslem brothers and sisters who "adore with us the one, merciful God."[14] Accept the effort of our Hindu brothers and sisters who seek freedom "by the asceticism of their lives, profound meditation and refuge in God with love and confidence."[15]

Are you not the universal Liberator? See also the offering of our Buddhist brothers and sisters in quest of light. Realize, Lord, for the entire world the prophecy of a light:

> The people who walk in darkness
> have seen a great light.
> Upon those who live in the land of death,
> a light has shown. Is 9, 1

When we look at the problem of the salvation of humanity, we risk losing heart. On the one hand is an immense crowd scattered throughout the ages, on the road to centuries, billions disseminated today over the entire earth. On the other hand is a newborn child lying in a manger, a young mother who looks at him with tenderness, a father who is seeking to make himself useful. These are the facts of the problem. Here also is the solution devised by God. The solution seems impossible. But is not our God precisely the God of the impossible? The salvation of all humanity is his problem. Should we give him advice for resolving his problems and show him how to realize the prophecy of Isaiah? We know that he is wise and that he will solve those problems according to the perfection of his heart and according to the infinity of his mercy.

Vatican II explains the Christian faith in this way:

> God is not far from those who seek him in
> darkness and under images…
> To those who have not yet arrived at an explicit
> knowledge of God, but who, not without divine
> grace, work to have an upright life, divine
> Providence does not refuse the help necessary
> for their salvation.[16]

To the degree that the human beings of prehistory progressed toward humanity, they advanced, without knowing it, toward the crèche of Jesus. The more they became men and women, the more they drew near to the perfect Man, the One who loved to call himself the "Son of Man."

We can suppose that this principle, which governed past times, is still valid in the present time for all those who are outside the light of revelation. Each time a man loves his wife and devotes himself to her with integrity, each time a woman loves her husband and respects him, each time parents raise their children—in the most beautiful sense of the word, each time that they raise them toward heaven!—each time people treat others as brothers and sisters, each time they follow their heart, they draw near to the crèche of Jesus—they enter into the salvation of God.

Paul affirms that our lives remains hidden in God with Christ.[17] We can think that the life of millions of people, those of centuries past and those of our time, remain hidden in God with Christ.

It is the heart that makes a Christian, not the inscription on the baptismal register.

For us who are inscribed on this register, what is our vocation today? We show others the path; we lead them to Jesus.

May our lives be for each one of our brothers and sisters a path toward the crèche, a road to Love!

3. The Genealogy of Jesus According to Matthew

The Titles of Christ

The prophecy of the book of Isaiah (first reading) gives the royal child marvelous names full of mystery:

> Wonderful Counselor, Mighty God,
> Everlasting Father, Prince of Peace. Is 9, 5

The angel of the Lord who appears to Joseph, according to the Gospel of Matthew, gives him the name of Jesus, "for he will save his people from their sins."[18]

The angel of the Annunciation, according to the Gospel of Luke, calls him "Son of God." And the angels in the fields of the shepherds sing to him as "Savior, Christ and Lord."[19]

Therefore, it would seem that with such prestigious names the genealogy of Jesus could cite only names of glory. Could a "Savior" be born from a sinful race? Could the Son of God be born from a race of slaves?

Human Misery and Divine Mercy

Matthew begins his gospel in this way: "Book of the genesis [as if he were describing a new creation] of Jesus Christ, Son of David, Son of Abraham." Then comes the genealogical list.

This genealogy is full of mystery. The gospel divides it artificially into three groups of fourteen generations each. The first goes from Abraham to David, from about 1800 to 1000, about eight centuries. The second goes from David to the deportation in 587, about four centuries. The last goes to Joseph, which is about six centuries. It is clear that Matthew follows a theological teaching across the facts of history. The fourteen generations call to mind the number of David. Indeed, by adding the letters of David's name (D=4, V=6, D=4), we obtain the number fourteen. (In Hebrew, letters also serve as numbers. Printed Hebrew words use no vowels, so David's name would be printed "Dvd.")

But this genealogy of glory is also a chain of human misery.

Ordinarily, women were not named in genealogical lists. Matthew cites four of them. All four of them are "strangers":

- Ruth, the Moabite, the "daughter" of a strange god.

• Tamar, the wife of Er, then of Onan, both born from the union of Juda with Shua, a Canaanite. Disguised as a prostitute, Tamar offered herself to her father-in-law Judah in order to conceive with him the children that Onan had refused her.

• Rahab, who did not pretend to be a prostitute but actually was one. She lived on the ramparts of Jericho and helped the people of God seize the city.

• Bathsheba, the wife of Uriah the Hittite, who committed adultery with David.

Those who believe that the blood of the Messiah of Israel is pure of all crossbreeding are mistaken. It is a blood mixed with Canaanite and Hittite blood. Those who think that the blood of the Savior of the world is a blood pure from all sinners are likewise mistaken: It is the blood of human sinners that flows in the veins of Jesus and of his mother. The blood of the Son of God is the blood of Ruth, the stranger! The blood of the Son of God is the blood of Tamar and of Rahab, the prostitute! The blood of the Son of God is the blood of Bathsheba, the adulteress!

Eucharist and Incarnation

Tradition liked to affirm that the Eucharist "is like a continuation and an extension of the mystery of the Incarnation."[20]

When I take the cup over which I will pronounce the words of consecration, I will remember, Lord Jesus, that your blood in that cup is the blood of the New Covenant, poured out for the multitude, for the remission of sins. But I will also remember all those who made the gesture of love a man and woman, so that your body might finally be born, so that their blood might flow in your veins. From prehistoric (Lucy) to Father (Abraham) to King (David) to Saint (Joseph), no one is missing. All are there who celebrate in you, son of Abraham and son of David, the eucharistic praise. I will especially remember the women named by Matthew.

Your blood, Lord Jesus, in this cup is also the blood of Tamar, the one who played the prostitute to seduce Judah, the son of Jacob, to have a child by him. You, Lord Jesus, who wanted to be born from Tamar, the child of a seductress, have mercy on the misery of all the Tamars and transfigure their transgressions—and ours!—into a cup of blessing.

Your blood, Lord Jesus, in this cup is also the blood of Bathsheba, the wife of Uriah the Hittite, who committed adultery with David. You, Lord Jesus, who wanted to be born of Bathsheba, a child of David's adulteress, have mercy on the misery of all Bathshebas and transfigure their life into a cup of blessing!

There is a fifth woman in Matthew's genealogical list, the last one names, the mother of Jesus. Your blood, Lord, in this cup of blessing is also the blood of the Virgin Mary, the "Full-of-grace" overshadowed by the Holy Spirit. You, Lord Jesus, who wanted to be born of Mary, a child of the sinless, have mercy on the sinners that we are and transfigure our lives into a cup of blessing. Amen.

CONCLUDING PRAYER

For those who give you a face,
Lord Jesus,
by spreading your love in the world,
we acclaim you.
Glory to God in the highest!
For those who give you hands,
Lord Jesus,
by defending the weak and the oppressed,
we acclaim you.
Glory to God in the highest!
For those who give you eyes,
Lord Jesus,
By admiring every particle of love
in the human heart,
we acclaim you.
Glory to God in the highest!
For those who give you a heart,
Lord Jesus,
by preferring the poor to the rich,
the weak to the powerful,
we acclaim you.
Glory to God in the highest!
For those who give your face of hope,
Lord Jesus,
Giving the kingdom to all poverty,
we acclaim you.
Glory to God in the highest!

For those who reveal you,
Lord Jesus,
simply by what they are,
reflecting your beauty in their lives,
we acclaim you.

Glory to God in the highest!

God our Father,
you are the God of a thousand faces,
and yet none can reveal you fully
except the face of the child of Bethlehem.
We pray to you:
Continue in our lives the mystery of Christmas.
Let your Son Jesus be embodied in us
so that we might be the revelation of your love
for all our brothers and sisters. Amen.

NOTES TO CHRISTMAS

1. See what are called the "We accounts" in the Book of the Acts of the Apostles (16, 10–17; 20, 2–15; 21, 1–18; 27, 1–28, 16.
2. 2 Cor 11, 26.
3. Acts 20, 5–15.
4. D. C. Johanson and Maitland A. Edey, *Lucy, The Beginnings of Humankind*, (New York: Warner Books, 1982).
5. Compare Eccl 1, 9 with Rev 1, 14–16.
6. Clement of Alexandria, *The Pedagogue III* 1, 2, 1. SC 158 (1970), p. 14.
7. *Discourse Against the Arians III*, 33–34. PG 26, 393–397.
8. *Discourse* 37, 2. SC 318 (1985), p. 272.
9. Ps 96, 11–13; Ps 98, 7–9.
10. 1 Tm 2, 4.
11. Hans Küng, *Le christianisme et les religions du monde* (Paris: Editions du Seuil, 1986), p. 211. We will take the numbers given with the ordinary approximations in these accounts. See also *L'état des religions* (Collective Work), (Paris: Editions La Découverte and Le Cerf, 1987).
12. Mk 1, 37.
13. Is 43, 21 and Rom 11, 20.
14. *Lumen Gentium*, 16.
15. Declaration of Vatican II *Nostra aetate*, 2, on Hinduism and Buddhism.
16. *Lumen Gentium*, 16.
17. Col 3, 3.
18. Mt 1, 21.
19. Lk 1, 35 and 2, 11.
20. Leo XIII, *Mirae Caritatis* (1902). –AAS, 34 (1902), p. 645.

HOLY FAMILY

SUNDAY IN THE OCTAVE OF CHRISTMAS

Reading I — Sir 3, 2-6. 12-14

A reading from the book of Sirach

The Lord sets a father in honor over his children;
a mother's authority he confirms over her sons.
He who honors his father atones for sins;
he stores up riches who reveres his mother.
He who honors his father is gladdened by children,
and when he prays he is heard.
He who reveres his father will live a long life;
he obeys the Lord who brings comfort to his mother.
My son, take care of your father when he is old;
grieve him not as long as he lives.
Even if his mind fail, be considerate with him;
revile him not in the fullness of your strength.
For kindness to a father will not be forgotten,
it will serve as a sin offering—it will take lasting root.

The Word of the Lord.

Responsorial Psalm — Ps 128, 1-2. 3. 4-5

R/. (1) Happy are those who fear the Lord
and walk in his ways.

Happy are you who fear the Lord,
who walk in his ways!
For you shall eat the fruit of your handiwork;
happy shall you be, and favored.

R/. Happy are those who fear the Lord
and walk in his ways.

Your wife shall be like a fruitful vine
in the recesses of your home;
Your children like olive plants
around your table.

R/. Happy are those who fear the Lord
and walk in his ways.

Behold, thus is the man blessed
who fears the Lord.
The Lord bless you from Zion:
may you see the prosperity of Jerusalem
all the days of your life.

R/. Happy are those who fear the Lord
and walk in his ways.

READING II — COL 3, 12-21

A reading from the letter of Paul to the Colossians

Because you are God's chosen ones, holy and beloved, clothe yourselves with heartfelt mercy, with kindness, humility, meekness, and patience. Bear with one another; forgive whatever grievances you have against one another. Forgive as the Lord has forgiven you. Over all these virtues put on love, which binds the rest together and makes them perfect. Christ's peace must reign in your hearts, since as members of the one body you have been called to that peace. Dedicate yourselves to thankfulness. Let the word of Christ, rich as it is, dwell in you. In wisdom made perfect, instruct and admonish one another. Sing gratefully to God from your hearts in psalms, hymns, and inspired songs. Whatever you do, whether in speech or in action, do it in the name of the Lord Jesus. Give thanks to God the Father through him.

You who are wives, be submissive to your husbands. This is your duty in the Lord. Husbands, love your wives. Avoid any bitterness toward them. You children, obey your parents in everything as the acceptable way in the Lord. And fathers, do not nag your children lest they lose heart.
The Word of the Lord.

GOSPEL — LK 2, 22-40

A reading from the holy gospel according to Luke

When the day came to purify them according to the law of Moses, Mary and Joseph brought Jesus up to Jerusalem so that he could be presented to the Lord, for it is written in the law of the Lord, "Every first-born male shall be consecrated to the Lord." They came to offer in sacrifice "a pair of turtledoves or two young pigeons," in accord with the dictate in the law of the Lord.

There lived in Jerusalem at the time a certain man named Simeon. He was just and pious, and awaited the consolation of Israel, and the Holy Spirit was upon him. It was revealed to him by the Holy Spirit that he would not experience death until he had seen the Anointed of the Lord. He came to the temple now, inspired by the Spirit; and when the parents brought in the child Jesus to perform for him the customary ritual of the law, he took him in his arms and blessed God in these words:

"Now, Master, you can dismiss your servant in peace;
you have fulfilled your word.
For my eyes have witnessed your saving deed
displayed for all the peoples to see:
A revealing light to the Gentiles,
the glory of your people Israel."

The child's father and mother were marveling at what was being said about him. Simeon blessed them and said to Mary his mother: "This child is destined to be the downfall and the rise of many in Israel, a sign that will be opposed —and you yourself shall be pierced with a sword—so that the thoughts of many hearts may be laid bare."

There was also a certain prophetess, Anna by name, daughter of Phanuel of the tribe of Asher. She had seen many days, having lived seven years with her husband after her marriage and then as a widow until she was eighty-four. She was constantly in the temple, worshiping day and night in fasting and prayer. Coming on the scene at this moment, she gave thanks to God and talked about the child to all who looked forward to the deliverance of Jerusalem.

When the pair had fulfilled all the prescriptions of the law of the Lord, they returned to Galilee and their own town of Nazareth. The child grew in size and strength, filled with wisdom, and the grace of God was upon him.

The gospel of the Lord.

INTRODUCTORY PRAYER

On this day when we celebrate the Holy Family:
Jesus, Mary and Joseph;
we bless you, God our Father,
source of every family in heaven and on earth.
It is you who created in the heart of Joseph
love for Mary, his wife.
It is you who united their mutual tenderness
in the service of Christ Jesus.

We pray to you:
Let the love which is at the heart of our earthly families
be for us a path to your Kingdom,
where together we will form the family
of all those who love you and bless you
through your Son Jesus, in the love of the Holy Spirit.
Amen.

HOMILY

The mystery of the Incarnation is one of unbelievable richness. It shines like a rising sun which at each moment changes the colors of dawn. Luke dares to make the following statements as if they would not cause a problem:

> Jesus grew in wisdom,
> in stature and in grace,
> before God and men. Lk 2, 52

And here we are projected into the midst of the mystery, into the fires of dawn.

We understand quite easily that Jesus grew in stature, that the newborn of Bethlehem became a child, then an adolescent, then a man. The ancient Latins used to say: *Filii matrizant*, boys resemble their mothers. As he grew, Jesus resembled his mother more and more.

We also understand that he grew in wisdom in the eyes of men. He learned to pronounce his first words: *abba*, papa, *imma*, mama. He learned to speak Aramaic with a Galilean accent that was easily recognized in Jerusalem, with the vocal intonations of Joseph and Mary.

Jesus also learned very early in life how to read and write. As a rule, one began to study scripture at the age of five, the *Mishna* (oral tradition) at ten, the practice of the commandments at thirteen and the *Talmud* at fifteen.[1] We can be sure that Joseph and Mary instructed their son in a manner consistent with their piety.

Joseph taught him the trade (*tektôn*) of carpenter. He taught him how to distinguish the wood of the trees that the Bible mentions: acacia, cedar, cyprus, pine, sycamore and thuya. He showed him how to use an axe, a chisel, a hammer, a saw, a square rule and a brace effectively without hurting himself.

Together, Joseph and Jesus made doors, windows, yokes and plows. Tradition in the middle of the second century still spoke about the yokes and plows that Jesus had made.[2] Such is the law of the Incarnation: The Artisan of the universe made wooden plows!

The trade of carpenter was esteemed. In the sayings of the *Talmud* it was said concerning something difficult to understand: "That is a thing that no carpenter—implying how well instructed he may be—can explain."[3]

Jesus undoubtedly also knew Greek. It was the dominant language in such centers as Caesarea. Greek influence was extensive itself, especially in Galilee. A number of the inscriptions in the synagogues were written in Greek. Even if he did not master the language perfectly, as Paul and Luke did, Jesus was able to carry on a conversation in Greek with the Syrio-Phoenician woman, with the centurion of Capernaum and his slave, with a group of Greeks whom Philip and Andrew brought to him and with Pilate at the time of the Passion.[4]

But the most marvelous thing in the formation of Jesus was his progression in grace before God. The familial intimacy of Joseph and Mary was the home where Jesus learned that there was a God of love who reigned over the world, that this God was the Father—the Abba!—of tenderness and mercy and that the first duty of all children of the Covenant was to love him with all their hearts, with all their souls, with all their spirits, and with all their strength. Such is once again an overwhelming law of the Incarnation: Joseph and Mary taught the One who was the face of God's love on earth to love God!

Of course, the mystery of Jesus remains impenetrable. It is the mystery of the heart that was formed not only in the school of Joseph and Mary but also in personal prayer. We know that Jesus liked to pray alone on the mountain until late at night or early in the morning.[5] No one can say what the intimacy of these dialogues were with the Father. But we can at least outline the influence of this family on what could be called the "religion of Jesus." It is a world of marvels.

A Soul of Praise and Blessing

The heart of Mary is revealed in a special way in the Magnificat. We can assume, however, that the text Luke gives to us does not reproduce word for word the canticle that Mary sang in the presence of Elizabeth. We can also rightly think that other factors, probably coming from tradition, influenced his writing. In any case, the text as Luke transmitted it to us had to correspond to the image of Mary that the early community, which had known the mother of Jesus, kept of her.

The very first word of Mary's song is a word of praise to God. Literally:

My soul magnifies the Lord;
My spirit exults in God my Savior. Lk 1, 46-47

Mary's soul is a soul of praise and also of joy: She exults with joy in God her Savior, that is, in Jesus whom she is carrying in her womb.

The soul of Jesus is likewise a soul of praise. The Hymn of Jubilation of Jesus corresponds to Mary's Magnificat. Just as Mary trembles with joy (*ègalliasen*) in God her Savior, so does Jesus tremble with joy *(ègallisato*) in the Holy Spirit and says:

I bless you, Father,
Lord of heaven and earth
for having hidden this (mystery) from the wise and learned
and for having revealed it to little children.
Yes, Father, for that was your good pleasure. Lk 10, 21

We have here the essence of the religion of Jesus. This religion is first of all praise and blessing of God. This praise that the prayer of his public life reveals to us is a direct echo of the prayer of the hidden life in Nazareth. In fact, the beginning of the Hymn of Jubilation reproduces the beginning of the Jewish prayer of the Eighteen Benedictions, a prayer that the Holy Family recited three times a day:

Blessed be you, Yahweh,
God of Abraham, Isaac, and Jacob,
Lord of heaven and earth,
our shield and the shield of our fathers.
Blessed be you, shield of Abraham.[6]

Thus, the dwelling of Nazareth was the school where Jesus learned to praise God. It was also the school of obedience to the will of the Father. This "Yes, Father," pronounced here in the jubilation of the Holy Spirit, announces the humble prayer of Gethsemane, where Jesus begged:

Abba! Father!
Everything is possible for you...
But not what I want,
but what you want. Mk 14, 36

Jesus had already taught his disciples this submission to the will of the Father in the Lord's Prayer.

Your will be done,
on earth as it is in heaven. Mt 6, 10

This "everything is possible for you" of the prayer of Gethsemane calls to mind the "nothing is impossible for God" of the Annunciation at Nazareth. The God of Jesus, like the God of Mary, is really the Master of the impossible, the one whose will is blessed by saying:

Here is the servant (literally: the slave) of
the Lord.
Let it be done to me according to your word! Lk 1, 28

If every family, in imitation of the Holy Family of Nazareth, could become a community of blessing and praise of the holy will of God, if they could say with Jesus in all circumstances: "Yes, Father, for that is your good pleasure," then, with Jesus, they would live forever in the jubilation of the Holy Spirit.

The God of Mercy

In order to bless the Almighty who did wonders for her, Mary commemorates his mercy:

His mercy extends from age to age
upon those who fear him.

He helped Israel, his child;
he remembers his mercy. Lk 1, 50. 54

The story of Mary is the story of the divine mercy that invades her soul; it is the story of her love for Jesus, the mysterious fruit that germinated from her virginal womb; it is the story of her nuptial love for Joseph, whom God had given to her as a husband. Mercy was the source from which her life had sprung forth and where her praise to God drank plentifully.

That mercy was often spoken about under the roof of the carpenter. And that mercy which had marked the soul of Mary likewise marked the soul of Jesus. He proposes it as the supreme rule of imitation of the Father:

Be merciful
as your Father is merciful. Lk 6, 36

Jesus also gives it as the rule of the Christian community: We must be merciful to our brothers and sisters, companions of service, as God himself is merciful to us.[7]

The very ministry of Jesus appears as the face of God's mercy on earth. The scribes and the Pharisees, the official interpreters of God's Law, thought that the goodness of Jesus exceeded the limits that their wisdom had fixed on the mercy of God. His ministry to sinners was, according to their judgment, not only open to criticism but sometimes even scandalous. He had gone as far as to feast with publicans, such as Zacchaeus of Jericho, who jumped from a sycamore tree—was that not ridiculous?—and then received Jesus in his home, at his table, with a whole group of sinners. Jesus had even enlisted a publican, a certain Matthew, among his closest companions and had dared to say on that subject:

I want mercy
and not sacrifice.
For I have not come to call the righteous,
but sinners. Mt 9, 13

Whereas an honorable rabbi who took even a little care of his reputation would abstain from speaking to his own wife in public, Jesus—good grief, what was the world coming to!—had engaged familiarly in a conversation with a Samaritan woman who had already been divorced five times and was living as a concubine. To another woman caught in the act of adultery he had declared that he did not condemn her. Instead of inflicting upon her a penance, he opened for her a path of freedom without even demanding a word of regret. Another woman, who was known in the city as a sinner, was allowed to weep on his feet, embrace them and wipe them with her hair. As for the prodigal son who had left to squander his inheritance with prostitutes, Jesus affirmed that it was simply not necessary to await his return; he told of the father running to meet him and embrace him.

God had revealed himself on Sinai as the God of mercy and compassion.[8] Never had that mercy and compassion appeared so close to the poor and to sinners as with Jesus. In him, mercy had come "to seek and save what was lost."[9]

If every family could be, in imitation of the Holy Family of Nazareth, the place where, with Mary, one unceasingly commemorated the mercy of God, then they too would be filled with that mercy; they would become, with Jesus, a revelation of God's mercy on earth.

The God of the Poor

The Magnificat is also the song of Yahweh's poor. The God of Mary is the Lord who casts his eyes on the humility of his servant but scatters hearts full of pride; the Lord who lifts up the humble but throws down the powerful from their thrones; the Lord who fills the hungry with good things but sends the rich away empty-handed. Therefore, in Nazareth, people knew that God loved the poor. Some even experienced a certain material poverty, since the Holy Family classified itself among the poor.[10]

This cult of poverty marked the conscience of Jesus. Mary's song of poverty became the spiritual environment in which the great themes of the symphony of the gospel unfolded. The first homily of Jesus in Nazareth, according to the tradition of Luke, begins with the affirmation that he came to bring Good news to the poor, the captives, the blind and the oppressed. And his first great discourse, according to the tradition of Matthew, begins with the proclamation of the beatitude of the poor.[11]

People used to say in Nazareth:

> The rich
> God sends away empty-handed. Lk 1, 53

Jesus will remember his mother's song of poverty when he will say in the Sermon on the Mount:

> Blessed are the poor,
> for theirs is the Kingdom of God.

Woe to you rich,
for you have received your consolation. Lk 6, 20. 24

Matthew has to specify, through catechetic concern, that it is (also) a matter of poverty "in spirit," of a spiritual disposition; for material poverty is "beatifying" only if it opens the heart to God. But the Virgin of Nazareth and the Christ of the Beatitudes speak about a universal poverty, one which includes material poverty, one which people experienced in the daily life of Nazareth.

Mary said further:

The hungry (*peinôntas*)
God fills with good things. Lk 1, 53

Jesus will remember the hungry that his mother spoke about when he will say in the Sermon on the Mount:

Blessed are those who hunger (*peinôntas*) now,
for you will be satisfied.
Woe to you who are full now,
for you will hunger. Lk 6, 21. 25

Matthew has to specify, through catechetic concern, that it is (also) a matter of a hunger for righteousness. But the Virgin of the Magnificat and the Christ of the Beatitudes think about a true bodily hunger, one that people asked God to satisfy when they prayed: "Give us today our daily bread."[12]

It has been affirmed that the text of Second Isaiah was "the favorite book of Jesus and of his disciples."[13] It was also his mother's favorite. We may suppose that during the long years at Nazareth, it was Mary, with Joseph, who gave to her son this preferential love for the message of Second Isaiah. Now one section of the Book of Isaiah corresponds directly to the Magnificat. It is a sublime text where God comments on the reconstruction of the Temple in this way:

Heaven is my throne,
and the earth is my footstool,
What house could you build for me
and in what place my resting place?...
But the one on whom I cast my eyes (*epiblepsô*)
is the humble (*tapeinon*) and contrite heart
that trembles at my word. Is 66, 1-2

At the Annunciation, Mary had appeared as the new Temple filled with the glory of God.[14] The marvel of this Temple was the humility of Mary. This was what attracted God to look upon the new Temple:

> He has cast his eyes (*epeblepson*)
> upon the humility (*tapeinôsin*) of his slave. Lk 1, 48

Pride, in return, had bad press in the dwelling of Nazareth. One said there:

> The Lord scatters proud hearts. Lk 1, 51

Literally: those who exalt themselves in the thinking of their heart. In reality it is the heart which is the altar upon which this liturgy of the humble is celebrated. If the heart is eaten up with pride, God deserts the altar and scatters its stones. If it is humble, God makes his dwelling in it.

Jesus will remember the meek and humble heart of his mother. He will imitate her. He will say this to his disciples:

> Learn from me,
> for I am meek and humble (*tapeinos*) of heart. Mt 11, 29

If every family could be, in imitation of the Holy Family, a school of meekness and humility; if all those who live in them could be, like Jesus, meek and humble of heart; then God's look of love would rest on each one of them and each one would be a revelation of the heart of Jesus.

Joseph and Mary

We have spoken a great deal about Mary and about her influence on Jesus. We have said little about Joseph. This is inevitable because Joseph never says anything in the gospels. We cannot cite one of his words. But Joseph is more than a word—for Mary, he is silent love; while for God, he is obedient love.

Jewish tradition affirmed that it was God who chose everyone's wife.[15] Never was this truer than for Joseph. It was God who had given Mary to him for a wife and had entrusted Jesus, born of the Holy Spirit, to him for a child.

It can be said that two people who love each other with tenderness and truth receive their heart from each other. Each one can say to the beloved: "You gave me my heart." Joseph's heart had to have been very beautiful in order to manifest such splendors in the heart of Mary. Without Joseph, without the long intimacy of the silent years in Nazareth, Mary would not have been that presence of love at the foot of the agony of Jesus. Without Joseph, she would not have been that praying presence at the heart of the Church being born on the eve of Pentecost. Without Joseph, Jesus himself would not have been that man so perfectly balanced as human and divine. For everything that Jesus had received from Mary, Mary had received in part from Joseph and had shared it with him.

The Family of Heaven

The last time Mary is mentioned by name in the New Testament, and also the only time she appears in the company of the Twelve, is when she prays with the early community in the "upper room" while awaiting the Holy Spirit.

> All (that is, the Apostles) with one heart
> were steadfast in prayer with some women and
> Mary, the mother of Jesus. Acts 1, 14

The Twelve form a crown of prayer around Mary. In the Book of Revelation, the Twelve will form a crown of twelve stars around the Woman clothed with the sun.[16] The family of Nazareth opened itself to the dimensions of the redeemed universe.

Thus, this story of love, the most extraordinary story that the earth has ever known and which began in the humility of Nazareth, is continued throughout the time of the Church. Each family, in the very measure that it welcomes Jesus, can become a Holy Family. Amen.

CONCLUDING PRAYER

For the father you gave us,
because you are our Father in heaven,
we bless you.
Help the men you call to fatherhood
to be the reflection on earth of your fatherly love,
we pray to you.

God of love,
hear our prayer!

Holy Family

For the mother who carries us,
because the Virgin Mary is our Mother in heaven,
we bless you.
Help each woman you call to motherhood
to be the song of your tenderness for her child,
we pray to you.

God of love,
hear our prayer!

For the husband or the wife that you gave to us
who is flesh of our flesh and a sign of your love,
we bless you.
Help each family to recognize
that their tenderness is a path toward heaven,
we pray to you.

God of love,
hear our prayer!

For the children that you gave to us,
because they are your adopted children
in your only Son,
we bless you.
Help us to recognize in every person
the image of Jesus, your firstborn Son,
we pray to you.

God of love,
hear our prayer!

Hear us, God our Father,
in the name of the love that you bear for Jesus,
child of the Virgin Mary, and our brother
forever and ever. Amen.

NOTES TO HOLY FAMILY

1. Strack–Billerbeck, *Kommentar*, vol. II, p. 146.
2. Justin, *Dialogue avec Tryphone*, 88.
3. G. Vermes, *Jésus le Juif* (Paris: Editions Desclée, 1978), p. 26.
4. Mk 7, 26 Lk 7, 1–10. Jn 12, 20–22; 18, 33–38; 19, 8–11. See M. Carrez, *Les langues de la Bible* (Paris: Editions du Centurion, 1983), p. 87.
5. Mk 1, 35; 6, 46; 14, 32–39.
6. J. Jeremias, *Théologie du Nouveau Testament*, Coll. "Lectio Divina," 76 (1973), p. 82. The text of the "eighteen Blessings" can be found in L. Deiss, *Springtime of the Liturgy* (Collegeville, MN: The Liturgical Press, 1979), pp. 9–14.
7. Mt 18, 32 (in the "Ecclesiastic Discourse").
8. Ex 34, 6.
9. Lk 19, 10.
10. At the presentation of Jesus at the temple, she offers the sacrifice of the poor: Lk 2, 23–24 and Lv 2, 8.
11. Lk 4, 18 and Mt 5, 5. On the early text of the Beatitudes, see *God's Word Is Our Joy, Sundays Ordinary Time*, Cycle A, cf. Lk 11, 3.
12. Lk 11, 3.
13. P. E. Bonnard, Le Second Isaie, p. 81. By "Second Isaiah" one means here what we call Deutero and Trito–Isaiah.
14. See p.
15. E. Fleg, *Anthologie juive* (Editions Flammarion–Sulliver) p. 164.
16. Rv 12, 1.

SOLEMNITY OF MARY, MOTHER OF GOD

Reading I — Nm 6, 22-27

A reading from the book of Numbers

The Lord said to Moses: "Speak to Aaron and his sons and tell them: This is how you shall bless the Israelites. Say to them:

The Lord bless you and keep you!
The Lord let his face shine upon you,
  and be gracious to you!
The Lord look upon you kindly
  and give you peace!
So shall they invoke my name upon the Israelites, and I will bless them."

The Word of the Lord.

Responsorial Psalm — Ps 67, 2-3. 5. 6. 8

R/. (2) May God bless us in his mercy.

May God have pity on us and bless us;
  may he let his face shine upon us.
So may your way be known upon earth;
  among all nations, your salvation.

R/. May God bless us in his mercy.

May the nations be glad and exult
  because you rule the peoples in equity;
  the nations on the earth you guide.

R/. May God bless us in his mercy.

May the peoples praise you, O God;
  may all the peoples praise you!
May God bless us,
  and may all the ends of the earth fear him!

R/. May God bless us in his mercy.

READING II — GAL 4, 4-7

A reading from the letter of Paul
to the Galatians

When the designated time had come, God sent forth his Son born of a woman, born under the law, to deliver from the law those who were subjected to it, so that we might receive our status as adopted sons. The proof that you are sons is the fact that God has sent forth into our hearts the spirit of his Son which cries out "Abba!" ("Father!"). You are no longer a slave but a son! And the fact that you are a son makes you an heir, by God's design.

The Word of the Lord.

GOSPEL — LK 2, 16-21

A reading from the holy gospel according to Luke

The shepherds went in haste to Bethlehem and found Mary and Joseph, and the baby lying in the manger; once they saw, they understood what had been told them concerning this child. All who heard of it were astonished at the report given them by the shepherds.

Mary treasured all these things and reflected on them in her heart. The shepherds returned, glorifying and praising God for all they had heard and seen, in accord with what had been told them.

When the eighth day arrived for his circumcision, the name Jesus was given the child, the name the angel had given him before he was conceived.

The gospel of the Lord.

INTRODUCTORY PRAYER

At the threshold of this new year,
we bless you, Lord God
Master of time and eternity.

For us you create each day anew,
filling it with the presence of your Son Jesus.
You create every moment of our lives,
and fill each of them with the love of your Holy Spirit.

Day after day, in our joys and in our pains,
help us progress on the way which is Jesus.

May we sing the songs of your Holy Spirit's love.
And, when the river of time stops flowing,
on the threshold of your eternity,
when our road has emerged
into the dawn of your eternal day,
welcome us into your arms, O Lord
at the eternal feast of your mercy,
forever and ever. Amen.

HOMILY

Formerly, the first song of this Mass—the Introit—began with the words *In nomine Jesu*, "in the name of Jesus."

It is in the name of Jesus that we begin this new year. It is also in his name that we offer to the Father each coming day, whatever may be its darkness or its brightness. It is also in his name that we hope to be received into the kingdom of his Father on the first day of our eternity.

1. The Christian Meaning of Time

We are immersed in time; we are almost imprisoned in it. We sometimes waste it off-handedly; we say that we are "killing" time. Most often we count it with avarice. We ascertain the inconsistency and the folly of human life. That is why we pray with the psalmist:

> Teach us to number our days.
> Let us open our hearts to wisdom. Ps 90, 12

How do we count our days? We count them in numbers, and we populate our life with souvenirs. We mark the dates that have scarred or enlightened our existence. We cultivate souvenirs, as one lovingly keeps a geranium, though each day it may grow yellow and wither away. And then, finally, we are obliged to throw everything into a "compost" of souvenirs.

Sometimes we seek to gain time. Let us think of the considerable risks that a driver takes to pass a car and thus "gain" some time. This may be a legitimate thing, but it ignores the problem: What is the person going to do with the time gained in this way? If it is to return home more quickly, to scold one's children, to argue with one's wife or husband, or simply to smoke a cigarette, that would really not be worth the trouble. Do we not all have examples of time gained in this way which we have lost afterwards?

The time given us for living is also a creation of God. It is only that. It is all that. It is said: "Time is money." This is to say that God esteems time, including our time to live, as much as he esteems money, including our own money, which is to say he does not esteem it. Time is good or bad according to whether we use it well or badly.

Our life is related first not to time, but to God.

What counts today, in this unique moment of this new year—unique because it is the only moment that I have at my disposal; the past no longer belongs to me, and the future is not here yet—is my position in relation to God, the manner in which I regard myself in this light.

Sometimes it is said that the young are lucky because they have life ahead of them. Peguy used to say that it was the old people who were lucky because they had eternity before them. For God, the young are not luckier than the old, nor the old luckier than the young. Rather, young and old have the opportunity to stand in God's presence. God calls some to die young, when their life has not yet seen a single flower bloom, such as the Holy Innocents who died at one or two years of age. Others die full of years, such as good Anna,[1] the prophetess about whom Luke speaks and whose wrinkled eighty-four-year-old face was illuminated by the smile of baby Jesus. Others die when they are thirty-three years old. The only thing that counts is our relationship with God.

On this first day of the New Year, when we wish each other so many good things, let us not forget to pray to God for this essential grace: the joy and peace of keeping us in his presence.

The Success of a Life

In biblical tradition each day is a new creation. There is no tacit renewal of existence. Each morning when we awake, God once again gives us the grace of existence. Each new year that he opens before us is a new gift of his love.

What is the goal of this creation that is unceasingly renewed? Each day is given to us not so that we might progress in years, as if the ideal were the greatest number of years, but so that we might progress in our knowledge of God. Jesus said:

> Eternal life
> is that they might know you,
> the only true God. Jn 17, 3

Now the present life is like an apprenticeship to eternal life. Thus, the success of a life, the most extraordinary adventure which is proposed to us, is to progress each day that God creates for us in our discovery of what he is, to know him better, to recognize him better in each one of his creatures.

Who is he, not first of all in the infinity of his splendor—for we know well that he lives in inapproachable light,[2] that he possesses all the names that can be known on earth but that no name can fully express his mystery—who is he according to the most mysterious, the most divine being? And also, who is he for me? How is he situated at the root of my being? Who am I for him?

Discovering the God of Mercy and Compassion

The pygmies of the Camaroon forest call God "the One who lives above the trees." The Bible knows many names for God which bear a familial resemblance to the names given by these pygmies.

During the time they settled in the Promised Land, the chosen people identified the God of Abraham, of Isaac, and of Jacob with *El*, the supreme god of Ougarit, "king and father of the years." Thus one invoked *El-Elyôn*, the God Most High, at Jerusalem; *El-Roi*, the God who sees, at Lahai Roi at Negeb; *El Shaddai*, the Mountain God at Sinai, and *El-Olam*, the God of eternity, at Mambre.[3] These are all, in some way, "pygmy" names. They venerated the God of cosmic forces while remaining open to a greater mystery.

The most divine name of God, if one dares to say it, is the one that he gave himself in the revelation at Sinai:

> Yahweh, Yahweh,
> God of mercy and compassion,
> slow to anger,
> rich in grace and faithfulness,
> who keeps his grace for thousands... Ex 34, 6-7

It is this name that John sums up and translates in this affirmation: "God is love."[4]

The success of a life, the luck of an existence which has not been lived in vain but in plenitude, is to discover that God is mercy and compassion and to discover that more profoundly each day.

The success of a life is to discover it not because we read it somewhere in a book, nor because others have told us, nor because we have sung it in canticles or heard it in a homily, but to discover it where there can be no lies, no trickery—I want to say first of all in the depths of our heart, at the most intimate part of our life. And then we venerate, we serve, and we love our God not simply as the God above the trees but as this immense reality of love which has invaded our life.

Because we are sinners, we must also discover the forgiveness of God. Jewish tradition affirmed that before creating the world, God created his mercy. The letter to the Ephesians says that God loved us "before the creation of the world."[5] And since we are sinners, he loved us in this way in spite of our sin.

On this first day of the New Year, let us ask ourselves some question about the success of our lives. What is my personal knowledge of God? Where am I in this, the most formidable adventure of my existence?

If I close all of my books, if I forget everything that I have learned from those who were given to me as teachers, from those whom I chose as teachers, from those whom I kept as friends, do I know you, Lord, as the God of mercy and compassion at the heart of my life? You alone, Lord, love me for myself, just as I am, even with my mediocrities, even with my faults. You alone know me and call me by name, for it is you who created me as I am. In return, do I love you simply for what you are, God of mercy and compassion?

The Value of the Present Moment

Each moment we live is not merely a moment interchangeable with another moment. All time is the time of Christ, each hour is the hour of Christ. Since Emmanuel, God-with-us, now dwells with us until the end of time, he is simultaneously not only the end of time, but also the path toward the end. This path has divine value. Through Jesus, the time of our life is deified in some way. For the believer walking with Christ, there is no "dead," empty or lost time. Each instant is unique. Each instant I love and God loves me is solemn, definitive, and irreversible in some way.

Neglecting to make today's time bear fruit while proposing to recover time lost tomorrow is foolish.

> Today, if you hear his voice,
> harden not your heart.
>
> Ps 95, 7-8

It is today that the Lord speaks to me. It is today that I must answer him. Biblical vocabulary likes to distinguish between *chronos*, which is common time, time which measures the years or senseless, pagan time, and *kairos*, which is favorable, opportune time, intelligent time in which God intervenes. It is about this time that Paul wrote:

> Now is the favorable time (*kairos*),
> now is the day of salvation. 2 Cor 6, 2

Pagan time measures the years of our life; God's time measures our relationship of love with him. It is up to us to transform senseless, pagan time into God's time.

Only Love Explains the World

Paul tells us that our knowledge of God is partial. The tradition of Sufism tells this story:

> One dark night, a dark elephant entered into a dark cavern. The inhabitants of this country had never seen an elephant. They sent people to explore this unknown animal.
>
> The first, the most courageous, entered into the cavern, felt in the dark the trunk of the dark elephant, and came out crying: "This ferocious animal is like a snake!"
>
> The second person entered into the cavern, felt in the darkness the foot of the elephant, and came out and said: "This animal is rather like a tree that would walk!"
>
> A third person entered into the cavern, caught the tail of the elephant and came out laughing: "No, this is not an animal at all! Would it not be rather a small broom?
>
> Another person, who had touched the end of the ear, reflected a long time. Then like a wise man, he frowned and said: "In my humble opinion, it is rather, I am sure, a cabbage leaf!"

So are we, groping in the darkness of the universe which surrounds us in order to decipher in it the name of God. With a thousand little pieces of truth, with a thousand fragments of knowledge, with a thousand names for God, we try to recompose in its totality the image of the One who is infinite Splendor and eternal Love. This is endless, exciting work, for God is infinite.

But we can also start from God as he reveals himself to us in his word. Of course, he is the Infinite One, but his infinity is the infinity of love. And through that infinite love we understand the universe. The psalms affirm that "the whole earth is filled with his love."[6] Upon each one of his creatures shines a ray of his love. He is really the God of the ancient mountains, *El-Shaddai*, but they are the mountains of his love, for if the whole earth is filled with his love, the mountains are also. He is the Most High God, *El-Elyôm*, but his transcendence is not simply the one that directs billions of galaxies, but the one that watches over each being and leads it on the path of love. He is the God of eternity, *El-Olam*; he fills the centuries with his love as he also fills this new year with his love. He is the God whose love lives in my intelligence, in my mind, in my heart, for if the whole earth is filled with his love, then my whole being and also my whole existence are filled with this love.

God created me as a reality of love, as a being of his tenderness, or further, as Paul says, as a vessel of his mercy.[7] The success of my life, the luck of this new year, is to discover this grace in my heart even more. Do not miss the success of your life. Do not miss the luck of this new year.

It has been said: "Only love is believable."[8] It must be added: Only love explains the world.

Live like Mary. Luke writes that she pondered all these words, all the events that she had shared with Gabriel, with Joseph, with Elizabeth, with the shepherds, with the magi, with Simeon and with Anna, events through which God spoke to her. And she concluded: "God has remembered his mercy."[9]

You can also imitate Joseph who, while planing his boards, thought about that marvelous child who, from heaven, had come into this poor carpenter's hands; and about Mary, the ideal spouse whom the Holy Spirit had sent into his house. And each time the angel disturbed him to tell him: "Get up and leave," Joseph got up and left, but always taking "with him the child and his mother." He took with him the source of his joy and his love.

Toward the Feast

There are two ways of envisioning the progression of time in our life. Both of them are biblical. Each one presents an aspect of reality.

The first way insists on the vanity of life and on the decrepitude of humanity. This is the view of Qoheleth. In a sumptuous page filled with incomplete sentences like images in a dream, he describes our walk toward old age:

Remember your Creator in the days of your youth
before the bad days come
and the years arrive when you will say:
"I do not like them..."

On the day when the keepers of the house tremble,
when strong men stoop,
when women cease to grind
because night is coming on in the windows
and because the door is already closed on the street;
when the sound of the grinding falls,
when the voice of the bird stops
and when the songs are silent:
when one is afraid of heights
and one has fears in the streets.

And the almond tree is in bloom,
and the grasshopper is slow,
and the caper-bush gives its fruit.

While man goes toward his eternal home
and mourners already turn in the street.

Before the silver cord is broken,
before the golden lamp is broken,
before the pitcher is broken at the fountain,
and the pulley breaks at the well,
and the dust returns to the earth from which it came
and the breath returns to God who gave it.

"Vanity of vanities," says Qoheleth,
"everything is vanity!" Eccl 12, 1. 3-8

Everything is lost, cries Qoheleth. Everything is gained, sings the Letter to the Hebrews. The walk toward the eternal home prepares, in reality, for the entrance into the heavenly Jerusalem; it inaugurates the celebration of the eternal feast. That is what this solemn litany sings:

You have drawn near to the mountain of Zion,
to the city of the living God, to the heavenly Jerusalem,
to myriad angels, to a solemn feast,

to the assembly of the firstborn
who are written in heaven,
to a God, the Universal Judge,
to spirits of the righteous made perfect,
to Jesus, the Mediator of a new covenant. Heb 12, 22-24

Therefore, "the eternal house" of Qoheleth is not our ultimate dwelling. It is only a place of passage, a temporary stop on the path toward the solemn feast with Christ Jesus and with myriad angels.[10] May each step on the road of the new year bring us closer to the eternal feast!

2. The Portal of the Virgin

Our most ancient cathedrals are full of mysteries and symbols. They are all "oriented," that is, the sanctuary is turned to the Orient, the east. The rising sun passing through the stained-glass window inundates the sanctuary with light and colors, and the prayer of the Christian community is "oriented" toward Christ, the rising sun who rises on the world. The west portal, on the contrary, is illuminated by the setting sun. It typically represents Christ in glory, the universal Judge who will come back in majesty at the end of time when the sun of this world will have set forever.

These old cathedrals ordinarily have a portal called "of the Virgin." Thus, when one enters the house of Jesus, one is welcomed by his Mother. One passes through her to worship the Lord.

No more than a threshold holds back one who is entering into a house, Mary does not hold back the pilgrim who is entering into the cathedral. She is quite simply the welcomer of the believer, the opening to the mystery of God.

It is in this way that Mary, like a portal of God, welcomes us at the threshold of this new year. The liturgy made the first of January "the Feast of Holy Mary, the Mother of God." It wants us to meet Mary first at the threshold of the new year, as we enter into the mystery of God.

The Virgin of Beginnings

Our Lady is really the Virgin of all beginnings.

She was at the beginning of the Incarnation. Her virginal womb was the door through which Jesus entered into the world on the day of the Annunciation.

She was also present at the beginning of the public life of Jesus. It was at her request that Jesus performed his first sign at Cana and manifested his glory to his disciples for the first time.

Present at the birth of Jesus, she was present also at what could be called "the birth of the Church." Her prayer with the apostles was the door through which the Holy Spirit, coming upon the early community, gave birth to the church at Pentecost.

Mary is not a possessive mother who would like to keep her children next to her. Rather, it is she who sends them on a pilgrimage with her Son to the Father. Each day, she invites us to joy by saying to us, as she did of old at Cana: "Do everything that he tells you!" Amen.

CONCLUDING PRAYER

Holy Mary, Mother of God,
Place in me a child's heart,
pure and transparent like the water of a spring.
Obtain for me a simple heart
which does not savor sadness,
a magnificent heart to be given,
tender to compassion:
a faithful and generous heart
which does not forget any good
and holds no grudge for any evil.
Make mine a meek and humble heart,
loving without asking for anything in return,
joyful to give to another heart
before your divine Son,
a large and indomitable heart
that no ingratitude closes,
that no indifference wears out;
a heart tormented by the glory of Jesus Christ,
wounded by his love,
and whose wound is healed only in heaven.[11]

Reverend Léonce de Grandmaison, c. 1886

NOTES TO MARY, MOTHER OF GOD

1. Lk 2, 36, 38.
2. 1 Tm 6, 16.
3. Gn 14, 18–22; 16, 13; 17, 1; 21, 33.
4. 1 Jn 4, 8, 16.
5. Eph 1, 4.
6. Ps 33, 5.
7. Rom 9, 23.
8. H.U. von Balthasar, cited by J. H. Nicolas in *Vie Spirituelle*, 1987, p. 336.
9. Lk 1, 54; 2, 19, 51.
10. Lk 2, 13–14, 20–21.
11. In J. Lebreton, *Le ère Léonce de Grandmaison* (Paris: Editions Beauchesne, 1932), p. 29.

EPIPHANY

Reading I — Is 60, 1-6

A reading from the book of the prophet Isaiah

Rise up in splendor, Jerusalem! Your light has come,
the glory of the Lord shines upon you.
See, darkness covers the earth,
and thick clouds cover the peoples;
But upon you the Lord shines,
and over you appears his glory.
Nations shall walk by your light,
and kings by your shining radiance.
Raise your eyes and look about;
they all gather and come to you:
Your sons come from afar,
and your daughters in the arms of their nurses.
Then you shall be radiant at what you see,
your heart shall throb and overflow,
For the riches of the sea shall be emptied out before you,
the wealth of nations shall be brought to you.
Caravans of camels shall fill you,
dromedaries from Midian and Ephah;
All from Sheba shall come
bearing gold and frankincense,
and proclaiming the praises of the Lord.

The Word of the Lord.

Responsorial Psalm — Psalm 72, 1-2. 7-8. 10-11. 12-13

R/. (11) Lord, every nation on earth will adore you.

O God, with your judgment endow the king,
and with your justice, the king's son;
He shall govern your people with justice
and your afflicted ones with judgment.

R/. Lord, every nation on earth will adore you.

Justice shall flower in his days,
and profound peace, till the moon be no more.

May he rule from sea to sea,
 and from the River to the ends of the earth.

R/. Lord, every nation on earth will adore you.

The kings of Tarshish and the Isles shall offer gifts;
 the kings of Arabia and Sheba hall bring tribute.
All kings shall pay him homage,
 all nations shall serve him.

R/. Lord, every nation on earth will adore you.

For he shall rescue the poor man when he cries out,
 and the afflicted when he has no one to help him.
He shall have pity for the lowly and the poor;
 the lives of the poor he shall save.

R/. Lord, every nation on earth will adore you.

Reading II — Eph 3, 2-3. 5-6

A reading from the letter of Paul to the Ephesians

I am sure you have heard of the ministry which God in his goodness gave me in your regard. God's secret plan, as I have briefly described it, was revealed to me, unknown to men in former ages but now revealed by the Spirit to the holy apostles and prophets. It is no less than this: in Christ Jesus the Gentiles are now co-heirs with the Jews, members of the same body and sharers of the promise through the preaching of the gospel.
The Word of the Lord.

Gospel — Mt 2, 1-12

A reading from the holy gospel according to Matthew

After Jesus' birth in Bethlehem of Judea during the reign of King Herod, astrologers from the east arrived one day in Jerusalem inquiring, "Where is the newborn king of the Jews? We observed his star at its rising and have come to pay him homage." At this news King Herod became greatly disturbed, and with him all Jerusalem. Summoning all of the chief priests and scribes of the people, he inquired of them where the Messiah was to be born. "In Bethlehem of Judea," they informed him. "Here is what the prophet has written:

'And you, Bethlehem, land of Judah,
are by no means least among the princes of Judah,
since from you shall come a ruler
who is to shepherd my people Israel.'"

Herod called the astrologers aside and found out from them the exact time of the star's appearance. Then he sent them to Bethlehem, after having instructed them: "Go and get detailed information about the child. When you have discovered something, report your findings to me so that I may go and offer him homage too."

After their audience with the king, they set out. The star which they had observed at its rising went ahead of them until it came to a standstill over the place where the child was. They were overjoyed at seeing the star, and on entering the house, found the child with Mary his mother. They prostrated themselves and did him homage. Then they opened their coffers and presented him with gifts of gold, frankincense, and myrrh.

They received a message in a dream not to return to Herod, so they went back to their own country by another route.

The gospel of the Lord.

INTRODUCTORY PRAYER

We bless you, God our Father.
By guiding the magi to the manger of the infant Jesus,
You open a path of hope for the nations.
In lighting the light of faith on their way,
you make the morning star rise in our hearts.
In receiving their offering of gold, frankincense, and myrrh,
you accept the homage of our love.

We pray:
To all those who seek you with uprightness, send a star—
a reason to hope and love—
which will guide them toward your house of light
where we will celebrate together your fatherly love
through your Son Jesus, in the joy of the Holy Spirit,
forever and ever. Amen.

HOMILY

Epiphany, Feast of the Nations

In his last appearance to his disciples, the risen Christ gives his disciples the commandment of the universal mission: "Make disciples of all nations."[1] This opening of the Church to the nations is anticipated from the beginning of the gospel in the visit of the magi to the royal child. Their entrance into the dwelling of Bethlehem announces the entrance of all peoples into the Church. And when the magi worship the God-Child, they walk at the head of the procession of all those who recognize Jesus as Lord.

Therefore, tradition is right to consider the magi as the "first fruits of the nations." In one of his homilies on Epiphany, Leo the Great (+461) explains:

> Recognize, my beloved brothers and sisters, in the magi worshipers of Christ, the first fruits of our vocation and of our faith. Our souls exulting with joy, let us celebrate the beginnings of our blessed hope. It is here that we began to enter into possession of our eternal inheritance.[2]

In order to celebrate the call of the nations to the inheritance of Israel, the liturgy has chosen as the first reading a poem from the third part of Isaiah (Trito-Isaiah). It says:

> Herds of camels will invade you,
> dromedaries of Midian and Ephah.
> All the people of Sheba will come,
> bearing gold and incense
> and singing the praises of the Lord. Is 60, 6

There is an obvious relationship between the texts of Isaiah and Matthew. This relationship, communicated through images, remains superficial and somewhat folkloric. What is more folkloric than camels at the manger? But on the level of the message itself, this relationship has the depth of the word of God.

What is the source of this poem? What is its date of composition? The poem comes from the time which saw Israel's great adventure as they returned from captivity. The date is rather easy to calculate. The poem mentions the altar which had been rebuilt to receive the offerings but allows us to understand that the restoration of the Temple was not yet finished.[3] Now we know that the altar was rebuilt from 538 and that the restoration of the

Temple was finished in 515. Therefore, the poem dates from the period between those years.

The Light of God Upon Jerusalem

The glory of Yahweh had formerly led the people of the Exodus across the desert of Sinai and had brought them into the Holy Land.[4] That glory is now gathering together the people formerly deported to Babylon, and it rests like a crown of light upon the Holy City:

> Arise! Shine, for here is your light
> and the glory of Yahweh rises upon you,
> whereas darkness extends over the earth
> and obscurity over the peoples!
>
> Lift up your eyes and look around you;
> all assemble and come to you.
> Your children come from afar
> and your daughters are carried in arms. Is 60, 1-2. 4

What a marvelous prophecy! The first time it was realized was at the end of the captivity, when the joy of their return illuminated the face of the repatriates.

Next, it was realized in Jesus. "We have seen his glory," say the disciple-witnesses.[5] It is also in Jesus that the glory of God was identified with God himself, according to the text of the Book of Isaiah:

> Yahweh rises upon you,
> and his glory appears over you. Is 60, 3

The prophecy continues to be realized throughout history, until the day when the Church on earth will be transfigured into the Church in heaven. The earthly Jerusalem will then become the heavenly Jerusalem.

Every believer, in the very measure that he or she is a living stone of the Church, is a bearer of the light of Jesus and becomes an epiphany of his glory. Isaiah says to each one of us today: "Arise! Get up! Shine the light of Jesus on your brothers and sisters! Be an epiphany for those who walk in darkness!"

It is this word from Isaiah that Jesus echoes in the gospel:

> Let your light shine before others
> so that they may see your good works
> and glorify our heavenly Father. Mt 5, 16

The Pilgrimage of the Nations to Jerusalem

As soon as the dawn of return rose upon Jerusalem, the nations set out toward the brightness of that morning:

> Nations walk toward the light,
> and kings toward your dawning brightness. Is 60, 3

Nations come in great quantity from everywhere. From the East come caravans of camels from Midian and Ephah, bringing—like the Magi of Matthew—offerings of gold and incense. From the West, like a flock of doves in the blue of heaven, comes a flotilla of white sails which, on the blue of the ocean, hastens toward the Promised Land:

> Who are those who fly like a cloud,
> like the doves toward their nests?
> Yes, ships are assembling for you;
> the ships of Tarshish are in the lead. Is 60, 8-9

In the Bible, Tarshish is, as one would say, the end of the world: It undoubtedly refers to Tartessus, in southwest Spain, at the mouth of the Guadalquiver River. That is where Jonah, the rebellious and grumbling prophet, wanted to flee from the presence of Yahweh in order not to have to preach repentance to the Ninevites. It is useless to ask oneself how Tarshish saw the dawn rise upon Jerusalem: This dawn is the dawn of God's light; it can be seen everywhere!

The pilgrims arrive in Jerusalem with hands full of presents. At the same time, with gold and incense, they bring "the treasures of the sea, the riches of the nations." They also think about the Temple. Here, then, is "the glory of Lebanon," the famous cedars, not to mention cypress, the platan and the box-wood "to adorn the sanctuary." Here also to be offered at the altar of sacrifice are the best offerings, "all the flocks of Kedar, the rams of Nebaioth,"[6] two semi-nomadic tribes of the Transjordan who were descendants of Ishmael.

Full of ardor for work, the pilgrims placed themselves immediately in the service of the chosen people and restored the enclosure of the Holy City:

> The children of strangers will rebuild your walls
> and their kings will be your servants. Is 60, 10

Finally, here is the most beautiful part: this pilgrimage of the nations becomes an immense fiesta of praise to God:

> All those from Sheba will come
> singing the praises of Yahweh. Is 60, 6

How was the prophecy realized?

When this prophecy was realized the first time at the return from Babylonian captivity, the realization was humble, and resembled an unfulfilled dream.

When it was realized a second time in Jesus, it was realized in plenitude. The light of the resurrection of Jesus rose upon the world, and on the day of Pentecost, "pious men from all the nations that are under the sun" entered into the church "while singing the marvels of God."[7]

As it continues to be realized throughout the era of the Church, this prophecy of joy becomes for us, on this day of Epiphany, a criterion for judgment. Indeed, the number of believers who walk toward the Church today bear witness to the intensity of the light that rose upon her. If this number is great, it is because the dawn of God that rose upon the Church is great. If this number is small, it is because the light is hazy. If people are not attracted by the Church, it is because the Church is not attractive. And the Church is each one of us.

We often tire ourselves by crying to our brothers and sisters: "Come with us! Enter into our church! Our community is the most beautiful! Our liturgy is the truest!" And their astonished eyes seem to ask us: "Where is your light? Where did your dawn rise? Where is the glory of God? Where, the joy? Where, the praise?"

As we look at ourselves we are filled with confusion as well as joy. We are confused by the mist that obscures our heaven. We are full of joy for the dawn that pierces it. We are full of admiration for the stars of Epiphany which Christ has made rise in the heaven of the Church throughout history. We are full of sadness for the stars that we have allowed to be extinguished.

We also know that the mistakes have not all been ours. Discussing with pagans, Theophilus of Antioch (+185) argues:

> If you say to me: "Show me your God," I would answer: "Show me your man and then I will show you my God! Show me if the eyes of your soul know how to see... All have eyes, but some have blinded them and do not notice the light of the sun."[8]

Lord, make our lives a light for our brothers and sisters, and open blind eyes.

The Future Jerusalem

How resplendent is the Jerusalem of the future! Her beauty is welcoming to all nations:

> Your doors will always be open;
> day and night, they will never be closed. Is 60, 11

Her inhabitants will be composed of only the righteous; her Judge will be called "Peace;" her Governor, "Justice;" her ramparts will be called "Salvation;" and her gates, "Praises." She herself will bear the name of "City of the Lord," "Zion of the Holy One of Israel."[9] She is totally transfigured by the splendor of God:

> Yahweh will be your eternal light,
> and your God will be your beauty. Is 60, 19

When will this marvelous Jerusalem be built? At the end of time, in heaven.

While waiting, the Church on earth serves as the path toward the church in heaven. All Christians, bearers of the Star, announce the light that comes from God to their brothers and sisters. Each ray of beauty that shines on their faces proclaims that God is the source of infinite splendor.

The continual temptation remains for the Church to mistake ourselves for the Kingdom when we are only the path, to think that the nations come to us when they are walking toward God (to "suck the milk of nations and the riches of kings," as the poem says[10]) to become the banker for people when we are only the trustees of offerings to the Lord.

In the face of this temptation, the prayer of the Church is the prayer of her humility:

> Not to us, Lord, not to us,
> but to your name belongs the glory. Ps 115, 1

In order to reduce the revelries of our pride and to prevent us from sculpting a statue to our glory in the clouds, the liturgy invites us to come back to the humility of Bethlehem. There is found the gate of heaven, but it is a stable. There stands the throne of the Messiah, but it is a manger. There is found Christ the Lord, but he is a small child, a newborn.

To that Child, the light of the world, be glory and praise, eternally. Amen.

CONCLUDING PRAYER

Today the magi come to Bethlehem.
With them, Lord Jesus,
we come to bow down before you.
We pray to you:
Christ, be our light of glory!

Today the star leads them to the manger.
With them, Lord Jesus,
we want to let ourselves be led by your light.
We pray to you:
Christ, be our light of glory!

Today, they find the little Child with Mary his mother.
With them, Lord Jesus,
we want to discover you in the midst of our brothers and sisters.
We pray to you:
Christ, be our light of glory!

Today they bow down before you and worship you.
With them, Lord Jesus,
we want to worship your holy will for us.
We pray to you:
Christ, be our light of glory!

Today they offer you their gifts.
With them, Lord Jesus,
we want to offer our own lives to you as a gift.
We pray to you:
Christ, be our light of glory!

You, Lord Jesus,
are the shining Star of the eternal morning.
Make rise upon our hearts that Day
when we come to see your splendor
in the Kingdom of your Father,
in the joy of the Holy Spirit, forever and ever. Amen.

NOTES TO EPIPHANY

1. Mt 28, 19.
2. On Epiphany, Second Sermon, 4. SC 22 bis (1964), p. 224.
3. Is 60, 7. 13 See P. E. Bonnard, *Le Second Isaiah*, p. 401. The liturgy only gives the beginning of the poem, Is 60, 1–6. Our analysis envisions the entire poem, Is 60, 1–22.
4. Ex 13, 21.
5. Jn 1, 14.
6. Is 60, 5. 7. 13.
7. Acts 2, 5. 11.
8. Lettre à Autolycus, I, 2. L. Deiss, *Printemps de la théologie*, (Paris: Editions Fleurus, 1964), p. 78.
9. Is 60, 14. 17. 21.
10. Is 60, 16.

BAPTISM OF THE LORD

READING I — Is 42, 1-4. 6-7

A reading from the book of the prophet Isaiah

Here is my servant whom I uphold,
my chosen one with whom I am pleased,
Upon whom I have put my spirit;
he shall bring forth justice to the nations,
Not crying out, not shouting,
not making his voice heard in the street.
A bruised reed he shall not break,
and a smoldering wick he shall not quench,
Until he establishes justice on the earth;
the coast lands will wait for his teaching.

I, the Lord, have called you for the victory of justice,
I have grasped you by the hand;
I formed you, and set you
as a covenant of the people,
a light for the nations,
To open the eyes of the blind,
to bring out prisoners from confinement,
and from the dungeon, those who live in darkness.

The Word of the Lord.

RESPONSORIAL PSALM — Ps 29, 1-2. 3-4. 9-10

R/. (11) The Lord will bless his people with peace.

Give to the Lord, you sons of God,
give to the Lord glory and praise,
Give to the Lord the glory due his name;
adore the Lord in holy attire.

R/. The Lord will bless his people with peace.

The voice of the Lord is over the waters,
the Lord, over vast waters.
The voice of the Lord is mighty;
the voice of the Lord is majestic.

R/. The Lord will bless his people with peace.

The God of glory thunders,
  and in his temple all say, "Glory!"
The Lord is enthroned above the flood;
  the Lord is enthroned as king forever.

R/. The Lord will bless his people with peace.

Reading II — Acts 10, 34-38

A reading from the Acts of the Apostles

Peter addressed Cornelius and the people assembled at his house in these words: "I begin to see how true it is that God shows no partiality. Rather, the man of any nation who fears God and acts uprightly is acceptable to him. This is the message he has sent to the sons of Israel, 'the good news of peace' proclaimed through Jesus Christ who is Lord of all. I take it you know what has been reported all over Judea about Jesus of Nazareth, beginning in Galilee with the baptism John preached; of the way God anointed him with the Holy Spirit and power. He went about doing good works and healing all who were in the grip of the devil, and God was with him."

The Word of the Lord.

Gospel — Mk 1, 7-11

A reading from the holy gospel according to Mark

The theme of John's preaching was: "One more powerful than I is to come after me. I am not fit to stoop and untie his sandal straps. I have baptized you in water; he will baptize you in the Holy Spirit."

During that time, Jesus came from Nazareth in Galilee and was baptized in the Jordan by John. Immediately on coming up out of the water he saw the sky rent in two and the Spirit descending on him like a dove. Then a voice came from the heavens: "You are my beloved Son. On you my favor rests."

The gospel of the Lord.

INTRODUCTORY PRAYER

We bless you, Lord Jesus Christ,
on this day when we celebrate your holy baptism.
As you descended into the waters of the river Jordan,
the prophecy of the psalmist was fulfilled.
The voice of God the almighty came over the waters,
and the whole earth became his temple
where every creature sings his glory.

We pray:
May the voice of your Father also come upon us,
may he say to each one of us:
"You also are my child
in whom I have placed all my love!"
Then our lives will be changed into your eternal life,
and we will celebrate your love forever and ever. Amen.

HOMILY

The Baptism of the Lord is the feast which celebrates the time when Jesus received his vocation, when he was confirmed in his vocation: He is the Servant of Yahweh of whom it is said in Isaiah:

> Behold my servant, whom I love,
> my chosen one in whom my soul delights.
> I have put my Spirit upon him. Is 42, 1

There are many ways, good ways, to celebrate this feast. We call to mind that each Sunday, the day we celebrate the Resurrection of the Lord, is also the anniversary of our own baptism, the day we were born into the life of the risen Christ. St. Basil (+369) writes:

> The beginning and the source of my life is my baptism. The first of my days is the day of my new birth. Also, the most precious word of all is the very one that was pronounced when I received the grace of adoption.
>
> That word introduced me into light; it conferred upon me the grace of knowing God. It is in this way that I became a child of God.[1]

The Witness of St. Hippolytus of Rome

Everybody knows how the baptism of little children is celebrated today in our churches. We have kept only a few symbols of the entrance of a child of God into the church, the new Promised Land where milk and honey flow, and those symbols are very weak.

But in the early church, baptism was celebrated with powerful symbols. We are fortunate to have the witness of St. Hippolytus of Rome, who describes baptism as it was celebrated in Rome around the year 215. Hippolytus was a priest of the church in Rome. Among his numerous writings, we have what is called the Apostolic Tradition.[2] It is one of the last books written in Greek before the Latin language became prevalent in Rome. The Apostolic Tradition also gives us the oldest eucharistic prayer, which is the source of the second eucharistic prayer in the Roman Missal.

1. The Catechumenate

The information given in the Apostolic Tradition describing the catechumenate as it existed in the Roman community at the beginning of the third century will certainly surprise the ordinary Christian of our day. Although the Church was expanding rapidly, nowhere do we find any trace of organized propagandistic activity. Although there was intense missionary activity, the church had no missionaries, that is, no believers who devoted themselves specifically to the task of evangelization. Although the church continually faced and overcame the paganism that surrounded her, she had no workers specially trained for this task. Reflecting on this marvelous expansion of Christianity during the first three centuries, A. von Harnack wrote:

> The most numerous and successful missionaries of the Christian religion were not the regular teachers but the Christians themselves, in virtue of their loyalty and courage... It was characteristic of this religion that everyone who seriously confessed the faith proved of service to its propaganda. Christians are to "let their light shine, that pagans may see their good works and glorify the Father in heaven." If this dominated all their life and if they lived according to the precepts of their religion, they could not be hidden at all; by their very mode of living, they could not fail to preach their faith plainly and audibly.[3]

That is the reason Hippolytus has no special name for priests or other members of the clergy whose task it would be to recruit catechumens, but he does speak readily about "those who introduce them." All members of the community engaged themselves in this apostolic task by virtue of their baptism, which deputed them for this mission.

Baptism of Blood

The time of Hippolytus was a time of persecution. Hippolytus himself was condemned to the mines of Sardinia during the persecutions by Maximus the Thracian (235-238). These mines were the extermination camps of that age, and Hippolytus gave his life there as a martyr. He writes about this baptism of blood:

> If catechumens are arrested for the name of the Lord, they are not to be left anxious about their testimony. For if they suffer violence and are put to death before receiving forgiveness for their sins, they will be justified, for they will have been baptized in their own blood.

We should never forget that our own baptism is linked with the death of Christ and with his resurrection. As it is said, we must keep in mind:

> If we die with the Lord,
> we shall live with the Lord.
> If we endure with the Lord,
> we shall reign with the Lord. 2 Tm 2, 11-12

The Time of the Catechumenate

How long was the time of the catechumenate? According to Hippolytus:

> The catechumens are to listen to the word for three years. If, however, a person is zealous and perseveres well in this undertaking, he or she is to be judged not by length of time but by conduct.
>
> Now this time of three years was not only a time of instruction, it was also a time of prayer and good works.
>
> When the catechist has finished an instruction, the catechumens are to pray apart, separately from the faithful... At the end of their prayer, the catechumens are not to exchange the kiss of peace, since their kiss is not yet holy.

It is sometimes debated today whether the time of the catechumenate should be only a time of learning the different articles of the Christian faith. Hippolytus would say that it must also be a time of Christian living.

> When those to be baptized have been selected, their life is to be examined: Have they lived uprightly during their catechumenate? Have they respected the widows, visited the sick, practiced all the good works?

Hippolytus presents a long list of trades which must be left behind if a pagan wants to become a Christian. Those whose professions were opposed to the law of God included sculptors and painters because they made images of idols, actors who gave performances of legends of gods and soldiers who had to venerate the emperor as a god. It was evident that the community took the words of the Lord very seriously:

> No one sews a patch of unshrunk cloth
> on an old garment,
> for the patch will pull away from the garment
> making the tear worse. Mt 9, 16

In the same way that the gospel could not patch the old Judaism, neither could it patch the pagan way of life. Life according to the gospel is really a new life.

The Giving of the Gospel

Of great importance was the *paradosis*, the giving of the Gospel. As we said, the candidates for baptism had their life examined to see if they were living lives of good works. The Apostolic Tradition states:

> If those who introduced the candidates testify that they have been living in this way, let them hear the gospel.

We know that at the time, Christians liked to keep little papers with them on which the beginnings of the four gospels were written. Sometimes they were even buried with these papers. The beginning pages of the gospels were considered the tickets to gaining entry into paradise.

The Daily Exorcisms

Hippolytus insists on these exorcisms:

> From the day they are chosen, hands are to be laid upon them daily in exorcism. As the day of their baptism draws near, the bishop is to exorcise each of them so that he may be certain of their purity. But if any of them are not good or pure, they are to be put aside, for they have not heard the word with faith, since it is impossible for the stranger (the demon) to remain hidden in them.
>
> Those who are to receive baptism must fast on the Friday and Saturday.
>
> On Saturday, the bishop shall assemble them all in one place and bid them all to pray and kneel.

> Then the bishop shall lay his hand on them and command all the foreign spirits to depart from them and never to return to them again.

The meaning of these exorcisms was not a matter of believing or not believing in the existence of bad spirits and devils. The point was to believe that evil can abide in our hearts. A bad spirit and evil can be expelled from our hearts only through the good Spirit, the Holy Spirit of the Lord. In the same way, darkness can be chased from our hearts only through the light of Christ. The Letter to the Ephesians cites a very old baptismal hymn drawn from the early liturgy, and Clement of Alexandria quotes the second part of this hymn:

> Awake, O you who sleep!
> Rise from the dead
> and Christ will shine on you! Eph 5, 14
>
> He is the sun of resurrection
> born before the morning star.
> He gives life by his rays.[4]

Baptism was called "illumination," and the baptized ones were called the "illuminated ones." Today this illumination is symbolized by the candle lighted from the paschal candle and is given to the newly baptized immediately after their baptism.

The Baptismal Vigil

Here is what Hippolytus writes about the baptismal vigil:

> When the bishop has finished exorcising, let him breathe on their faces, make the sign of the cross on their foreheads, ears and noses, and then bid them stand. They are to spend the entire night in vigil, listening to readings and instruction.
>
> Those who are to be baptized are to bring nothing with them except what each person brings for the eucharist. For it is fitting that those who are worthy of baptism should bring their offering at that time.

Notice the importance of the sign of the cross. Hippolytus speaks about it later in the following way:

> If you are tempted, hasten to sign yourselves on the forehead in a worthy manner. For this sign manifests the Passion which stands against the devil, provided you make it with faith, not for men to

see but knowing how to use it like a breastplate. Then the adversary, seeing the power that comes from the heart, will flee. This is what Moses imaged forth through the passover lamb that was sacrificed when he sprinkled the thresholds and smeared the doorposts with its blood. He was pointing to a faith that we now have in the perfect Lamb.

By signing our forehead and eyes with our hand, we repulse him who seeks to destroy us.

2. The Giving of Holy Baptism

The following instructions from the Apostolic Tradition govern the conferring of Holy Baptism.

Running Water

When the cock crows, prayer is first said over the water.

The water is to be water flowing from a fountain or running water. This rule is to be observed except when impossible. If the impossibility is permanent and the need pressing, use whatever water is available.

The candidates are to remove their clothes.

The children are to be baptized first. If they can answer for themselves, let them answer. If they cannot, let their parents or someone from their family answer for them.

Then baptize the men, and last, the women, who will have unbound their hair and laid aside their jewels of gold and silver.

The ordinary rite consisted in total immersion in the blessed water. It is easy to understand that this rite of immersion, as well as the rite of anointing, posed delicate problems when they involved young girls and women. The *Didascalia of the Apostles* (beginning of the third century) explains the necessity of the deaconesses in this way:

When women descend into the water (to receive baptism), it is required that those who thus descend into the water be anointed by the deaconess with the oil anointing. Where there is no woman, and especially no deaconess, the minister of baptism must himself be the one who anoints the woman being baptized. But if there is a woman present, and above all a deaconess, it is not fitting that the woman (being baptized) be seen by men.[5]

An example of the problems posed by the baptism and anointing of women is given by John Moschus (+619). In *The Spiritual Meadow* he tells the story of a monk named Conan who had been ordained a priest especially for the administration of baptism. This priest was acutely disturbed by a beautiful young Persian woman to whom he had to give the rite of anointing. He decided to leave his monastery and seek refuge in solitude in order to avoid further embarrassing situations, but John the Baptist appeared to him and strengthened him. After that, Conan continued to baptize for another twelve years without ever being troubled again.[6]

The Oil of Thanksgiving and the Oil of Exorcism

> At the hour set for baptism, the bishop will pronounce a prayer of thanksgiving over the oil and collect it in a vessel: this is called the "oil of thanksgiving."
>
> He will take another oil and exorcise it: this is called the "oil of exorcism."
>
> A deacon will carry the oil of exorcism and stand at the priest's left. Another deacon will take the oil of thanksgiving and stand at the priest's right.

Renunciation of Satan

> The priest will take each of those who are to be baptized and will order each one to turn to the west and renounce, saying:
>
> I renounce you, Satan, and all your undertakings, and all your works.

Those who are to be baptized make their abjuration facing the west, the place where the devil is supposed to dwell. Christian antiquity, as we know, attached great importance to "orientation" (facing the east) in prayer, since the rising sun was regarded as the symbol of Christ. The *Didascalia*, which has already been cited, gives the following rule:

> You should pray facing the East. For you know that it is written: "Give thanks to God, who rides on the heaven of heavens, on the eastern side."

The orientation of prayer influenced the orientation of the churches. This practice became general in the East in the fifth century and traditional in the West in the sixth. All our ancient cathedrals are oriented this way, with the sanctuary turned to the east.

The Anointing of Exorcism

Hippolytus of Rome distinguishes between two anointings. The first one is before baptism, after the renunciation of Satan. Hippolytus explains:

> After this abjuration, he (the priest) anoints them with the oil of exorcism, saying: "Let every evil spirit depart from you!"

The Triple Immersion

The heart of baptism is the triple immersion. Here is what Hippolytus says:

> The person to be baptized lays aside his clothes, then is brought to the bishop or priest who stands near the water of baptism. A deacon descends into the water with the one to be baptized.
>
> The one doing the baptizing lays his hand on the one being baptized and asks:
>
> Do you believe in God,
> the Father Almighty?
>
> The one being baptized is to answer "I believe." Keeping his hand on the person's head, let him baptize him once.
>
> Then he asks:
>
> Do you believe in Christ Jesus, the Son of God, who was born of the Holy Spirit and the Virgin Mary, who was crucified under Pontius Pilate, who died and rose on the third day living from the dead, who ascended into the heavens, who sits at the right hand of the Father, who will come to judge the living and the dead?
>
> When the one being baptized answers "I believe," let him be baptized a second time.
>
> And again the one baptizing says:
>
> Do you believe in the Holy Spirit, in the Holy Church, and in the resurrection of the flesh?
>
> The one being baptized is to answer "I believe." Then he baptizes him a third time.

Here we have the perfect meaning of baptism. The verb "to baptize," in Greek, *baptizein*, means precisely "to plunge," "to immerse," "to dip." The ones who are baptized are plunged into the blessed waters to signify that they die with Christ. They rise from the waters to signify that they come back to life with Christ. Paul sums up this symbolism admirably when he explains that we are baptized, plunged into the death and resurrection of Christ:

> Do you not know that all of us who were baptized into Christ Jesus were baptized into his death? We were therefore buried with him through baptism into death in order that, just as Christ was raised from the dead... we too may live a new life. Rom 6, 3-4

Thinking about the original meaning of the verb "to baptize," we see that we have a problem today with symbolism. Pouring out a little stream of water over the forehead of the one who is being baptized reduces the symbolism greatly. We understand well that in very cold countries, this may be the only possible way to baptize. But today, with our technology, we should be able to build beautiful baptismal pools or at least beautiful fountains with running water. The baptismal corner of our churches should not be lonely and friendless. On the contrary, it should be the image of the source of life.

The Anointing with the Oil of Thanksgiving

After baptism, Hippolytus presents the second anointing, the one with the oil of thanksgiving:

> After the one being baptized comes up again, the priest will anoint him with the oil of thanksgiving and say:
>
> I anoint you with oil that has been sanctified in the name Jesus Christ.
>
> After drying themselves off, they will put on their clothes again and enter the church.

It is this anointing which gives us the name "Christian." The word "Christian" comes from Christ. Christians are the followers of Christ. According to Luke in the Acts of the Apostles "The disciples (of Christ) were first called Christians in Antioch."[7]

The name of "Christ" comes from the Greek *Christos*, which comes from the verb *chriein*, which means "to anoint." *Christos* is the One who is anointed, consequently, who is consecrated as Messiah.

Therefore, to receive the baptismal anointing is to enter into the vocation of Christ and to become one in him. Paul explains:

> All of you who were baptized into Christ have been clothed with Christ... for you are all one in Jesus Christ. Gal 3, 27. 28

When Christians are anointed with the oil of thanksgiving, they enter into the royal, prophetic and kingly people of God.

Conclusion

St. Ambrose (+397) spoke admirably about the mystery of the baptism of Christ and its universal value:

> One alone—that is, Christ—was plunged into the water. But he raised us all. One alone descended. But it was in order that we all reascend. One alone took upon himself the sins of all. But it was in order that the sins of all be purified.[8]

This means that the celebration of our own baptism never ends. Once, we made the adjuration of Satan. But every day we have to renounce the evil which abides in our heart.

Once, we received the gospel which was proclaimed to us. But every day we have to listen again and follow this gospel of the Lord.

Once, we came out from the darkness of sin and were enraptured by the light of Christ. But every day we have to keep this light of Christ shining in our hearts.

Once, we were immersed into the death of Christ. But every day we have to destroy once again the sin in our life and abandon our mediocrity.

Once, we rose in the Resurrection of Christ. But every day we have to live this new life of the risen Lord.

Once, we were anointed with the oil of the thanksgiving. But every day we have to thank the Lord for this heavenly salvation.

Once, we received the Holy Spirit. But every day we have to let this Spirit lead us in the new way of heaven.

Once, we were baptized. But every day we have to celebrate our baptism until the day comes when we will be baptized—that is, immersed—into the eternal joy and peace of our heavenly Father, with his Son Jesus Christ and with the Holy Spirit, forever and ever. Amen.

CONCLUDING PRAYER

We were baptized in you,
Lord Jesus Christ;
immersed in your death.
Help us now to die to sin;
free us from the slavery of our faults.

Save us, O Lord,
in your great love.

We were baptized in you,
Lord Jesus Christ;
dressed with the garments of your life.
help us now to live your Resurrection
and to give glory to our Father.

Save us, O Lord,
in your great love.

We were baptized in you,
Lord Jesus Christ;
receiving the gift of your Spirit.
May your Spirit guide us in your ways
and awaken us on the day of your love.

Save us, O Lord,
in your great love.

We were baptized in you,
Lord Jesus Christ;
hearing the voice of your Father upon you.
May this voice now say to each one of us:
"You, too, are my beloved Child.
In you I place all my love!"

Save us, O Lord,
in your great love.

God our Father, give us the grace
to live according to the light of our baptism.
Then our lives will praise you forever,
and the whole earth will be filled
with the glory of your Son Jesus
and with the song of your Holy Spirit. Amen.

NOTES TO BAPTISM OF THE LORD

1. Basil of Caesarea (+379), *On the Holy Spirit*, X, 26, trans L. Deiss. Cf. SC 17 bis (1968), p. 336.
2. We will be quoting the *Apostolic Tradition* extensively in this homily. For a more complete translation of the text, see L. Deiss, *Springtime of the Liturgy*, pp. 136–144 and p. 153.
3. *The Mission and Expansion of Christianity in the First Three Centuries*, trans. J. Moffatt (New York, 1908), 1:336–68.
4. The second stanza is cited by Clement of Alexandria in Protrepicus IX, 84, 2. PG 8:196 A–B.
5. See L. Deiss, *Springtime of the Liturgy*, p. 177.
6. See R. de Journel, Jean Moschus: Le Pré spirituel SC 12 (Paris, 1946), pp. 48–50.
7. Acts 11, 16.
8. Ambrose of Milan, *Treatise on the Gospel of Luke*, II, 91, trans. L. Deiss. Cf. SC 45 (1956), pp. 115–116.

Seasons of Lent and Easter

ASH WEDNESDAY

Reading — Jl 2, 12-18

A reading from the book of the prophet Joel

Even now, says the Lord,
return to me with your whole heart,
with fasting, and weeping, and mourning;
Rend your hearts, not your garments,
and return to the Lord, your God.
For gracious and merciful is he,
slow to anger, rich in kindness,
and relenting in punishment.
Perhaps he will again relent
and leave behind him a blessing,
Offerings and libations
for the Lord, your God.

Blow the trumpet in Zion!
Proclaim a fast,
call an assembly;
Gather the people,
notify the congregation;
Assemble the elders,
gather the children
and the infants at the breast;
Let the bridegroom quit his room,
and the bride her chamber.
Between the porch and the altar
let the priests, the ministers of the Lord, weep,
And say, "Spare, O Lord, your people,
and make not your heritage a reproach,
with the nations ruling over them!

Why should they say among the peoples,
'Where is their God?'"
Then the Lord was stirred to concern for his land and took pity on his people.
The Word of the Lord.

Responsorial Psalm — Ps 51, 3-4. 5-6. 12-13. 14, 17

R/. (3) Be merciful, O Lord, for we have sinned.

Have mercy on me, O God, in your goodness;
  in the greatness of your compassion wipe out my offense.
Thoroughly wash me from my guilt
  and of my sin cleanse me.

R/. Be merciful, O Lord, for we have sinned.

For I acknowledge my offense,
  and my sin is before me always:
"Against you only have I sinned,
  and done what is evil in your sight."

R/. Be merciful, O Lord, for we have sinned.

A clean heart create for me, O God,
  and a steadfast spirit renew within me.
Cast me not out from your presence,
  and your holy spirit take not from me.

R/. Be merciful, O Lord, for we have sinned.

Give me back the joy of your salvation,
  and a willing spirit sustain in me.
O Lord, open my lips,
  and my mouth shall proclaim your praise.

R/. Be merciful, O Lord, for we have sinned.

Reading II — 2 Cor 5, 20 – 6, 2

A reading from the second letter of Paul to the Corinthians

We are ambassadors for Christ, God as it were appealing through us. We implore you, in Christ's name: be reconciled to God! For our sakes God made him who did not know sin to be sin, so that in him we might become the very holiness of God.

As your fellow workers we beg you not to receive the grace of God in vain. For he says, "In an acceptable time I have heard you; on a day of salvation I have helped you." Now is the acceptable time! Now is the day of salvation!

The Word of the Lord.

Gospel **Mt 6, 1-6. 16-18**

A reading from the holy gospel according to Matthew

Jesus said to his disciples: "Be on guard against performing religious acts for people to see. Otherwise expect no recompense from your heavenly Father. When you give alms, for example, do not blow a horn before you in synagogues and streets like hypocrites looking for applause. You can be sure of this much, they are already repaid. In giving alms you are not to let your left hand know what your right hand is doing. Keep your deeds of mercy secret, and your Father who sees in secret will repay you.

"When you are praying, do not behave like the hypocrites who love to stand and pray in synagogues or on street corners in order to be noticed. I give you my word, they are already repaid. Whenever you pray, go to your room, close your door, and pray to your Father in private. Then your Father, who sees what no man sees, will repay you.

"When you fast, you are not to look glum as the hypocrites do. They change the appearance of their faces so that others may see they are fasting. I assure you, they are already repaid. When you fast, see to it that you groom your hair and wash your face. In that way no one can see you are fasting but your Father who is hidden; and your Father who sees what is hidden will repay you."

The gospel of the Lord.

INTRODUCTORY PRAYER

On this Ash Wednesday, the Church invites us
to begin our time of Lent.
Through the voice of our friend, the prophet Joel,
the Lord calls to us today:

"Come back to me with all your heart...
Come back to the Lord your God,
for he is tender and merciful,
slow to anger and full of love."

Our path of Lent is a path of return,
and this return is an encounter with the tenderness of God.
What exile would not rejoice upon returning home?
What prisoner would not rejoice to regain freedom?
What child would not rejoice to come back home?
Who among us would not rejoice to encounter
the tenderness and the mercy of God?

Blessed be our Father in heaven!
He offers us this opportunity of forty days
to discover his mercy once again.
He gives us this Ash Wednesday
as a door of hope and the path of return.
To him be glory forever and ever. Amen.

HOMILY

Each time Jesus speaks to us, joy rises up in our lives. It is like the morning sun making our hearts rejoice.

The Good News that God gives us today is the following: we are dust, and we are sinners. But God is seeking us. He loves us. He says to us today:

> Return to the Lord your God,
> for he is tender and merciful,
> slow to anger and full of love. Joel 2, 13

For this road of return, today Jesus proposes to us three paths of joy: prayer, almsgiving and fasting. In the days of Jesus, these were important works of piety and Jewish observance. These three works invite all Christians to the joy of the gospel.

Prayer

This Good News first concerns prayer.

To pray to God is a feast. But for this feast to succeed, Jesus tells us: withdraw into your room. Close the door of your heart. And there you will find your Father. With him, close to him, you will rejoice. Like a bird close to its nest. Like a lover close to his beloved. Like a child close to its Father.

A thousand difficulties can await you on the path of your Lent, of your life, in your walk toward the Lord's Passover. A thousand waves of sadness or discouragement can threaten to engulf your boat. But prayer will keep you in peace close to your Father. As the psalm says:

> I keep my soul in peace and silence
> like a weaned child close to its mother.
> My soul is within me like a weaned child. Ps 131, 2

A longer time of prayer is suggested during Lent. How long? We must all decide according to our own hearts and according to the feast that we wish to offer our hearts. We are all so busy! We sometimes think we are indispensable. And yet, look at our cemeteries: they are filled with people who were very busy, who sometimes thought they were indispensable! I am not a prophet but a simple priest; however, I can assure you of this before God: when you finally lay aside your indispensable occupations, terminate the Lent of your life and present yourself before your Father in heaven to take part in the resurrection of Jesus, you will not regret the time that you will have dedicated to prayer during this Lent.

Starting today, prayer can be the joy of your life. It is a feast with your Father! Do not deprive yourself of the joy of this feast!

Almsgiving

Secondly, this Good News concerns almsgiving.

To give alms for the love of God is a feast.

Share with your brothers and sisters. Do not give them something useless that you do not want but give them something that you like and that will make them happy.

We live in times of inflation. Therefore, save your money by investing it where it will not lose its value. Jesus says to us: "Make for yourselves purses that will not wear out; make a treasure in heaven."[1]

Above all, share the bread of love with your brothers and sisters. Give the alms of a smile to one who is grumpy. Give the alms of joy to one who is sad.

For your feast of almsgiving to be successful, Jesus tells you, do not look at what you give, look only at your Father. And you will rejoice with him.

Fasting

To fast for the love of God is a feast! Jesus says to you: "Anoint yourself!" Let your assembly be fragrant. For when you fast, when you deprive yourself for your brothers and sisters, you enrich your heart.

If there are some among you who want to acquire a youthful figure, if there are pounds to be lost, the liturgy says to you today: "Now is the acceptable time!" It is now that the diet must begin.

Once, when I was in Morocco, I traveled on the road that leads to the holy city of Fez. My Muslim driver was a very holy man, with a faith as solid as granite. Along the way we discussed everything and nothing. I asked him: "Is it hard for you to fast during Ramadan?" Ramadan is the ninth month of the Moslem year, spent in fasting from sunrise to sunset. He answered me: "Yes, sometimes very hard. Every Ramadan I lose eleven pounds." Then he asked me: "And you Christians, when you fast during the forty days of Lent, how many pounds do you lose?" I did not dare to answer him.

And you, would you have dared?

Let us not disregard the humble practice of fasting. Of course, as in all things, one must use moderation. That is common sense. Saint Francis de Sales, who was not only a great saint but also a man full of humor, said that the deer of the forest run badly in two seasons: the season when they are too fat and the season when they are too thin. Therefore, to run briskly in the forest of the Lord, do not be too fat or too thin. Do what is necessary to fill your Lent with the joy of the Lord.

Now is the Acceptable Time

To conclude, I would like you to hear a voice that resounded in Jerusalem toward the middle of the fourth century, in the Church of Anastasis where the Tomb of the Resurrection is found. This text comes to us from the mystagogic catechism attributed to Cyril of Jerusalem (314-387). He is addressing himself to candidates for baptism and, through this marvelous voice, he speaks to us:

> As for us, the ministers of Christ, we have welcomed each of you, and, like men filling the office of porters, we have left the door open. Perhaps you entered with a soul defiled by sins and with a perverse intention. You did enter, however; you have been welcomed, and your name has been registered.

See the venerable appearance of our assembly. Do you observe its order and discipline, the reading of the Scriptures, the presence of religious, the sequence of instructions? Let the place fill you with a holy fear, and allow yourselves to draw instruction from what you see. Go forth today in good time, and return tomorrow with even better dispositions.

If you are wearing the robe of avarice, don another garment and return. Get rid of your lust and uncleanness, and put on the sparkling robe of purity. I give you this warning before Jesus, the Spouse of souls, comes in and sees the garments you are wearing. A lengthy stay is granted you: You have forty days in which to repent; you have plenty of time to put off your garments, wash yourself, put on new robes and then return.

If you persevere in your evil intention, he who is speaking to you is not responsible for that. But then you must not expect to receive grace. The water may receive you, but the Spirit will not accept you.

If anyone is conscious of wounds, let him seek healing! If anyone has fallen, let him get up! Let there be no Simon among you,[4] no hypocrisy, no prying curiosity!

Perhaps you have come for some other reason? A man may want to please a woman and may come for that reason. The same may be true of a woman. Often too, a slave wants to please his master, or a friend a friend. I take whatever is on the hook, I pull you in, you who came with an evil intention but will be saved by your hope of the good. Doubtless you did not know, did you, where you were going, and did not recognize the net in which you have been caught? You have been caught in the Church's net! Let yourself be taken alive, and do not flee! Jesus has you on his hook, not to cause your death but to give you life after putting you to death. For you must die and rise again. You have heard the Apostle's words: "Dead to sin but alive to righteousness" (Rom. 6, 11). Begin today to live!...God has called; it is you he has called!...You who have enrolled yourselves have become the sons and daughters of a single Mother.[2]

"Now is the acceptable time," Paul affirms. To tell the truth, it is always the "time" (*kairos*) of God. But some times are more decisive than others. What would you do if this Lent were the last that the patience of God offered to you?

Now, if this were truly your last Lent, this time would no longer be feast days that the Father would be offering to you. It would truly be the threshold of the feast, the feast where your misery will meet his mercy, the feast where the Lent of your life will meet his eternal Passover.

Blessed be you, Father, for that day when the dust that we are, on this Ash Wednesday, will meet your eternity on the day of Resurrection.

CONCLUDING PRAYER

"Now is the acceptable time;
Now is the day of salvation."
Let us then pray that our lives
will be worthy of the Gospel of Christ.

Remember us, O Lord, in your loving care.

For the prayers on our lips
while our hearts are far from you
and for all our vain celebrations
when we make a spectacle of your Church,
forgive us, Lord.
For our secret prayers, indwelt by your Spirit,
offered in living praise to your glory,
thank you, Lord.

Teach us to pray according to your gospel.

Remember us, O Lord, in your loving care.

For the alms we give with ostentation,
when we make a spectacle of your Church,
forgive us, Lord.
For our secret almsgiving transfigured by your love,
offered in living praise to your glory,
thank you, Lord.
Teach us to give according to your gospel.

Remember us, O Lord, in your loving care.

For our works of piety and our fasting like the Pharisees,
when we make a spectacle of your Church,
forgive us, Lord.
For our secret sacrifices joined to your sacrifice,
offered in living praise to your glory,
thank you, Lord.
Teach us to fast according to your gospel.

Remember us, O Lord, in your loving care.

Let us pray again for all our personal intentions.

Look, O Lord, at the dust
that marks our foreheads
and recognize us as your children.
From the clay of the earth
you fashioned the earthly Adam
and the beautiful Eve, his companion.
From the dust of our earth you raised
the blessed body of your Son, Jesus.
You took him from the dust of the grave;
you made him rise in the glory of the Resurrection.
When the day comes that we will sleep
in the land of dust
and you will make the eternal Day dawn,
recognize then on our foreheads
the sign of your Son Jesus,
and awaken us for the eternal feast. Amen.

NOTES TO ASH WEDNESDAY

1. Lk 12,33.
2. *Procatechesis to the Candidates for Baptism.* L. Deiss, *Springtime of the Liturgy,* Collegeville, MN: The Liturgical Press, 1979, p. 271-273.

FIRST SUNDAY OF LENT

Reading I — Gen 9, 8-15

A reading from the book of Genesis

God said to Noah and to his sons with him: "See, I am now establishing my covenant with you and your descendants after you and with every living creature that was with you: all the birds, and the various tame and wild animals that were with you and came out of the ark. I will establish my covenant with you, that never again shall all bodily creatures be destroyed by the waters of a flood; there shall not be another flood to devastate the earth." God added: "This is the sign that I am giving for all ages to come, of the covenant between me and you and every living creature with you: I set my bow in the clouds to serve as a sign of the covenant between me and the earth. When I bring clouds over the earth, and the bow appears in the clouds, I will recall the covenant I have made between me and you and all living beings, so that the waters shall never again become a flood to destroy all mortal beings."

The Word of the Lord.

Responsorial Psalm — Ps 25, 4-5. 6-7. 8-9

R/. (10) Your ways, O Lord, are love and truth,
to those who keep your covenant.

Your ways, O Lord, make known to me;
teach me your paths,
Guide me in your truth and teach me,
for you are God my savior.

R/. Your ways, O Lord, are love and truth,
to those who keep your covenant.

Remember that your compassion, O Lord,
and your kindness are from of old.
In your kindness remember me,
because of your goodness, O Lord.

R/. Your ways, O Lord, are love and truth,
to those who keep your covenant.

Good and upright is the Lord;
thus he shows sinners the way.
He guides the humble to justice,
he teaches the humble his way.

R/. Your ways, O Lord, are love and truth,
to those who keep your covenant.

Reading II — 1 Pt 3, 18-22

A reading from the first letter of Peter

This is why Christ died for sins once for all, a just man for the sake of the unjust: so that he could lead you to God. He was put to death insofar as fleshly existence goes, but was given life in the realm of the spirit. It was in the spirit also that he went to preach to the spirits in prison. They had disobeyed as long ago as Noah's day, while God patiently waited until the ark was built. At that time, a few persons, eight in all, escaped in the ark through the water. You are now saved by a baptismal bath which corresponds to this exactly. This baptism is no removal of physical stain, but the pledge to God of an irreproachable conscience through the resurrection of Jesus Christ. He went to heaven and is at God's right hand, with angelic rulers and powers subjected to him.

The Word of the Lord.

Gospel — Mk 1, 12-15

A reading from the holy gospel according to Mark

The Spirit sent Jesus out toward the desert. He stayed in the wasteland forty days, put to the test there by Satan. He was with the wild beasts, and angels waited on him.

After John's arrest, Jesus appeared in Galilee proclaiming God's good news: "This is the time of fulfillment. The reign of God is at hand! Reform your lives and believe in the good news!"

The gospel of the Lord.

INTRODUCTORY PRAYER

On this First Sunday of Lent,
the Church celebrates the Old Covenant
that God established with Noah the righteous,
his servant,
when he saved him from the waves of the Flood,
and the New Covenant,
the victory that he accorded to Jesus the Holy, his Son,
when he took him away from the temptations of Satan.

God our Father, we humbly pray to you:

Save the ark of your church,
tossed about in the waves of sin,
and give us, in the triumph of Jesus,
victory over the evil that lives in us.

Give us the grace to not live in vain
during these forty days of Lent, gift of your patience.
Let us use them to truly convert ourselves
and to return to you with all our love.

You are the God of forgiveness,
the Lord of tenderness.
To you be the praise of our love forever and ever. Amen.

HOMILY

1. The Flood

Until the year 1872, not much more than a hundred years ago, we knew only one account of the flood, the one found in the Bible. At that time we thought it was a historical account. Since then, a number of legends about the flood have been found in the sands of the Middle East. These legends go back to about the second millennium before Christ.

Between 1844 and 1854, during the excavation of the archeological site at Nineveh, in Mesopotamia, about twenty-five thousand tablets were discovered in the royal library of King Ashurbanipal (668-626). These tablets were brought to the British Museum in London where they were classified as "decorated pottery" because no one knew how to decipher the inscriptions found on them. In 1857 we penetrated the secret of cuneiform writing, and in 1872 George Smith, an engraver of bank notes who was very interested in Orientalism, succeeded in classifying and deciphering the tablets. He then published his findings in *The Chaldean Account of the Deluge*. This made a dazzling impact on the religious and archeological worlds.

On the historical level, these mythical accounts of the flood testify to an extraordinary cataclysm that ravaged the flat countries of Mesopotamia when, as the Bible says, "all the fountains of the deep burst forth and the floodgates of heaven were opened."[1] But conclusive and precise contact with the historical event, in Genesis as well as in the Sumerian and Akkadian accounts, is lost.

However, on the level of faith, there is in the Bible the marvelous revelation of the plan of God for humanity, the revelation of his plan for each one of us. The account of the flood concerns us because it is our own life that is judged there. For almost three thousand years, the people of God meditated on the parable of the flood. Today the liturgy invites us to continue that meditation.

The Flood, the Judgment of God on the World

The flood is the judgment of God on the world. This judgment is twofold. It is first the condemnation of sin, and secondly, the judgment of God's love.

The Condemnation of Sin

In Genesis, sin is presented not simply as a state but as a power, as the force of evil that is at work in the world.

Sin first entered into the heart of Adam and obscured his outlook on the earth, which changed from fraternal to hostile and became full of brambles and thorns.

Next, sin devoured the heart of Cain, who killed his brother.

Like cancer, it spread into the hearts of the people in the days of Noah. "Great was the wickedness of people upon the earth," says Scripture.[2]

Noah, the righteous man, is opposed to Adam, the sinner. We can picture Noah building his boat of gopherwood while the impious jeered at him: "What do you think you are doing with this boat of gopherwood? Where is your God?"

All of a sudden, the judgment of God came upon sin. Jesus spoke of this judgment in these terms:

> In those days of Noah which preceded the flood, people were eating, drinking and marrying until the day Noah entered the ark. They did not suspect anything until the arrival of the flood, which carried them all away.
>
> Watch, therefore, for you do not know which day your Master is coming. Mt 24, 37, 42

The lesson of the flood, then, is this: yes, there is a judgment of God on sin. God intervenes brutally in the wickedness of sinners. He seizes them in their total madness. And he condemns them.

The Judgment of God's Love

God condemns all sins, but not all sinners. He condemns only those sinners who refuse to convert. For the others, his judgment is that of his love, that of his forgiveness.

There is no doubt that those sinners who are converted are just as sinful as those who are not. But converted sinners carry sin like a wound in their hearts. For them, God creates a time of conversion, a time "where the patience of God is prolonged," as Peter's letter says.[3] For converted sinners, that is, for each one of us, the Book of Wisdom presents these wonderful words:

> You bequeathed to your children the sweet hope that after sin, you leave room for forgiveness. Wis 12, 19

The time of Lent is the time of that chance, of that love, of that forgiveness which God offers us.

The lesson of the flood is this: Great is our sin. But greater is God's forgiveness. His love triumphs over our wickedness.

One man alone was enough, one upright man alone was enough, one Noah alone was enough for God to renew his covenant with all people.

Through one upright man—Jesus—God offers you an eternal covenant.

It is here that this story of a legend, of a flood, of a rainbow, touches the depths of our hearts. Whatever our sin may be, today God offers us his forgiveness. A thousand times we may fall, but if we cry out a thousand times, a thousand times he will lift us up. What am I saying? A thousand times? Eternally, he offers us his Covenant! How marvelous are these words from the Book of Isaiah:

> "With everlasting love,
> I will have compassion on you,"
> says the Lord, your Redeemer.
> "To me this is like the days of Noah...
> Though the mountains depart
> and the hills be removed,
> my unfailing love will not depart from you,
> nor the covenant of my peace be removed,"
> says the Lord, who has compassion on you. Is 54, 8-10

Oh, Lord! Prolong for us sinners the time of your patience! Keep your compassion for us higher than the highest mountains, more lasting than the hardest granite, more luminous than your bright rainbow after the storm. Grant that we may come back to you during this Lent, the time of the patience of your love!

2. The Flood and Baptism

As Peter's letter teaches us, the flood is also the symbol of baptism.

The abyssal waters that drown sinners, save the upright and create the world anew represent the waters of baptism that drown sin, purify our conscience and create in us a new heart and a new spirit. Noah's ark is the image of the boat of the Church. To be baptized, it is said, is

> to pledge oneself to God with a good conscience, to participate in the resurrection of Jesus Christ, who has gone into heaven...at God's right hand. 1 Pt 3, 21-22

Stay in the boat of the Church; stay with your brothers and sisters. As we say: "We are all in the same boat." This boat is the ark of God. There you are safe. Jesus is the pilot. Trust him, for the breeze that billows your sail is his Holy Spirit. He is pushing you toward the shores of eternity.

Look at Noah in his boat of gopherwood, cast on the dark and tumultuous waves of the flood. The Bible gives us a final and marvelous detail. It is written that God closed the door of the ark on Noah.[4]

God does not abandon those who love him. Yes, God often closes the door on us and pushes our ark onto the sea of solitude, of distress or of pain. But he never abandons us. He is the one who is going to welcome our boat after leading it to the shore of the New Land.

God never forgets us—on the condition, of course, that we stay in his hand, that we do as Saint Noah did. It is written about him:

> Noah was a righteous man and blameless...
> He walked with God. Gn 6, 9

Happy are those who have made of their lives a walk with God. Happy are we, especially during this time of Lent, if we put our hand in the hand of Jesus, if we walk in his Covenant. Then, as it is written in the psalm, "his breath of goodness will lead you to a level land."[5] That is to say, his Holy Spirit, who is goodness, will lead us to a land of light.

3. The Temptation of Jesus

Mark's gospel speaks to us about the temptation of Jesus.[6] We know that Matthew and Luke describe the three temptations of Jesus extensively. But Mark just mentions them. He does it with sobriety, without pathos but with power. He never uses the word *diabolos* (devil) but the word that makes us tremble, Satan, which is translated in Hebrew as "Adversary" or "Accuser." We find ourselves here in the presence of the one who is the eternal Adversary of the love of God on earth.

"Prepare Yourself for Trials"

Do not be astonished at having to undergo temptation. It is a completely normal trial for every believer. It was even more of a trial for Jesus at the beginning of his apostolic ministry. Scripture informs us, in fact, as if to give us courage:

> My son, if you intend to serve the Lord,
> prepare yourself for trials...
> Make your heart right;
> arm yourself with courage. Sir 2, 1-2

There is a certain foolish and naive ideal of spiritual comfort which is to want to live safe from all temptation. In order to avoid the cold wind that chills and the tornado that shakes, some people close forever the windows of their hearts and die asphyxiated in their mediocrity. They never fall while walking because they never walk at all. They never love badly because they never love at all. And they die without ever having really lived.

> Jesus was completely different.
> He was tempted in every way, just as we are,
> yet never sinned. Heb 4, 15

He knew the temptation of an easy messianism by which he could have announced the Kingdom without the cross, the love of neighbor without the obligation to serve him, the grace of heaven without paying for it with the price of his life. He could have possessed a home of tranquil peace, but he did not even have a rock on which to rest his head. He could have loved and married a woman—were there not sweet and lovable girls in Nazareth?—and had children, for he loved them. When they were brought to him, he embraced them.[7] But he wanted to have a family as big as the world, the family of all those who do the will of the Father. He refused miraculous bread, the bread of the devil, for his food was always to do the will of the Father.[8]

Blessed be you, Lord Jesus. You wanted to walk on the humble path of trial and temptation. Each time we are tempted to give up and stop on the side of the road, give us the courage to start out again and walk on the path with you.

The Purpose of Temptations

What is the purpose of temptations? Why does God permit them? Deuteronomy explains to us with certain candor:

> Remember how the Lord your God led you all the way in the desert for forty years to humble you, to test you, to know what was in the depths of your heart: whether or not you would keep his commandments. Dt 8, 2

The trial of temptation is the trial of love. "To know what was in the depths of your heart..."

Not that God needs to know what is in our hearts. He knows his creature.

"Lord, you search me and you know me" we say in the psalm (Psalm 139, 1). But it is we who need to touch the depths of our hearts, to experience how vulnerable and fragile we are and how much we need his grace.

Among the Wild Beasts, with Angels

Mark ends his account of the temptation in a wonderful way:

> Jesus lived among the wild beasts, and angels ministered to him.
> Mk 1, 13

I dream of a world where I, too, will be able to live with angels, where I will make a covenant with wild beasts. I dream of a new world where I will live in peace with the rose, where I will be able to sing to the dawn with the nightingale of the thicket, where I will be able to speak to the evening dew with the doe of the woods, where I will be able to frolic among the waves with the dolphins of the ocean.

Foolishness? No, because the covenant made with Noah wants to gather into one family all the creatures of God:

God said to Noah: "Here I am establishing my covenant with you...and all the living beings which are around us—the birds, the domestic animals and all the wild beasts.[9]

Make peace with your heart and then you will live with the angels; with them you will be able to celebrate the Lord: "I will sing to the Lord in the presence of angels."[10] Drive away the devil who lies in wait for you on the path of your life—the devil of whom I speak is not the devil with horns who makes faces to frighten children but the evil that seeks to invade your soul—and then you will be at peace with the rose, the flower of the field will be your brother, the violet of the woods will be your companion; you will live like Francis of Assisi in a world filled with the laughter of birds, filled especially with your love for all your brothers and sisters.

Your life is the life of Jesus. Your victory is his victory in you.

At his baptism, Jesus was proclaimed Son of God.[11] Then he was tempted by the devil. At your baptism, you became a child of God; prepare yourself, therefore, to meet the devil.

At his baptism, Jesus received the Spirit, who rested upon him and then drove him into the desert.[12] At your baptism, the Spirit invaded your soul and now is driving you into the desert for combat.

No one is a child of God who must not then submit to the insults of the demon. And no one can proclaim, like Jesus, the Kingdom of God,[13] if he does not first conquer the devil who is in his heart.

On this First Sunday of Lent, the door of eternal hope is opened before you. God is welcoming you. Enter into his covenant. Look at the rainbow that unites heaven with earth. Let your life take root thus in heaven. Let it burst forth in a thousand colors of joy. A new world must rise out of the flood. A new world must rise in your heart. Take the hand that Jesus extends to you. Walk with him. Fight at his side with him. Be triumphant with him.

If you do this, you will put joy into your life. An eternal joy.

PRAYER TO THE GOD OF THE COVENANT

For the living water that springs forth
from the heart of the mountain
and washes the rock,
and for the holy water of our baptism
that washes our hearts of stone,

blessed be you,
God of the Covenant.

For the wheat that germinates
in the heart of the earth
and prepares the bread of tomorrow,
and for the bread that germinates
in the heart of our Eucharist
and gives us the bread of eternity,

blessed be you,
God of the Covenant.

For the rainbow after the storm
that unites heaven with earth,
and for the forgiveness after sin
that opens for us a path to heaven,

blessed be you,
God of the Covenant.

For the ark of Noah that on the waters of the deep
floated to a new land,
and for the ark of the Church that in the tempest
guides us to the shore of the eternal Land,

blessed be you,
God of the Covenant.

For the dove that came back to the ark
carrying the olive branch,
and for the Holy Spirit
who hovered over the waters of our baptism
and brought us peace,

blessed be you,
God of the Covenant.

For Noah the righteous, your friend,
who offered you a sacrifice of thanksgiving,
and for Jesus the Holy, your Son,
who offered himself in sacrifice
for an eternal Covenant,

blessed be you,
God of the Covenant.

Yes, we want to bless you eternally,
God of all marvels,
for the Covenant that you give us
is Jesus, the Son of your love.
To you be glory forever and ever. Amen.

NOTES TO FIRST SUNDAY OF LENT

1. Gn 7, 11. About the Flood and archeology, see A. Parrot, *Bible et archeologie*, vol. 1-2 (Paris: Delachaux et Niestle, Neuchatel, 1970)
2. Gn 6, 5.
3. 1 Pt 3, 20.
4. Gn 6, 5.
5. Ps 143, 10.
6. Mk 1, 13.
7. Mk 9, 36 and 10, 16.
8. Mk 12, 50; cf. Mk 3, 35. Jn 4, 34.
9. Gn 9, 9-10. Cf. Hos 2, 16-20.
10. Ps 138, 1.
11. Mt 3, 17.
12. Mk 1, 13.
13. Mk 3, 14.

SECOND SUNDAY OF LENT

Reading I — Gen 22, 1-2. 9. 10-13. 15-18

A reading from the book of Genesis

God put Abraham to the test. He called to him, "Abraham!" "Ready!" he replied. Then God said: "Take your son Isaac, your only one, whom you love, and go to the land of Moriah. There you shall offer him up as a holocaust on a height that I will point out to you."

When they came to the place of which God had told him, Abraham built an altar there and arranged the wood on it. Then he reached out and took the knife to slaughter his son. But the Lord's messenger called to him from heaven, "Abraham, Abraham!" "Yes, Lord," he answered. "Do not lay your hand on the boy," said the messenger. "Do not do the least thing to him. I know now how devoted you are to God, since you did not withhold from me your own beloved son." As Abraham looked about, he spied a ram caught by its horns in the thicket. So he went and took the ram and offered it up as a holocaust in place of his son.

Again the Lord's messenger called to Abraham from heaven and said: "I swear by myself, declares the Lord, that because you acted as you did in not withholding from me your beloved son, I will bless you abundantly and make your descendants as countless as the stars of the sky and the sands of the seashore; your descendants shall take possession of the gates of their enemies, and in your descendants all the nations of the earth shall find blessing—all this because you obeyed my command."

The Word of the Lord.

Responsorial Psalm — Ps 116, 10. 15. 16-17. 18-19

R/. I will walk in the presence of the Lord,
in the land of the living.

I believed, even when I said,
"I am greatly afflicted."
Precious in the eyes of the Lord
is the death of his faithful ones.

R/. I will walk in the presence of the Lord,
in the land of the living.

Oh Lord, I am your servant;
  I am your servant, the son of your handmaid;
  you have loosed my bonds.
To you will I offer sacrifice of thanksgiving,
  and I will call upon the name of the Lord.

R/. I will walk in the presence of the Lord,
  in the land of the living.

My vows to the Lord I will pay
  in the presence of all his people,
In the courts of the house of the Lord,
  in your midst, O Jerusalem.

R/. I will walk in the presence of the Lord,
  in the land of the living.

Reading II — Romans 8, 31-34

A reading from the letter of Paul to the Romans

If God is for us, who can be against us? Is it possible that he who did not spare his own Son but handed him over for the sake of us all will not grant us all things besides? Who shall bring a charge against God's chosen ones? God, who justifies? Who shall condemn them? Christ Jesus, who died or rather was raised up, who is at the right hand of God and who intercedes for us?

The Word of the Lord.

Gospel — Mk 9, 2-10

A reading from the holy gospel according to Mark

Jesus took Peter, James and John off by themselves with him and led them up a high mountain. He was transfigured before their eyes and his clothes became dazzlingly white—whiter than the work of any bleacher could make them. Elijah appeared to them along with Moses; the two were in conversation with Jesus. Then Peter spoke to Jesus: "Rabbi, how good it is for us to be here. Let us erect three booths on this site, one for you, one for Moses, and one for Elijah." He hardly knew what to say, for they were all overcome with awe. A cloud came, overshadowing them, and out of the cloud a voice: "This is my Son, my beloved. Listen to him." Suddenly looking around they no longer saw anyone with them—only Jesus.

As they were coming down the mountain, he strictly enjoined them not to tell anyone what they had seen before the Son of Man had risen from the dead. They kept this word of his to themselves, though they continued to discuss what "to rise from the dead" meant.

The gospel of the Lord.

INTRODUCTORY PRAYER

Today we celebrate this Second Sunday of Lent,
the sacrifice of Abraham, our father in faith,
and the Transfiguration of Jesus, our brother according to grace.

We praise you and we bless you, God our Father.
You call us to share
the blessing promised to your servant Abraham,
and you give us your Son Jesus
as our Savior and our brother.

We pray to you:
Give us the grace to live in such a way
that you will say to us, as you did to Jesus transfigured,
"You also are my Son.
In you I have placed my love."
And on the last Day, transfigure our mortal life
into the eternity of your joy and your love.

HOMILY

1. The Sacrifice of Abraham

For the three great monotheistic religions of the world—Judaism, Christianity and Islam—Abraham is the Father of all believers. He is preeminently "the faithful one," the one who lives by faith.

This faith of Abraham culminates in the sacrifice of his son Isaac. It is that sacrifice that we celebrate today in the first reading.

"Take Your Son, Your Only One, the One Whom You Love, Isaac"

Like a litany of tenderness, each word is chosen intentionally and bruises the heart of the aged father:

• "Your son," the child of the miracle, the son of Abraham's golden anniversary, who was promised to him when he was seventy-five years old and who was given to him twenty-five years later.[1]

• "Your only one," that is, the child of the Covenant, the only one on whom rested the fulfillment of the promise.

• "The one whom you love," because he was born not of Hagar, the servant, but of Sarah, the wife whom Abraham loved.

• "Isaac," whose name means "He (God) smiles." It is the smile of God in Abraham's old age; it is the laughter of his joy.

From the first call, when Abraham left Ur in Chaldea, God gave him only vague information: "Leave your country...for the country that I will show you." Here he says: "Offer your son as a holocaust...on the mountain that I will point out to you."[2] Obviously, God takes pleasure in leaving us in situations where everything is vague for us but everything is clear for him!

Three Days' Journey

Abraham left for a journey of three days. The biblical account, with austere grandeur and total detachment, says nothing about the innermost feelings of Abraham. But tradition has always emphasized the agony of the patriarch during this journey toward the mountain.

There remained only three more days of familiarity with Isaac, the child of his laughter. All the gestures of daily life became gestures of agony: the tent unrolled at each stop, the bread torn apart to be shared and the goatskin containing water to drink passed from one to the other. During the night, under the desert stars, Abraham gazed upon his little child sleeping against him and felt his heart beat against his own.

Then only two days remained.

Then only one day remained.

Then it was the last night, and the child smiled, feeling safe near his father.

Finally, it was the dawn of that day when Abraham was able to say: "This evening, I will have killed my child Isaac: I will have reduced him to ashes."

It is here that Abraham is great. He is alone with God. Alone with his tenderness. In anticipation, Abraham was obeying the words of Jesus: "Anyone who loves his son or his daughter more than me is not worthy of me."[3]

As you know, God stopped Abraham's arm and restored to the aged father the joy of his faith as well as the life of his son.

The Blessing of the Covenant

This ancient account is rich in many meanings. There is first a violent criticism of human sacrifices, especially the sacrifice of children as practiced by the Phoenicians, the Ammonites and the Moabites, or even in the Canaannite religions and in Egypt. In the ruins of the ancient East, one often finds at the base of the wall foundations or the city gates—at Jericho, for example—skeletons of children who had been sacrificed.[4]

God affirms to us here that he rejects such sometimes heroic but barbaric sacrifices.

But he accepts the offering of the heart. For, we must add, the principles that govern Abraham's love for Isaac are always valid. No child belongs exclusively to its parents; it belongs first to God. A child is a gift that God places in the hands of parents so that they can return it to him later, along with their heart. How true are these words of Jesus:

> Whoever welcomes a little child in my name welcomes me.
>
> Mt 18, 5

Between Abraham and Isaac is God and the blessing of the Covenant.

Between all parents and their children is God and the blessing of the Covenant.

However, there is more between you and the mother of your child or the father of your child is God and the blessing of the Covenant. And it is there that this story, which is nearly four thousand years old, touches you in the depths of your heart. For at the heart of the love of Abraham and Sarah is the God of the Covenant. At the heart of your gestures of love with your wife or with your husband is the God of the Covenant and his blessing. No religion is more concerned with the human heart than the Christian religion. And no love is dearer to God than your love for your wife or for your husband and your love for your children.

Through their love, Abraham and Sarah became the ancestors of a billion faithful; for today, Jews, Christians and Moslems consider themselves their descendants. The promise made nearly four thousand years ago to an obscure tribal leader:

I will make your descendants as numerous
as the stars of the sky,
as the sands of the seashore Gn 22, 17

was fulfilled with marvelous superabundance. If I were not Christian, such an accomplishment would pose questions for me. As a believer, I am enraptured by it. Yes, God is faithful to his word.

We must add this marvel: through that love, Abraham and Sarah became the ancestors of Jesus, the Son of God. In Jesus, their love—spiritual and physical—touches the shores of divinity. In Jesus, their tenderness becomes truly eternal. In Jesus, the whole of humanity—that of prehistory, that of the future, and that of the four billion brothers and sisters with whom we live today—is invited to become sons and daughters of God, children of the Father. In Jesus, as Mary, the daughter of Abraham, sings,

God remembers his mercy,
as he had promised to Abraham
and to his descendants forever. Lk 1, 54-55

With Jesus, Abraham and Sarah also enter into your home. Or rather, it is you who enter into the heavenly home with them and with all those whom God loves and blesses.

By Faith

How should we respond to God? Like Abraham — by faith. "God will provide," said Abraham in the deepest agony of his heart.[5]

To believe is to answer with Abraham to each call of God: "Here I am!"

To believe is to have confidence that our entire life, and especially that which we love most in the world, is under the watchful eye of God.

To believe is to have assurance that even our death is a blessing, a path of life. The Letter to the Hebrews explains:

By faith Abraham...offered Isaac...It was his only son that he offered as a sacrifice, he who had received the promises...He reasoned that God was able to raise the dead. Heb 11, 17. 19

God provided for Abraham. God provides for each one of us. Faith is a blank check that we sign for God. In business affairs it is very dangerous to sign blank checks. In the affairs of God, on the other hand, it is very wise. We gain at all times. For God fills in the check with his love.

A Prophecy and a Revelation

Biblical tradition has identified the hill where Abraham offered his son as Mount Moriah, the place where the Temple of Jerusalem would later be built.[6] All the old sacrifices were a continuation of Abraham's.

Abraham loved God so much that he offered his only son. Abraham is a "type," a prophecy of the Father who so loved the world that he gave his only Son. Paul comments in the second reading: "How could he not, along with him, give us all things?"[7]

There is a difference, however, between the sacrifice of Isaac and that of Jesus. Abraham received Isaac back again. How he must have embraced him after that adventure! And how the aged Sarah must have cried with joy upon hearing their story. But Mary, receiving Jesus in her arms, could only kiss the dead body of her Son. God goes further than Abraham. He goes as far as the death of Jesus, as far as his Resurrection. God's love always surpasses ours.

Everyone admires Abraham's courage. Jewish biblical tradition also admires Isaac's courage. Here is a wonderful text, one of the most beautiful stories that Jewish tradition has handed down to us and one that Mary and Joseph might have told to the child Jesus:

Isaac spoke to his father Abraham and said: "My father!" He said: "Here I am, my son!" Isaac said: "Here are the fire and the wood. But where is the lamb for the holocaust?" Abraham said: "Before Yahweh has been prepared for him a lamb for the holocaust. However, you are the lamb of the holocaust." And they both went on together with a perfect heart.

They arrived at the place that Yahweh had told Abraham and he built an altar there. He arranged the wood, bound his son, and placed him on the altar, on top of the wood. Then he stretched out his hand and took the knife to sacrifice his son Isaac.

Isaac began to speak and said to Abraham his father: "My father, tie me well lest I resist you..." Abraham's eyes were fixed upon the eyes of Isaac and Isaac's eyes were turned toward the angels on high. Abraham did not see them. At that moment a voice came down from heaven saying: "Come, see two unique (people) in my universe. One sacrifices and the other is sacrificed: The one who sacrifices does not hesitate and the one who is sacrificed extends his throat."[8]

Isaac, with his eyes smiling toward heaven, is the image of the sacrifice of Jesus. Paul affirms: "He gave himself up for us as an offering to God in a fragrant sacrifice."[9]

Each of us has an Isaac to offer to God. We each have ourselves to offer like Isaac. Let us do it, like Isaac, in the joy of giving, with our eyes fixed toward heaven.

Every year, the Muslim faithful celebrate the sacrifice of Abraham on the tenth day of the month of Dhu 1-Hijja. Every day, we Christians commemorate this same sacrifice and we pray thus to our Father in heaven:

> Look with favor on these offerings
> and accept them as once you accepted…
> the sacrifice of Abraham, our father in faith.[10]

3. Nothing Useless in a Sacrifice

A Hasidic story:

Some people said, "This story of sacrifice had a happy ending for Isaac, but not for the ram…Poor animal," They sighed! "It was sacrificed, but it had not done anything!"

A sage replied: "This ram had an extraordinary destiny. Indeed, God created it precisely to take Isaac's place, and since creation it spent happy days in Paradise. In its sacrifice, nothing was lost. Indeed, its ashes were placed in the foundations of the altar of the Temple. Of its tendons, David made six chords for his harp. Of its skin, Elias made his cloak. As for its two horns, the smallest served to gather together the Israelites at Sinai for the celebration of the Covenant. As for the largest, it will resound on the day of the Messiah!"

Therefore, in this sacrifice, nothing was useless.[11]

In your sacrifice, also, nothing is lost. Everything is transfigured by the love of God who receives you as he received his Son, Jesus.

You know the word fiancé. The root of this word is "faith" (fiancé is old French). The fiancé is someone to whom we have given our faith. We are in some way the fiancés of God. Like Abraham, we have given God our faith. Each time God calls us, we need to answer with Abraham: "Here I am!"

4. The Transfiguration

All through his life, Jesus reveals to us the mystery of his person. The Resurrection is the magnificent and ultimate revelation of his mystery: It is then that we learn fully who he is. As Paul says, Jesus "is proclaimed Son of God with power by his Resurrection from the dead."[12]

The Transfiguration is also the glorious, but transitory, revelation of this mystery. It takes place midway between Jesus' baptism, when he was proclaimed Son of God on earth, and the Resurrection, when he was established Son of God in heaven.

The Transfiguration is the answer to the concept that the believing community had of the final destiny of the just. In the *Apocalypse of Baruch*, an apocryphal book from the end of the first century, one reads:

> (The just) will live on the summits of this world,
> they will resemble the angels,
> they will be comparable to the stars.
> (They will pass) from beauty to splendor,
> from light to the brightness of glory.[13]

The Transfiguration of Jesus Is Our Transfiguration

The transfiguration of Jesus is the pledge of our own future transfiguration. It includes our own destiny in his glorious destiny. Paul explains:

> Our citizenship is in the heavens from where we eagerly await the Savior and Lord Jesus. It is he who will transfigure our body of misery by making it conform to his body of glory, with that power that he has of being able to subject even the universe to himself. Phil 3, 20-21

We are children of this earth. Jesus transfigures us into children of heaven. Our earthly body is a body of misery: Jesus transfigures it into a body clothed with his glory. Our heart is sometimes heavy and often runs after falsehood: Jesus transfigures it into a heart resplendent with his truth. Our intellect is sometimes opaque and gloomy, a prison where a thousand mysteries run around seeking escape: Jesus invades it with his light and opens the prison, and we see God in his splendor.

May we live in such a way that we may take part in the Transfiguration of Jesus! Happy are those to whom God the Father will say, when the Lent of their lives is finished and the day of the eternal Passover rises in their hearts: "You also are my beloved child!" Happy are those whom God will welcome into his arms as a father welcomes his child and to whom he will say: "You have the same face as my Son Jesus. You have walked on the same path as he; you have loved with the same love as he. In you, also, I place all my love!"

Around the second century, this is what was sung in the Odes of Solomon:

> Because I love the Son,
> I myself will become son.
> For the one who is bound to the Immortal,
> will himself become immortal.
> And the one who delights in life,
> that one will become living in turn.[14]

To Transfigure

What does it mean to transfigure? It is not to exchange our "figure" for another (as, for example, one would exchange one part of a motor for another). God loves us just as he created us! His creation ignores all standardization. To transfigure is to keep our "figure" but to embellish it with a thousand splendors through the beauty of God. Paul explains nicely:

> We who are in this tent (that is, in our body, our earthly dwelling)...do not wish to be unclothed but to be clothed from above with our heavenly garment, so that what is mortal may be swallowed up by life. 2 Cor 5, 4

A mother who loves her child, flesh of her flesh and fruit of her tenderness, does not want to be stripped of that love. She wants, on the contrary, to save it, to transfigure it. She can only do it in the Transfiguration of Jesus.

And the man who loves his wife and gives his life for her as Christ does for his Church does not want to be stripped of that love. He wants, on the contrary, to save it from mediocrity; he wants to enrich it with the beauty of heaven. He can only do it in the Transfiguration of Jesus.

And those who have joy in their hearts do not want to be impoverished of that joy, as if to love God means to be stripped of what one loves. On the contrary, they want to eternalize it, so to speak. They can only do it in the Transfiguration of Jesus.

It is in that Transfiguration that our death itself will be transfigured into his eternity.

Icons of the Transfiguration

We know how much Eastern tradition insists upon the importance of icons, reflections of God's beauty on earth, and especially the icon of the Transfiguration.[15] Tradition required that those who devoted themselves to the vocation of painting icons begin by painting the Transfiguration. The meaning of that requirement was the following: It is in the light of the transfigured Christ that one must contemplate and paint all other images. The whole creation, and especially the saints who shine like stars in it, must be clothed with the light of the transfigured Lord.

May our eyes be filled with light. May we also be, for our brothers and sisters, icons of the beauty of God. "They no longer saw anything but Jesus alone," it is said about the apostles. May we see in all things, and especially in the faces of all those who travel with us, a face resplendent with beauty and peace, the face of Christ Jesus.

CONCLUDING PRAYER

Jesus risen is at the right hand of the Father
and intercedes unceasingly on our behalf.
With confidence, let us then present to him our prayer
for the salvation of all our brothers and sisters.

Remember us, O Lord, in your loving care.

We bless you, God our Father,
for your servant Abraham, for his wife Sarah,
and for the Covenant that you made with them.
Like them, help us to discover,
at the heart of our human tenderness,
the presence of your love.

Remember us, O Lord, in your loving care.

We bless you, God our Father,
for your servant Isaac, the child of the Promise,
who carried the wood for the sacrifice up the mountain.
Help us to carry our crosses with courage;
make our life a path of light toward you.

Remember us, O Lord, in your loving care.

We bless you also, God our Father,
for your humble servant, the Virgin Mary.

In her you remembered your mercy
as you had promised to our father Abraham.
Give to us a soul of praise and blessing
to sing with her the marvels of your love.

Remember us, O Lord, in your loving care.

We bless you especially, God our Father,
for Jesus, your beloved Son.
God who is for us,
how would you not give us everything with him?
Transfigure our life as a child of this earth
into the life of your risen Son.

Remember us, O Lord, in your loving care.

We also commend to your tenderness
all our personal intentions.

We bless you, God our Father.
In giving us your Son, Jesus,
you gave us all your love.
We want to thank you
forever and ever. Amen.

NOTES TO SECOND SUNDAY OF LENT

1. See Gn 12, 4 and 21, 5.
2. Gn 12, 1 and 22, 2.
3. Mt 10, 37.
4. See 2 Kgs 3, 21; 2 Kgs 16, 34. Cf. R. de Voux, *Les Institutions de l'Ancien Testament*, vol. 2 (Paris: Editions du Cerf, 1960), p. 326-333.
5. Gn 22, 8.
6. 2 Chr 3, 1.
7. Rom 8, 32.
8. This text comes from the *Targum of Genesis*. See A. Diez Macho, Ms. Neophyti 1(Madrid-Barcelona, 1968), p. 1250127. I use the translation established by R. le Déaut, in SC, 245 (1978) p. 216-218. (The Targum is the Aramaic translation of the Hebrew text used in the liturgical celebrations of the synagogue).
9. Eph 5, 2.
10. Eucharistic Prayer I.
11. Some elements of this story are found in L. Ginzberg, *The Legends of the Jews*, vol. 1 (Philadelphia: The Jewish Publication Society of America, 1909-1937), p. 283.
12. Rom 1, 4.
13. *Apocalypse de Baruch*, LI,10, trans. P. Bogaert, SC 145 (1969), p. 499.
14. Odes of Solomon, III, 7-9.
15. See P. Evdokionov, *L'art de l'icône Theologie de beauté* (Paris: Desclee de Brouwer, 1972), On the Transfiguration, p. 249-256.

THIRD SUNDAY OF LENT

READING I — EX 20, 1-17 OR 20, 1-3. 7-8. 12-17

A reading from the Book of Exodus

God delivered all these commandments:

"I, the Lord, am your God, who brought you out of the land of Egypt, that place of slavery. You shall not have other gods besides me.

"You shall not take the name of the Lord, your God, in vain. For the Lord will not leave unpunished him who takes his name in vain.

"Remember to keep holy the sabbath day.
"Honor your father and your mother, that you may have a long life in the land which the Lord, your God, is giving you.
"You shall not kill.
"You shall not commit adultery.
"You shall not steal.
"You shall not bear false witness against your neighbor.
"You shall not covet your neighbor's house. You shall not covet your neighbor's wife, nor his male or female slave, nor his ox or ass, nor anything else that belongs to him."

The Word of the Lord.

RESPONSORIAL PSALM — PS 19, 8. 9. 10. 11

R/. (Jn 6:69) Lord, you have the words of everlasting life.

The law of the Lord is perfect,
 refreshing the soul;
The decree of the Lord is trustworthy,
 giving wisdom to the simple.

R/. Lord, you have the words of everlasting life.

The precepts of the Lord are right,
 rejoicing the heart;
The command of the Lord is clear,
 enlightening the eye.

R/. Lord, you have the words of everlasting life.

The fear of the Lord is pure,
enduring forever;
The ordinances of the Lord are true,
all of them just.

R/. Lord, you have the words of everlasting life.

They are more precious than gold,
than a heap of purest gold;
Sweeter also than syrup
or honey from the comb.

R/. Lord, you have the words of everlasting life.

Reading II — 1 Cor 1, 22-25

A reading from the first letter of Paul to the Corinthians

Jews demand "signs" and Greeks look for "wisdom," but we preach Christ crucified, a stumbling block to Jews, and an absurdity to Gentiles; but to those who are called, Jews and Greeks alike, Christ is the power of God and the wisdom of God. For God's folly is wiser than men, and his weakness more powerful than men.

The Word of the Lord.

Gospel — Jn 2, 13-25

A reading from the holy gospel according to John

As the Jewish Passover was near, Jesus went up to Jerusalem. In the temple precincts he came upon people engaged in selling oxen, sheep and doves, and others seated changing coins. He made a [kind of] whip of cords and drove them all out of the temple area, sheep and oxen alike and knocked over the moneychangers' tables, spilling their coins. He told those who were selling doves: "Get them out of here! Stop turning my Father's house into a marketplace!" His disciples recalled the words of Scripture: "Zeal for your house consumes me."

At this the Jews responded, "What sign can you show us authorizing you to do these things?" "Destroy this temple," was Jesus' answer, "and in three days I will raise it up." They retorted, "This temple took forty-six years to build, and you are going to 'raise it up in three days'!" Actually he was talking about the temple of his body. Only after Jesus had been raised from the dead did his disciples recall that he had said this, and come to believe the Scripture and the word he had spoken.

While he was in Jerusalem during the Passover festival, many believed in his name, for they could see the signs he was performing. For his part, Jesus would not trust himself to them because he knew them all. He needed no one to give him testimony about human nature. He was well aware of what was in man's heart.

The gospel of the Lord.

INTRODUCTORY PRAYER

On this Third Sunday of Lent,
the holy liturgy celebrates
the gift of the Law at Sinai,
and the purification of the Temple.

Blessed be God our Father:
In giving his Law to the people of the Exodus,
he opened for them a path to heaven.
Blessed be Jesus, our Savior and our brother:
By driving away the vendors from the Temple,
he purified his Father's house
and made of it a dwelling of praise and of prayer.
Blessed be the Spirit of love:
By arousing in our hearts
passion for the beauty of his Church,
he lights a love that, today, creates our eagerness
and that, tomorrow, will be our eternal joy
in his heavenly home.

HOMILY

1. The Ten Words of the Covenant

In Rome on Wednesday of the third week of Lent,[1] the catechumens were "given" the "Ten Commandments." This was the Law according to which they had to conduct their future Christian life. Today, on this Third Sunday of Lent, the liturgy reminds us also of the Decalogue. It tells us that we are, in a certain way, catechumens walking toward the fullness of the grace of baptism and reminds us of the law we have to follow on the path to heaven.

The Ten Words of the Covenant

Our first question is the following: What is the significance of the Decalogue for us today?

We could ask the question in another way: How is the Decalogue original? Does it even have any originality?[2] It was not necessary for Israel to go to Sinai to learn that one must not kill, steal or commit adultery. It is not necessary to go to church today to know that. Those are laws common to all humanity; they are written on the heart of every person.

It is here that the word of God gives us a precise answer.

The word Decalogue is the transcription of the Greek *déka logoi* (ten words). We find the word Decalogue for the first time in the works of Irenaeus of Lyon[3] (c. 202) and Clement of Alexandria[4] (c. 215). But the Bible never uses the term. Clearly, the word of God never, never spoke of the Decalogue as one would speak of the ten commandments or a collection of taboos and laws. It speaks rather of "Ten Words," or better yet, of the "Ten Words of the Covenant."[5]

Therefore, what we call the Decalogue is really the Covenant dialogue between God and his people. God seems to say: "If you want to enter and walk in my Covenant, here is the path that I open before you." And because these laws regulate all human life, that is, all contact with neighbors, every relationship with another person becomes first a relationship with God. Between my brother or sister and me, there is the God of the Covenant.

Likewise, Israel, looking at the Ten Words of the Covenant, does not sigh as if they would be a burden, does not groan as if the Ten Words would be a weight, but gives thanks to God and praises him. God's Law is comfort for the soul, joy for the heart, light for the eyes, more desirable than gold, sweeter than honey.[6] In welcoming God's Law, Israel did not receive a set of police regulations but a deliverance; not chains, but a bond of tenderness. Israel did not submit to a forced labor of slaves but affirmed itself as the people of God.

A Path of Freedom

This path that God opens for us is a path of freedom. In the Decalogue, God presents himself not simply as a legislator but first as a liberator:

> I am the Lord your God
> who made you come out of the land of Egypt,
> out of the house of slavery. Ex 20, 2

For God, to give laws is to open the doors out of slavery; it is to lead the people on the path of freedom. Inversely, according to the word of God, to disobey his laws is to turn into a street with no outlet; it is to see one's way blocked.[7]

In order to hear this word which liberates, we must take off our own chains. Commenting on the words "I am the Lord your God who made you come out of the land of Egypt, out of the house of slavery," Origen, in his homilies on the Exodus (given at Caesaria in Palestine between 238-254), explains:

> These words are addressed not only to those who, of old, came out of Egypt; they are addressed much more to you who are listening to them now. If only you come out of Egypt and are no longer slaves of the Egyptians...See if the affairs of the century and the acts of the flesh are not that house of slavery, just as...life according to God is a house of freedom.[8]

Those words still judge us today. How do we receive your Law, O Lord? Like a word of Covenant or like taboos that bind our freedom?

How do we proceed on your path? Do we walk there as on a path of freedom, or do we really turn in circles as in a prison?

May your commandments, Lord, be the joy of our hearts; your laws, the light of our eyes; and your word, the path to heaven!

A Progressive Revelation of God's Will

Tradition has linked numerous codes of law from diverse dates to the feast of Sinai and has thus placed them under the authority of Moses.[9] Biblical tradition, however, has given preferential treatment to the Decalogue. In the gospels, Jesus himself refers to the Decalogue.[10] It is from the Decalogue also that Augustine borrows the outline of his statement on Christian ethics. Finally, we know the place the Decalogue occupied in the old catechisms.

Few people think any longer that, in its present form, the Decalogue goes back to Moses. The oldest, primitive nucleus undoubtedly springs from the fixation of an old, unwritten law sanctioned by usage in the nomad tribes before and after the installation of Israel in Canaan. It could also reflect aspects of the Pharanic culture practiced in Egypt during the reign of Ramses, a culture to which Moses, through his education, had access.[11]

The encounter with the God of Sinai involved above all a progressive discovery of the demands of Yahwism. As Israel advanced in its history, its conscience became refined, illuminated. Mainly under the guidance of the prophets—who appeared like a shower of stars in the heaven of Israel—the people understood more clearly God's will for them. They discovered also that to respect one's neighbor was to honor God.

I would like to insist on this progressive discovery of the Law. It is advisable to distinguish two levels: The principal affirmation that one must do good and avoid evil, an affirmation written in the heart of every man and woman; and the progressive discovery of what is good and what is evil.

In other words, we know that we must do good and avoid evil. But we also discover progressively what is good and what is evil.

Examples are numerous. There is the story of Lot's daughters.[12] They got their father drunk and then slept with him in order to conceive a child. They knew well that they should do good, that is, that they should not take a husband from among the pagan nations so as not to pollute the Yahwist faith. But, the holy girls did not know that their method, based on wine and incest, was, in this case, an evil. Now Genesis does not have one word of blame for them, and God protects the people issued from that union.[12]

There is the story of Jacob who cunningly takes by surprise the blessing which was coming to Esau, the eldest. When old, blind Isaac asks Jacob: "Are you really my son Esau?" he lies shamelessly and answers: "I am!" He wanted something good: To obtain the blessing. But at the time he did not think that the lie was an evil.[14]

Without doubt, one could say that those are very old stories. But the progressive discovery of God's Law continues even into modern times. For instance, up to the eighteenth century the act of loaning money for interest was considered a sin.[15] But today everyone goes to the bank to put his or her money there at better interest. Let us bear in mind also, in the domain of conjugal ethics, how certain points are still discussed in our days.

There is, therefore, a progressive discovery of God's Law and God's will for us. That is to say that certain consciences, even today, can live as in the time of Abraham. They know well the principle: One must do good. But they sometimes do not know what is good. They know well the law: One must avoid evil. But they sometimes do not know what is evil. One can even affirm that all human conscience is slightly wrapped in darkness and discovers God progressively on the path of its life. Our own Christian conscience, even illuminated by the sun of the gospel, sometimes still has shadowy areas. Our conscience can also be obscured by sin. And with respect to the infinitely limpid and sparkling conscience of Jesus, one can say that all human conscience is wrapped in darkness.

Walk toward God! Gropingly, if necessary, but walk. Discover each day what is to be desired above all things: His will for you. It is a will of love.

How suitable for the present time is this prayer of Paul for the Colossians:

> We do not cease to pray for you and to ask God to bring you to the full knowledge of his will, in all wisdom and spiritual understanding. Col 1, 9

A Path of Perfection

The laws of the Decalogue are barriers, limits outside of which one cannot live in the Covenant.

The Decalogue is a minimal path, for we do not have to guard against murder, robbery or adultery at each moment. The essential part of our life is not spent in defending ourselves against these temptations.

But we have to live each moment in the sight of God. Of course, it is important not to steal your neighbor's ox or ass, but it is even more important to come to his aid through your love. It is important not to desire your neighbor's wife, but it is even more important to love your own wife tenderly. It is important not to do anything on the Sabbath, but it is even more important to do good on the Lord's Day. It is important not to speak the Lord's name in vain, but it is even more important to invoke his blessed name each moment of your life.

More important than the Decalogue is the will of God for your own life, that personal Decalogue that God proposes to you. Let me speak about something I know very well: the Decalogue of the Book of Exodus does not mention the Lord asking me to become a priest in the service of his Church, but it was stamped in my heart. How could I ignore it? And the tablets of Moses do not mention the illness that the Lord sent to you who are listening to me, the illness with which you must live and die, nor do they mention that personal trial which no one can understand except you alone, that trial that you must try to accept as best you can because it is engraved on the tablets of your heart.

The goal of the Decalogue is to make you come back to your heart. Come back to your heart; it is there that you will discover God's will for you!

Toward a Single Law

The more one advances toward God, the more the Decalogue is simplified. It is placed under a single law, the law of love.

In the Louvre Museum in Paris, there is a column upon which is engraved the code of Hammurabi, the king of Babylon (1792-1750). This code is contemporaneous with Abraham. It is from the same source as the Covenant Code in Exodus. It contains 282 regulations; that is a great many. The Dodecalogue of Shechem (Dt 27) contains twelve. The Decalogue of Sinai contains ten. The law of love in Deuteronomy (6, 5) contains only one: "You shall love the Lord your God with all your heart." It is the Law that the pious Jews, at the time of Jesus, recited three times a day. It is that Law which is also the fundamental law of the gospel, the "great commandment," said Jesus.[16] It is about that Law that Paul the Pharisee, who knew well what legalism was, said triumphantly: "The fulfillment of the Law is love."[17] And, finally, that interior law which dwells in us is the Spirit of the Father. Paul even said:

> Those (only) are sons of God who are led by the Spirit of God.
> Rom 8, 11

Marvel, then, that there are no longer ten commandments that you have to observe; you will only have to follow your heart. Your life will be unified and placed under the movement of the Spirit, and each moment will be simple and peaceful, like a look of love toward your Father.

Question: Am I a child of God under the guidance of the Spirit? Am I a child of this New Covenant? Has the Decalogue led me to that land of freedom where each response to the Law is a word of love?

The Good God and the Police

Our God is marvelous. God invites us to an ideal, the law of love, but he rewards even the minimum, simple obedience to his commandments.

I returned home one evening after six hours of driving. Throughout the whole trip, I had carefully respected the speed limits. I had stopped cautiously at all the stop signs. At the highway exit, there were three police. They were doing their job. It is good that they do their job. When I passed in front of them, I glanced in their direction; I was suspicious of them because they are so clever that they will find you at fault when you think you are blameless! I was thinking, "Lucien Deiss, you are a good driver. That is good. You have respected all the speed limits. We congratulate you. You stopped at all the stop signs. The President of the Republic is pleased with you!" Of course, they did not tell me anything at all.

I also thought: God is entirely different. He rewards the simple observation of the Code of his road, his laws. When I end the journey of my life and return to my eternal home, God will welcome me and say to me: "Lucien, you are my child. You observed the essential points of my will. And if you sometimes did not stop perfectly at all my stop signs, if you sometimes neglected some of my priorities, I forgive you. I am not the policeman of the Decalogue. I am your Father."

Blessed be you, Lord! You make the Ten Words of your Covenant sing all along your road and you will welcome me one day into your home!

2. The Purification of the Temple

I like this account of the purification of the Temple. It has a popular and picturesque note that enraptures me.

I adore Christ when he presents himself as the Messiah, meek and humble of heart, and I know that to make an effort to resemble him on that point is not always easy for me. But I adore him also when he strikes out at the merchants of the Temple, and there I feel quite at ease and ready to imitate him. It delights me to know how the merchants were thrashed by the meek and humble Messiah, to remember the little time that the Lord had to clean up all of that breed, to remember the solid attachment that all people have for their money, and to imagine them trying to flee like hornets caught in jam.

However, the anecdote must not make us bypass the essential point.

Actually, it is a question of the Good News. And this news is good for all people, including merchants. Here are a few remarks.

A Purified Church

John places the episode at the beginning of Jesus' public life. The Synoptics place it at the end. It is not possible to determine with certainty who—John or the Synoptics—is the closest to history. The point of the accounts is theological. But, it is possible to understand easily how this account, in the Gospel of John, serves as an "overture" to Jesus' public life.

Just as the Synoptics do, John prefaces the public ministry of Jesus with the preaching of John the Baptist and Jesus' baptism. The Baptist is the messenger who precedes the Messiah. In Matthew 11,10, Jesus himself is supposed to cite and apply to himself this text from Malachi:

> Behold that I send my messenger ahead of you,
> who will prepare the way before you. Mal 3, 1

This prophecy was wonderfully suitable to describe the dawn of messianic times. Indeed, it continues in this way:

> "And suddenly, he will enter into his sanctuary,
> the Master whom you are seeking,
> the Angel of the Covenant whom you desire,
> here he is coming,"
> says the Lord Almighty…
> He will purify the sons of Levi,
> he will refine them like gold and silver.
> And they will become for the Lord
> those who present suitable offerings. Mal 3, 1. 3

In the purification of the temple, Jesus then fulfills the prophecy.[18] He appears as the Angel—that is, the Messenger—of the Covenant; enters into the Temple, purifies it and thus prepares the offering pleasing to the Lord.

What do these passages mean for us today?

The Church is the temple where Jesus, Messenger of the Covenant, never ceases to make the Good News resound. We always need to be purified. Who can be sure that the bad cooks of religious tidbits—sellers of revelations, keepers of spiritual profits, and all the other dealers of dreams and promoters of a cheap paradise—who can be sure, I ask, that they are definitively expelled from our Church?

Who can affirm, on the other hand, that without the buyers in the Temple, there would not be the sellers in the Temple? Let us then not place all the wrong only on the sellers!

Who can pretend, finally, that our own hearts do not need, even today, to be purified in expectation of the Lord's Passover?

"Zeal for Your House Consumes Me"

John cites the words of the Psalm that, he says, come back to mind after the Resurrection:

Zeal for your house consumes me. Ps 69, 10

One can understand this to mean: Zeal for the House of God will consume Christ and lead him to death. One can understand also: Zeal for the House impels Christ to purify the Temple. One can notice, finally, that these two interpretations complement each other in some way: It is truly zeal for the House of God that will consume by the hatred of the enemies of the Gospel.

What do these passages mean for us today?

The most spiritual and the most dis-incarnate love for God cannot be separated from the love for the House of God, which today is the Church of Jesus Christ.

In that love, no one can confuse the institution itself, with its weight and its sins, with the mystery of Jesus. Neither can anyone separate the one from the other.

Finally, this love for the Church, a spiritual mystery, expresses itself also, quite naturally, in the love for the place itself where the faithful gather and where the mystery of the Church is celebrated materially.

I love the house where you live, O Lord,
The dwelling place of your glory. Ps 26, 8

affirms the Psalmist. And the Greek version translates in this way:

I love the beauty of your House,
the dwelling place of your glory.

Jesus gives witness admirably to that love. Mark—who is the only one to have kept this feature—relates:

He would not let anyone transport an object through the Temple.
Mk 11, 16

The Temple, a place of prayer and of beauty, could not be used as a common shortcut.[19]

All through her history, the Spirit raised up in the Church her lovers of beauty, her architects of cathedrals, her makers of stained-glass windows at Chartres, her Silbermanns to build her organs and her J. S. Bachs to play them, her Josquin des Pres to write her masses and the innumerable crowd of anonymous musicians who, while singing, would contemplate what is beyond all music, the Lord of all beauty.

Let us give thanks to the Lord who has put in our hearts passion for his beauty and allows us to continue his praise.

The Sign of the Temple

The construction of the Temple had been begun in the years 20/19 before the Christian era. In speaking about the forty-six years needed to construct the Temple, the Jews let us know that we are in the years 27/28 of our era.

The "sign of the Temple" is one of the major themes of New Testament literature. Jesus clearly makes allusion to his Resurrection when he says:

> Destroy this temple and in three days I will raise it up (*égéró*).
>
> Jn 2, 19

He does not say: "I will rebuild it" but uses the verb *égérein*, which is applied to the Resurrection of the Lord. John notes later that the disciples remembered those words when "he was raised (*égèrthé*) from the dead" (2, 22).

What do these passages mean for us today?

The body of Jesus took the place of the Temple. And that body is also his Church, the community of the faithful. The cultural life that was developing in the Old Testament has ceased. The Christian priesthood is in no way the continuation of the levitical priesthood, and the eucharistic celebration does not take the place of the bloody sacrifices of the Temple. The time has come for worship "in spirit and truth."[20] This worship is not tied to the mountain Gerizim, as the Samaritans thought, nor to Rome, nor any place else. It is the community—even the smallest and most humble—assembled in faith which is the only place worthy of the celebration of Christ. Jesus lives in it "as in his house."

Blessed be the Lord who makes us his house, who purifies it through his word, who makes his praise sing in it, in the Spirit! To him be our song and our love forever and ever.

CONCLUDING PRAYER

Let us pray now
that God may incline our hearts
to the love of his holy will.

Give us your Word, O Lord;
give us Jesus Christ.

Your Word, O Lord, is joy for our hearts,
more jubilant than a feast day.
May it make us sing on the path to heaven.

Give us your Word, O Lord;
give us Jesus Christ.

Your Word, O Lord, is truth in our lives,
clearer than the glance of a child.
May it deliver us from the chains of falsehood.

Give us your Word, O Lord;
give us Jesus Christ.

Your Word, O Lord, is tenderness for our souls,
sweeter than a word of love.
May it fill us with your peace and joy.

Give us your Word, O Lord;
give us Jesus Christ.

Your Word, O Lord, is foolishness for the world
but supreme wisdom for those whom you call.
May it fill us with the strength of the gospel.

Give us your Word, O Lord;
give us Jesus Christ.

Your Word, O Lord, is pure beauty,
more transparent than a mountain spring.
May it clothe our souls with your splendor.

Give us your Word, O Lord;
give us Jesus Christ.

In the silence of our hearts,
we also commend to you our personal intentions.

We pray to you, God our Father,
for those who ignore the word of your love,
for those who refuse to receive it,
even for us who do not know it well enough.
To all, manifest the splendor of your love
in the face of your Son, Jesus,
he who reigns with you in heaven
and dwells in our midst
forever and ever. Amen.

NOTES TO THIRD SUNDAY OF LENT

1. Cf. A. Chavasse in A. G. Martimort, *L'Eglise en prière*, 3rd ed. (Paris: Desclée et Cie, 1965), p. 723. The text of the readings was Ex 20, 14-24 (the lectionary proposes for today Ex 20, 1-17).
2. The only originality is in the properly cultural laws, like that of the observance of the Sabbath, for example (Ex 20, 8-11).
3. Cf. *Against the Heresies*, IV, 15,1. Cf. SC (1965) 100, p. 548.
4. Cf. *The Pedagogue*, III, 12, 89. Cf. SC 158 (1970), p. 168.
5. Ex 34, 28.
6. Ps 19.
7. Lam 3, 9.
8. *Homélies sur l'Exode*, VIII,1. Trans. P. Fortier, SC 16 (1946), p. 184-185.
9. By way of information, one can cite:
   - The Code of the Covenant (Ex 20, 22-23. 19), which seems to be the oldest collection of laws. It seems to go back in its present form to the ninth or eighth centuries, even to the seventh century.
   - The second Decalogue, the one that Moses is supposed to have presented to the people after having broken the first tablets of the Law (Dt 5, 6-18). It goes back to the seventh century.
   - Among the sacerdotal laws, the Law of Holiness (Lv 17-26), whose composition takes place around the Exile (about 570) and whose refrain is the following: "Be holy because I am holy"; the ritual of sacrifices (Lv 1-7); and the Law of purity (Lv 11-16).
   - The Deuteronomic Code (Dt 12-26) which, in its present form, goes back perhaps to the seventh century and recalls the reform of Josias in 622.
10. Cf. Mk 10,19.
11. See H. Cazelles, *A la recherche de Moise* (Paris: Ed. du Cerf, 1979), p. 97-98.
12. Gn 19, 30-38.
13. Cf. Dt 2, 9, 19. See Cl. Westermann, *Genesis*, Coll. Biblischer Kommentar, Altes Testament, I, 2 (Neukirchener Verlag, 1981), p. 384-385.
14. Gn 27. One can still add to these examples taken from Genesis, the episode of Abraham in Egypt (GN 12, 10-19) and the story of Tamar (Gn 38).
15. See Benoit XIV, Encycl. Vix pervenit, November 1, 1745; cf. Denzinger-Schönmetzer, *Enchiridion Symbolorum, definitonium et declarationum*; 32nd ed. (Barcelona: Herder, 1963), nn. 2546-2550. (Based on Ex 22, 25; Lv. 25, 35-37 and Dt 23, 19-20.) See A. Bernard, G. Le Bras, H. Du Passage, art. "Unsure" in D.T.C., vol. 15/2 (1950), col. 2316-2390. A good bibliography on the subject will be found in *The Oxford Dictionary of the Christian Church*, 2nd ed. (1974), p. 1420.
16. Mt 23, 27.
17. Rom 13, 10.
18. I would cite also this text that closes the Book of Zechariah: "There will no longer be any merchants in the Temple of the Lord Almighty" (Zec 14, 21).
19. Jesus forcefully delivers an interdiction that is found in the Cf. Strack-Billerbeck, *Kommentar zum Neuen Testament*, vol. II (Munich: C. H. Beck, 1961), p. 27.
20. See Jn 4, 23.

FOURTH SUNDAY OF LENT

Reading I 2 Chron 36, 14-17. 19-23.

A reading from the second book of Chronicles

All the princes of Judah, the priests and the people added infidelity to infidelity, practicing all the abominations of the nations and polluting the Lord's temple which he had consecrated in Jerusalem.

Early and often did the Lord, the God of their fathers, send his messengers to them, for he had compassion on his people and his dwelling place. But they mocked the messengers of God, despised his warnings, and scoffed at his prophets, until the anger of the Lord against his people was so inflamed that there was no remedy. Then he brought up against them the king of the Chaldeans, who slew their young men in their own sanctuary building, sparing neither young man nor maiden, neither the aged nor the decrepit; he delivered all of them over into his grip. Finally, their enemies burnt the house of God, tore down the walls of Jerusalem, set all its palaces afire, and destroyed all its precious objects. Those who escaped the sword he carried captive to Babylon, where they became his and his sons' servants until the kingdom of the Persians came to power. All this was to fulfill the word of the Lord spoken by Jeremiah: "Until the land has retrieved its lost sabbaths, during all the time it lies waste it shall have rest while seventy years are fulfilled."

In the first year of Cyrus, king of Persia, in order to fulfill the word of the Lord spoken by Jeremiah, the Lord inspired King Cyrus of Persia to issue this proclamation throughout his kingdom, both by word of mouth and in writing: "Thus says Cyrus, king of Persia: 'All the kingdoms of the earth the Lord, the God of heaven, has given to me, and he has also charged me to build him a house in Jerusalem, which is in Judah. Whoever, therefore, among you belongs to any part of his people, let him go up, and may his God be with him!'"

The Word of the Lord.

Responsorial Psalm — Ps 137, 1-2. 3. 4-5. 6

R/. (6) Let my tongue be silenced,
if I ever forget you!

By the streams of Babylon
we sat and wept
when we remembered Zion.
On the aspens of that land
we hung up our harps.

R/. Let my tongue be silenced,
if I ever forget you!

Though there our captors asked of us
the lyrics of our songs,
And our despoilers urged us to be joyous:
"Sing for us the songs of Zion!"

R/. Let my tongue be silenced,
if I ever forget you!

How could we sing a song of the Lord
in a foreign land?
If I forget you, Jerusalem,
may my right hand be forgotten!

R/. Let my tongue be silenced,
if I ever forget you!

May my tongue cleave to my palate
if I remember you not,
If I place not Jerusalem
ahead of my joy.

R/. Let my tongue be silenced,
if I ever forget you!

Reading II — Eph 2, 4-10

A reading from the letter of Paul to the Ephesians

God is rich in mercy; because of his great love for us he brought us to life with Christ when we were dead in sin. By this favor you were saved. Both with and in Christ Jesus he raised us up and gave us a place in the heavens, that in the ages to come he might display the great wealth of his favor, manifested by his kindness to us in Christ Jesus.

I repeat, it is owing to his favor that salvation is yours through faith. This is not your own doing, it is God's gift; neither is it a reward for anything you have accomplished, so let no one pride himself on it. We are truly his handiwork, created in Christ Jesus to lead the life of good deeds which God prepared for us in advance.

The Word of the Lord.

Gospel — Jn 3, 14-21

A reading from the holy gospel according to John

Jesus said to Nicodemus:

"Just as Moses lifted up the serpent in
the desert,
so must the Son of Man be lifted up,
that all who believe
may have eternal life in him.

Yes, God so loved the world
that he gave his only Son,
that whoever believes in him may not die
but may have eternal life.
God did not send the Son into the world
to condemn the world,
but that the world might be saved through him.
Whoever believes in him avoids condemnation,
but whoever does not believe is already condemned
for not believing in the name of God's only Son.
The judgment in question is this:
the light came into the world,
but men loved darkness rather than light
because their deeds were wicked.
Everyone who practices evil
hates the light;
he does not come near it
for fear his deeds will be exposed.
But he who acts in truth
comes into the light,
to make clear
that his deeds are done in God."

The gospel of the Lord.

INTRODUCTORY PRAYER

God our Father,
We want to bless you unceasingly.
Your mercy is the richness that shines like a sun in our hearts.
And the strength that builds the house of our lives
is the great love you give us.
Keep us in the love of your Son Jesus
and in the joy of the Holy Spirit
forever and ever. Amen.

HOMILY

This Fourth Sunday of Lent is dominated by these marvelous words from the Gospel of John:

> God so loved the world
> that he gave his only Son,
> so that whoever believes in him shall not perish
> but have eternal life. Jn 3, 16

These words of faith dominate the history of our lives. They dominate the history of Israel. They dominate the history of the world.

However, the first reading, which relates the fall of Jerusalem, raises insurmountable questions not only in the history of Israel but also in our own lives.

1. The Fall of Jerusalem

In January 588, Nebuchadnezzar, the king of Babylon, laid siege to Jerusalem. Eighteen months later, in July 587, the Chaldean battering rams broke open a hole in the walls of the Holy City. It went down in fire and blood. Under the cover of night, King Zedekiah, a descendant of David, tried to escape the massacre by fleeing with his family to the desert of Judah. The Chaldeans caught sight of him while he was passing through the Jordan Valley, near Jericho. They captured him and dragged him off to Riblah, where Nebuchadnezzar had set up his field headquarters and harem. They killed all his children in front of him, then pierced his eyes and deported him to Babylon. The bloody corpses of his children — that was the last image that the most unfortunate of David's descendants saw in the light of the sun; that was the image that he carried with him forever in the darkness of his captivity. And then, in Babylon, the most beautiful song of love rose up for Zion:

> By the rivers of Babylon,
> we were seated and crying,
> remembering Zion. Ps 137, 1

This story is presented in detail in the last chapter of the Second Book of Kings (2 Kgs 25).

God speaks to his people through the words of his prophets, through everything that is written in the Bible. God also speaks to his people through the events of their lives, through the fall of Jerusalem which was agony for Israel. The fall was one of the most powerful and stupendous words that God had ever spoken to his people. What did the fall of Jerusalem mean for Israel? What does it mean for us today?

God Punishes Sin

God judges sin. He punishes sin if there is no conversion. If the Chaldeans overthrew and defiled the Temple, it was because Israel had already overthrown and defiled it through its sin. It is written:

> All the leaders of the priests and the people
> became more and more unfaithful...
> They defiled the temple of Jerusalem
> consecrated by the Lord. 2 Chr 36,14

God condemns and punishes sin. However, let us understand this punishment correctly. There is no need for God to send a punishing or destroying angel. God does not destroy anyone. He loves all people and wants them to be saved. But God punishes them by abandoning them to themselves. Left to themselves, they become like wolves with each other. Hell is people with people, without God. That is why we pray so often in the psalms:

> Do not forsake me, O Lord, my God,
> do not be far from me!
> Come quickly to help me,
> O God, my Lord and my Savior! Ps 38, 22-23

But He Saves the Sinner

God punishes sin. But he saves the sinner.

We all have a fall like that of Jerusalem written in our lives. This fall is the distress of being exiled in our mediocrity and sometimes even in the bitterness of sin.

But as soon as we weep in our Babylonian exile, as soon as the canticle of Zion rises to the surface of our hearts, God looks upon us and saves us. God allows us to be imprisoned in a history of distress so that our lives may become a history of salvation. He puts this history in despair so that it will open itself to hope. He allows our history to go astray so that we may seek our way to God somewhere other than on the roads of this world. Our greatness is to be people of hope. Our wealth is our hearts wide open to God.

Without a doubt, it is in our most profound distress that our prayer becomes the most intense. Then our praise to God, even silent praise, is strengthened in hope, filled with love. Is it not when we are the closest to our definitive fall of Jerusalem, our death, that we are closest to God? It was when Jesus prayed these words of intense desolation:

> My God, my God,
> why have you forsaken me?[2]

that he also offered the prayer of the most profound abandonment to God, a prayer that we can make our own each moment of our lives:

> Father, into your hands
> I commit my spirit.[2]

An Interpretation of History

The fall of Jerusalem is also the most fantastic lesson of exegesis that God gave to his people, that he continues to give to his Church, that he continues to give in my life. Let me explain.

God had promised to Abraham a line of descendents innumerable as the sands of the seashore, countless as the stars in heaven. Israel multiplied, certainly, but always remained a little people nestled in the Palestinian mountains, wedged between the giants Egypt and Syria and tossed about in the waves of their history. Here is Israel now almost erased from the map. But since the word of God must be fulfilled without fail, since the people of God had to become that people innumerable as the sands on the seashore and the stars in heaven, and since Jerusalem was agonizing under its ruins, we truly have to admit that the incomparable grandeur of that people was no longer situated on the political level but had to be sought elsewhere, on the level of faith. An immense people, most certainly, but a people of faith. How difficult it was for Israel to admit that it was erased from the map as an earthly power and that it no longer existed except as a power of faith. How difficult it is for the Church of today to admit that we are not a temporal power, that our value in the eyes of God is only the power of our faith and love! How difficult it is for me to accept that my strength, in this hostile world, is only the strength of my faith and of my love. That is the exegesis, the explanation that the fall of Jerusalem makes of history.

God had promised to David an eternal house, a throne as stable as the sun.[3] See how, according to the poignant words of the prophet Amos (9, 11), the royal palace had become a fallen tent. By the powerful hand of the Chaldeans, Israel had been stripped of the cloak of royalty. Zedekiah was rotting, blind, in a Babylonian prison. But since the word of God stands forever, we have to admit that this royalty was no longer a temporal royalty but a spiritual one. It was the royalty about which Jesus, the true son of David, would say: "My kingdom is not of this world."[4] How difficult it was for Israel to understand this interpretation. How difficult it is even for the Church of today, even for each one of us!

God had promised to Israel the possession of a land where each one, resting under his fig tree, could savor the messianic peace with his wife, a like charming doe, and with his children, like olive branches around his table.[5] Now that land had become an occupied land. To live there in peace in the days of Christ, one had to pay a tribute to the Roman occupier. But now that the land of Israel was trampled under the feet of pagan nations, one had to truly dream—since the promise of God is infallible—about a spiritual land that is conquered not by the strength of the sword, but by the spiritual arms of holiness. It is the land about which the Lord will say:

> "Happy are the meek, for they will inherit the land." Mt 5, 5

Of course, it was difficult for Israel to think about a spiritual land. It is very difficult to pass from the milk and honey of the Promised Land—from real honey that one eats, from real milk that one drinks, from real cows making real calves who dance in the midst of the daisies—to pass to spiritual milk, to spiritual honey, to spiritual cows (who do not make calves). Yes, it is difficult, even today, to detach oneself from this world in order to cling only to the heaven of Jesus Christ. God had promised to reside forever among his own people on the mountains of Zion, in the Temple of Jerusalem. Now the Temple had been razed to its foundations: The only part of it that would remain is what we call today the "Wailing Wall." The ark itself, the most precious symbol of the presence of God in the midst of his people, had perished in flames. However, God remains faithful to his word. On the smoking ruins of the Temple of Jerusalem, a new Temple will be built. God will no longer live in a house of stone; he will live in the heart of each believer. The most marvelous dwelling of divine glory is the heart of the poor. The prophet says this in a superb text:

> Thus says the Lord:
> "Heaven is my throne
> and the earth is my footstool.
> What house will you build for me?
> Where will my resting place be?
> All that, my hand has made.
> But the one whom I look upon
> is poor and contrite in heart
> and trembles at my word!" Is 66, 1-2

The fall of Jerusalem arises like a sign in the history of Israel. It rises into the sky of Israel exactly like the cross rises in the life of Jesus. The sacking of Jerusalem is not a blind alley in its history but a door of hope. It teaches us that it is necessary to die in order to live a new life. Each cross that the Lord sends to us is a path of tears, but it must become a path of hope. It is upon the ruins of our pride and upon the debris of our self-sufficiency that God can build the New Jerusalem. But this New Jerusalem is not built on earthly foundations; it comes from heaven. It is the "Holy City" about which it is said in the Book of Revelation:

> I saw the Holy City, the new Jerusalem,
> come down from heaven, from God,
> beautiful as a bride
> adorned for her husband. Rv 21, 22.

2. God So Loved the World

On the path that goes from the fall of Jerusalem to the resurrection of Jesus, or even, if you will, on the road that goes from our own ruin to what will be our Passover morning, there are these words full of mystery:

God so loved the world
[that is to say, God so loved you]
that he gave his only Son
[that is to say, that he gave you Jesus]. Jn 3, 16

The Mystery of the Love of God

Words full of mystery. Incomprehensible words. As incomprehensible as God. For who can understand love? God loves you. And he gives you his only Son. In the marvelous text of the second reading, Paul says:

- In this Son and with him, you come back to life (Eph 2, 5).
- In this Son and with him, you rise from the dead (2, 6).
- In this Son and with him, you reign in heaven (2, 6).

But for what reason does God love you in this way? Surely not because of your works. In a text of unbelievable audacity, a text that should be memorized, Paul explains: "It is by grace that you have been saved." Then he insists: "It is truly by grace that you have been saved, through faith."[6] Finally, to avoid any misunderstanding, he emphasizes heavily:

This does not come from you; it is the gift of God.
This does not come from your works;
there is nothing about which to boast. Eph 2, 8-9

Then, you will ask, why does God save us? Simply, because "God is rich in mercy, because of the great love with which he has loved us."[7] Simply, because he is merciful, and we are miserable. Simply, because he is the Savior, and we are lost. Simply, because he is Living, and we are dead. Simply, because he is Love. Because he is God!

Let our pride be shattered and destroyed before him! Let our humility sing in his presence! Let our thanks bless him!

What a joy for us to be able to say: "Lord, we are coming back from the fall of Jerusalem, from our own fall. We are coming to meet you. As we advance, we have lost all illusions about our own value, about our good works, about what we are worth; we have nothing more to present to you than our miseries, our wounds, our bruises and the remnants of our broken hearts." And the Lord will answer each of us: "My dear child, did you not hear what my apostle Paul said:

It is by grace that you have been saved...
This does not come from you;
it is the gift of God.
This does not come from your works;
There is nothing about which to boast!" Eph 2, 6-8

Then together we shall say: "What joy, O Lord, for us to have nothing. Because now we know that you save us for nothing, simply because you are God!"

A Story about Serpents...

I must say a last word concerning the bronze serpent about which the gospel speaks to us:

Just as the bronze serpent was lifted up by Moses in the desert,
so must the Son of Man be lifted up. Jn 3, 14

This comparison is not easy for our modern mentality to understand. It seems to me that three levels of interpretation must be distinguished.

There is first the level of history. The people of the Exodus, in the desert, murmured against God and against Moses. They were then attacked by serpents. To escape the death brought on by their bites, Moses fashioned a bronze serpent and fastened it on a standard. Whoever looked at it saved his life. Such is the fact that the book of Numbers 22, 4-9 tells us. The elements of this account come from diverse sources[8] and give it a more or less legendary ring. Let us note that this bronze serpent fashioned upon a post calls to mind the Sumerian image, so frequent in the Middle East, of two serpents twisted around a stick. That image, in the East as among the Greeks and Romans, was the special symbol of two healers. Today still, it is the emblem of doctors.

There is, secondly, the level of the spiritual interpretation of this story. The Book of Wisdom explains well:

(That serpent) was a sign of salvation that reminded them of the commandment of your Law. He who turned to it was not saved because he was contemplating, but by you, the universal Savior.
Ws 16, 6-7

The date of the Book of Wisdom is approximately the year 50 BCE. It is, therefore, almost contemporaneous with Jesus. It reveals that the pious hearts had exorcised the serpent from the Book of Numbers. It is the contemplation of God, the universal Savior, that healed.

There is, finally, on the third level, the image that the gospel uses. John says to us: Just as the bronze serpent was raised in the desert and those who looked at it were saved, so Jesus is raised today upon the cross: look at him and be saved.

Look, then, at the cross of Jesus: it is already an exaltation. The atrocious suffering of the Lord is the path to the resurrection; it is the road to heaven. Look at the cross of Jesus: in that suffering, you will see the image of all the sufferings of the world, the reflection also of your own suffering. Your suffering also, if you will, can become a path of resurrection. It is written in the psalm:

> Whoever looks at him will be radiant. Ps 34, 6

We are looking at you, Lord. Let your cross of light shine brightly in our hearts!

CONCLUDING PRAYER

Our wealth, God our Father, is your mercy.
Our hope is the love you give us.
With confidence, then, we present our prayer to you.

Save us, O Lord,
in your great love.

Look, O Lord, at your Church,
the Dwelling of your glory.
You are rich in mercy;
keep her from the sin that threatens to ruin her,
from the division that destroys her unity.

Save us, O Lord,
in your great love.

Look, O Lord, at the priests and leaders
and all the people whom you have chosen
to form your Church.
You are rich in mercy;
keep us from the infidelities
that threaten to profane her beauty.

Save us, O Lord,
in your great love.

Look, O Lord, at those who are deported
far from your Church
for the sake of the gospel.
You are rich in mercy;
give them soon the power to sing
the song of return and deliverance.

Save us, O Lord,
in your great love.

Look, O Lord, at those who are exiled
in the place of sin and sadness.
Place in their hearts the remembrance of Zion;
convert their hearts and ours.

Save us, O Lord,
in your great love.

Look, O Lord, at our community:
We are your Church.
You are rich in mercy;
turn our eyes toward your crucified Christ
and keep us all in your love.

Save us, O Lord,
in your great love.

We also commend to your mercy
all our personal intentions.

We were lost:
You saved us, Lord,
according to your great love.
We were dead:
You brought us to life again
according to the riches of your grace.
Marvelous is your mercy
in your Son Jesus, our Savior and our brother,
forever and ever. Amen.

NOTES TO FOURTH SUNDAY OF LENT

1. Concerning that date, see H. Cazelles, *Histoire politique d'lsraël* (Paris: Desclée, 1982), p 191, note 104.
2. Ps 22, 2 1 = Mk 15, 34. Ps 31, 6 = Lk 23, 46.
3. Cf. 2 Sm 7, 5-16. Ps 89, 37.
4. Jn 18-36.
5. Cf. Prov 5, 18-19. Ps 128.
6. Eph 2, 5. 8.
7. Eph 2, 4.
8. See M. Noth, *Das vierte Buch Mose*, Coll. Das Alte Testament Deutsch (Gottingen, Vendenhoeck & Ruprecht, 1966), pp 137-138.

FIFTH SUNDAY OF LENT

READING I — JER 31, 31-34

A reading from the book of the prophet Jeremiah

The days are coming, says the Lord, when I will make a new covenant with the house of Israel and the house of Judah. It will not be like the covenant I made with their fathers the day I took them by the hand to lead them forth from the land of Egypt; for they broke my covenant, and I had to show myself their master, says the Lord. But this is the covenant which I will make with the house of Israel after those days, says the Lord. I will place my law within them, and write it upon their hearts; I will be their God, and they shall be my people. No longer will they have need to teach their friends and kinsmen how to know the Lord. All, from least to greatest, shall know me, says the Lord, for I will forgive their evildoing and remember their sin no more.

The Word of the Lord.

RESPONSORIAL PSALM — PS 51, 3-4. 12-13. 14-15

R/. (12) Create a clean heart in me, O God.

Have mercy on me, O God, in your goodness;
  in the greatness of your compassion wipe
  out my offense.
Thoroughly wash me from my guilt
  and of my sin cleanse me.

R/. Create a clean heart in me, O God.

A clean heart create for me, O God,
  and a steadfast spirit renew within me.
Cast me not out from your presence,
  and your holy spirit take not from me.

R/. Create a clean heart in me, O God.

Give me back the joy of your salvation,
  and a willing spirit sustain in me.
I will teach transgressors your ways,
  and sinners shall return to you.

R/. Create a clean heart in me, O God.

Reading II — Heb 5, 7-9

A reading from the letter of Paul to the Hebrews

In the days when Christ was in the flesh, he offered prayers and supplications with loud cries and tears to God, who was able to save him from death, and he was heard because of his reverence. Son though he was, he learned obedience from what he suffered; and when perfected, he became the source of eternal salvation for all who obey him.

The Word of the Lord.

Gospel — Jn 12, 20-33

A reading from the holy gospel according to John

Among those who had come up to worship at the feast of Passover were some Greeks. They approached Philip, who was from Bethsaida in Galilee, and put this request to him: "Sir, we should like to see Jesus." Philip went to tell Andrew; Philip and Andrew in turn came to inform Jesus. Jesus answered them:

"The hour has come
for the Son of Man to be glorified.
I solemnly assure you,
unless the grain of wheat falls to the earth and dies,
it remains just a grain of wheat.
But if it dies,
it produces much fruit.
The man who loves his life loses it,
while the man who hates his life in this world
preserves it to life eternal.
If anyone would serve me,
let him follow me;
where I am,
there will my servant be.
Anyone who serves me,
the Father will honor.
My soul is troubled now,
yet what should I say—
Father, save me from this hour?
But it was for this that I came to this hour.

Father, glorify your name!"
Then a voice came from the sky:
"I have glorified it,
and will glorify it again."

When the crowd of bystanders heard the voice, they said it was thunder. Others maintained, "An angel was speaking to him." Jesus answered,

"That voice did not come for my sake, but for yours.
"Now has judgment come upon this world,
now will this world's prince be driven out,
and I—once I am lifted from earth—
will draw all men to myself."

(This statement of his indicated the sort of death he was going to die.)

The gospel of the Lord.

INTRODUCTORY PRAYER

We bless you, God our Father,
for the New Covenant that you offer to us
in your Son, Jesus.
Give us a new heart
so that we may welcome the love
that you renew for us each day.
Put in us a new spirit
so that we may understand your Word
and make it bear fruit in our life.
Keep us in this New Covenant,
through Christ, our Savior and our brother.

HOMILY

1. The New Covenant

Of all the good things that God had bequeathed to his people, the Covenant of Sinai was the most precious. The sages of Israel explained that it was like the marriage of love between God and Israel. It is that Covenant, a true chain of tenderness that bound God to his people, that the prophet Jeremiah attacked. He declared it broken, shattered like a worn-out chain whose rusted links are corroded by sin.

> This is not like the covenant
> that I made with their fathers
> the day I took them by the hand
> to bring them out of Egypt:
> they broke my covenant. Jer 31, 32

It is to that Covenant that Jeremiah opposes a new covenant that would no longer be engraved on the stone tablets of Sinai but on the heart of each believer:

> The days are coming when I will make
> a new covenant
> with the house of Israel…
> I will put my law in their innermost being;
> I will write it on their hearts… Jer 31, 31. 33

When Jeremiah issued the term "new covenant" around the year 600 BCE, he undoubtedly had no idea how much he was going to unsettle the face of the world or change the course of human history. Without that extraordinary prophet, humanity would not be what it is today; it would not know God as it knows him today. In reality, Jeremiah proclaimed a renewed religion, a completely interior religion. He invented a relationship of love with God, a relationship where each believer, even the least one, would be able to converse with the Creator not as a creature would but as a friend with the One who loves him.

The Border

We sometimes say, and we often think, that the Old Covenant is what we call in our Bible the "Old Testament," whereas the New Covenant is the gospel. This manner of thinking is not correct because this New Covenant, according to Jeremiah, already exists in the Old Testament.

Sometimes we also think that the Old Testament is dominated by the law of fear while the New is governed by the law of love. This manner of thinking is totally false because the gospel's law of love comes to us precisely from the Old Testament, from Deuteronomy![1]

We are sometimes tempted to believe that the people of Israel belong to the

Old Covenant, while we, good Christians, fortunately belong to the New Covenant. This is equally false and, moreover, manifests insupportable pride, since we are judging our brothers and sisters.

In reality, the border that separates the Old Covenant from the New does not pass between Jews and Christians nor even between non-Christians and believers. It passes through the heart of each person. It is in the heart of each believer that the founding of the New Covenant and the prophecy of Jeremiah are realized or lost. This text, about twenty-six centuries old, still poses a fundamental question: to which covenant do I belong? What is my relationship with God, or rather, what is the quality of my relationship with God? Indeed, was there ever a more timely question?

To tell the truth, sometimes we belong to the Old Covenant and sometimes to the New. It depends on the day…

I was invited to visit a kindergarten in Humbolt, Iowa. The children there had prayed a great deal and had made sacrifices for the success of a liturgical workshop that I was to lead in the diocese. One is really obliged then—since one is supposed to be on the side of God—to thank the children with a visit. They sang and also danced for me. I congratulated them and then asked them: "Are you good girls? Are you good boys?" A little girl who was standing in front of me, and was as pretty as a doll, tossed her head of angel curls and said: "Sometimes…" This is really true. Sometimes we belong to the New Covenant and sometimes to the Old Covenant.

What are the characteristics of the New Covenant?

"I Will Write My Law on Their Hearts"

To live in the New Covenant is to carry the Law of God engraved on one's heart. Indeed, it is written:

> I will put my law in their innermost being;
> I will write it on their hearts. Jer 31, 33

There is still a Law, but it is a word of Covenant. And we carry it in our hearts.

To carry the Law of God as one carries a book of driving regulations, for example, in one's pocket or in the glove compartment of one's car, is to live in the Old Covenant. To have branded one's heart with the Word of Jesus, to think about God while waking up in the night and while working or walking during the day, is to be of the New Covenant. The law of love of Deuteronomy said exactly:

> You will say these words of love when sitting at home, when walking on the road, when lying down and when getting up.
>
> Dt 6, 7

While the Word was engraved on the stone tablets of Sinai, it could be forgotten. That is really what we do from time to time. Now that it is engraved in our hearts, how could we no longer think about it? How could we forget our heart?

"All Will Know Me"

To live in the New Covenant is also to know God. It is written:

> They will no longer need to teach one another,
> each one saying to his brother:
> Learn to know the Lord!"
> For all will know me,
> from the least to the greatest. Jer 31, 34

What good luck then! No more need to give homilies: each one will know God personally. Each one will know Beauty. Each one will know Love. Each one will know the One who alone knows your heart because he held it in his hands before giving it to you...

In biblical vocabulary, "to know" implies most often not only a notional understanding but an experiential dimension, an existential relationship. One says, thus, that the country of Israel "knew" peace, which means that it had the experience of living in peace. One also says that the people "knew" sin, which means that they lived in sin. Concerning the Servant of Yahweh, one affirms that he "knew" suffering, which means that he experienced it. One also speaks of "knowing" a woman, which involves more than knowing her identity. It implies very precisely to live with her in love and to have children with her.[2]

To know God is thus to live a life of love with him.

As for me, if I close all my books, if I forget everything that I learned from those who were assigned to me as teachers or those whom I chose as teachers, what do I know of God? What is my personal experience of God? of his tenderness? of his patience to forgive me? Do I know him because I live a life of love with him? To know God is, so to speak, to recognize him at each step of our lives, at each meeting with our brother or sister. It is to recognize him not through laborious reasoning, as we would solve an algebraic problem, but by intuition as we recognize in the night the voice of the one we love. "Without seeing you, we love you."[3]

Do I know you in this way, O Lord? Or do I know about you only what I have learned in my books? only what I have heard others say about you? Or do I truly know you because I live a life of love with you?

"I Will Forgive Them All Their Sins"

To live in the New Covenant is to know that you are forgiven. If you are afraid of God, if you fear his vengeance because you have sinned, if you count on your merits to atone for your faults, as a mercenary counts on his salary then you are still under the law of fear. If, from time to time, you fearfully glance toward heaven while asking yourself: "What is God plotting against me? Because of my mediocrity, will he not inflict a serious illness upon me? Will he not pass judgment on me by attacking my family? Quick, I am going to do some good deeds and say some good prayers. If I do that, he will not plot anything disagreeable against me." If that is the case, then you are surely still under the law of fear; you are surely not in the New Covenant.

But if you hope for the forgiveness of everything by recognizing that you are a sinner, if you hope for this forgiveness precisely because you know that you are lost, if you accept it because God, in forgiving you, not only washes away your sins but actually creates for you a new heart—"Create in me a pure heart, O my God," we pray in the Psalm[4]—then you have entered into the New Covenant.

Jesus, the New Covenant

Finally, what is this New Covenant? Where can we see it? Where can we attain it?

When we celebrate the eucharist, when we priests hold in our hands the consecrated bread—the risen body of Christ Jesus—and the cup of blessing, we remember Jeremiah, and taking the words of Jesus, we say: "This is the New Covenant"[5] The New Covenant is Christ Jesus himself.

Of course this New Covenant is eternal because you, Lord, are eternal and you joined forever our humanity to your divinity.

Of course this New Covenant brings us the forgiveness of sins because you, Lord Jesus, came among us not to judge and condemn but to forgive and save.

Of course this New Covenant is a law engraved on our hearts since you, Lord, live in our hearts and you make your eternal dwelling there.[6]

Of course this New Covenant is definitive knowledge of God since you, Lord Jesus, are the friend who reveals to us the secrets of your Father.[7]

2. The Gospel

I would have liked to speak to you about this Sunday's Gospel, about its connection with the agony of Gethsemani as the Synoptics tell it.[8] But the time is going too fast. However, I will present to you two little stories that will establish, I hope, this gospel in your minds.

"If Grain Falling on the Ground Does Not Die..."

The first story is about a little grain of wheat. Do you know that story?[9]

Once upon a time, there was a little grain of wheat that spent happy days in the hayloft. Sheltered from the cold and damp, it rolled around in perfect happiness in the midst of all its friends, the other little grains of wheat. In short, happiness—beatitude in a pure state.

From time to time, among the grains of wheat, they told of the great adventures of their existence: frightful storms, clouds torn by lightning and huge hailstones. The neighboring field of alfalfa: completely slashed, ravaged, on the ground. While they, the wheat in the field, had, of course, bent under the tornado, they then straightened up just when the rainbow appeared. They also called to mind one Sunday evening, when an amorous couple passed by them and gathered a poppy. My, how touching that had been!

The grain of wheat was pious. It sang canticles. Not boring canticles, but new songs, even some psalms: "How good it is, how pleasant, to live as brothers and sisters—all together" with the other little grains of wheat![10] And it said: "Thank you, Lord, for keeping me sheltered, thus, from the cold of winter, for protecting me from the snow. Thank you also for sending us from time to time Felix, the big cat, to protect us from the mice who want to devour us. I am so happy in this hayloft that I would like to live here forever and ever. Amen."

From time to time, the farmer would go up into the hayloft. He looked with pride at his little grains of wheat. Then he would leave smiling. One would hear him say: "Now that is grain!" The little grain of wheat was happy — happy on the level of a lowly dandelion, without opening itself to heaven, without any future. The happiness of a hayloft. If we pray to God to keep us in this type of happiness, that is good. If we pray to God to give us only that type of happiness, that happiness of a hayloft, then we are making happiness an idol and God an illusion.

One day, however, the happiness of the little grain of wheat ended. Without a second thought, the little grain was taken out of the hayloft, loaded onto a cart, onto a tractor, across the damp field bathed in dew, thrown on the damp, cold, tilled ground and finally covered up with black, dirty earth: a burial. As it began to rot, the little grain of wheat cried. It said: "If God existed, such things would not happen!" But it is precisely because God does exist that such things happen! It is really what Jesus explains:

> Amen, amen, I say to you:
> If a grain of wheat falls on the ground
> and does not die,
> it remains just a grain of wheat.
> But if it dies,
> it bears much fruit. John 12, 24

How many have lost their lives for lack of having offered them for a great cause? They lost them because they wanted to save them for themselves instead of giving them for the gospel.

And how many who gave everything, who gave themselves completely, have saved everything by saving with themselves all their brothers and sisters?

Is not this little grain of wheat that dies in the earth and bears much fruit the very image of the One who was placed in the heart of the earth the evening of Good Friday and rose on Easter morning for the salvation of the universe?

"We Want to See Jesus..."

My second story is very short. I had been invited, for an ecumenical celebration, to give a homily in an Anglican church. I went up to the pulpit. It was very big, of sculptured wood, and magnificent. When I started to speak, I saw some words engraved in the wood on the stand. The listeners could not see them, but I had them constantly before my eyes. They were the words of today's gospel: "We want to see Jesus!"

Those words have never left my mind. I think about them sometimes right in the middle of my homilies. You who are listening to this homily, pray for us priests, pray for me, so that we can always respond to that request: "We want to see Jesus!" We priests have only one duty all through our homilies: to show you the Lord. And you have only one duty: to seek the Lord in them. All the rest are empty words. Wind.

Moreover, it is not only to us ministers of the Word but to each one of you that the request is addressed: "We want to see Jesus!" The whole world calls to us: "We want to see Jesus!" May our lives reveal Christ! May they be an epiphany of the Lord.

To him alone, glory forever and ever!

CONCLUDING PRAYER

> "From among the Greeks who had gone up to Jerusalem to worship God during Passover, some came to Philip who was from Bethsaida in Galilee. They made this request of him: 'We want to see Jesus.'" Jn 12, 20-21

As at the time of the gospel,
the world unceasingly renews this request:
"We want to see Jesus!"

Let us then pray with all our heart:
May the Church be the epiphany of the Risen!
May we reveal the tenderness of God
in the face of Christ Jesus.
Let your face smile on us.
Save us in your steadfast love.

They all say to us:
"We want to see Jesus!"

How could they recognize in us
the splendor of your risen face
if you yourself, Lord Jesus,
did not illumine our eyes through your Resurrection?

Let your face smile on us.
Save us in your steadfast love.

They all say to us:
"We want to see Jesus!"

How could they recognize on our lips
your word that gives courage to the hopeless
if you yourself, Lord Jesus,
did not proclaim the Good News through our mouth?
Let your face smile on us.
Save us in your steadfast love.

They all say to us:
"We want to see Jesus!"

How could they see in our hands
your hands of love, open to the poor,
if you yourself, Lord Jesus,
did not continue to pour out goodness through our hands?
Let your face smile on us.
Save us in your steadfast love.

They all say to us:
"We want to see Jesus!"

How could they recognize in our smile
the joy of forgiveness that comes from heaven
if you yourself, Lord Jesus,
did not forgive through our goodness?
Let your face smile on us.
Save us in your steadfast love.

They all say to us:
"We want to see Jesus!"

How could they recognize in our lives
the grain of wheat fallen to the ground
that dies to bear fruit
if you yourself, Lord Jesus,
did not transform our death into your Resurrection?
Let your face smile on us.
Save us in your steadfast love.

Let us also pray for all our personal intentions.

Fifth Sunday of Lent

How we long to meet you, Lord,
for we also want to see your face.
When you have made the light of your face shine on us
and when we contemplate you in your dazzling beauty,
our eyes meeting your eyes,
we will celebrate for eternity
the marvels of your love. Amen.

NOTES TO FIFTH SUNDAY OF LENT

1. Dt 6, 4-9. Insisting on the newness of the gospel, one will speak willingly of the new covenant. That is what Heb 8, 13 does: "In saying New Covenant he (God) makes obsolete the first. Now that which is obsolete and worn out is about to disappear." But insisting on the continuity that exists between the two Testaments one will speak more willingly of the First Testament (instead of the Old Testament). There is here a question of vocabulary to which it is advisable to be attentive.
2. On the other hand, "not to know someone" is to reject him: that is the judgment of God on those who stay outside of his love. Thus, the bridegroom in the parable of the Ten Virgins says to the five foolish ones who had neglected to bring some oil and who were knocking on the door of the wedding banquet: "Amen, I say to you: I do not know you!" (Mt 25, 12). He knew those bridesmaids very well, but he rejected them as guests of the feast.
3. Cf. 1 Pt 1, 8: "Without having seen him you love him. Without seeing him now, you tremble with an inexpressible joy full of glory."
4. Ps 51, 12.
5. Lk 22, 20.
6. See Jn 14, 23.
7. See Jn 15, 15.
8. See M. E. Boismard, A. Lamouille, *Synopse de Quatre Evangiles*, vol. 3, L'Evangile de Jean (Paris: Cerf, 1972), pp. 310-320.
9. This story has been developed often; cf., for example, F. Varillon, Joies de croire, Joies de croire, Joie de vivre (Paris: Centurion, 1981), pp. 38-39, from whom came the inspiration for this story.
10. See Ps 133,1.

PASSION SUNDAY

Reading I — Is 50, 4-7

A reading from the book of the prophet Isaiah

The Lord God has given me
  a well-trained tongue,
That I might know how to speak to the weary
  a word that will rouse them.
Morning after morning
  he opens my ear that I may hear;
And I have not rebelled,
  have not turned back.
I gave my back to those who beat me,
  my cheeks to those who plucked my beard;
My face I did not shield
  from buffets and spitting.

The Lord God is my help,
  therefore I am not disgraced;
I have set my face like flint,
  knowing that I shall not be put to shame.

The Word of the Lord.

Responsorial Psalm — Ps 22, 8-9. 17-18. 19-20. 23-24

R/. (2) My God, my God, why have you abandoned me?

All who see me scoff at me;
  they mock me with parted lips, they wag their heads:
"He relied on the Lord; let him deliver him,
  let him rescue him, if he loves him."

R/. My God, my God, why have you abandoned me?

Indeed, many dogs surround me,
  a pack of evildoers closes in upon me;
They have pierced my hands and my feet;
  I can count all my bones.

R/. My God, my God, why have you abandoned me?

They divide my garments among them,

and for my vesture they cast lots.
But you, O Lord, be not far from me;
O my help, hasten to aid me.

R/. My God, my God, why have you abandoned me?

I will proclaim your name to my brethren;
in the midst of the assembly I will praise you:
"You who fear the Lord, praise him;
all you descendants of Jacob, give glory to him."

R/. My God, my God, why have you abandoned me?

Reading II — Phil 2, 6-11

A reading from the letter of Paul to the Philippians

Your attitude must be Christ's:
though he was in the form of God
he did not deem equality with God
something to be grasped at.

Rather, he emptied himself
and took the form of a slave,
being born in the likeness of men.

He was known to be of human estate,
and it was thus that he humbled himself,
obediently accepting even death,
death on a cross!

Because of this,
God highly exalted him
and bestowed on him the name
above every other name,

So that at Jesus' name
every knee must bend
in the heavens, on the earth,
and under the earth,

and every tongue proclaim
to the glory of God the Father:
JESUS CHRIST IS LORD!

The Word of the Lord.

GOSPEL MK 14, 1-15, 47 OR 15, 1-39

The Passion of our Lord Jesus Christ according to Mark

(Long Form)

The feasts of Passover and Unleavened Bread were to be observed in two days' time, and therefore the chief priests and scribes began to look for a way to arrest Jesus by some trick and kill him. Yet they pointed out, "Not during the festival, or the people may riot."

When Jesus was in Bethany reclining at table in the house of Simon the leper, a woman entered carrying an alabaster jar of perfume made from expensive aromatic nard. Breaking the jar, she began to pour the perfume on his head. Some were saying to themselves indignantly: "What is the point of this extravagant waste of perfume? It could have been sold for over three hundred silver pieces and the money given to the poor." They were infuriated at her. But Jesus said: "Let her alone. Why do you criticize her? She has done me a kindness. The poor you will always have with you and you can be generous to them whenever you wish, but you will not always have me. She has done what she could. By perfuming my body she is anticipating its preparation for burial. I assure you, wherever the good news is proclaimed throughout the world, what she has done will be told in her memory."

Then Judas Iscariot, one of the Twelve, went off to the chief priests to hand Jesus over to them. Hearing what he had to say, they were jubilant and promised to give him money. He for his part kept looking for an opportune way to hand him over.

On the first day of Unleavened Bread, when it was customary to sacrifice the paschal lamb, his disciples said to him, "Where do you wish us to go to prepare the Passover supper for you?" He sent two of his disciples with these instructions: "Go into the city and you will come upon a man carrying a water jar. Follow him. Whatever house he enters, say to the owner, 'The Teacher asks, Where is my guest room where I may eat the Passover with my disciples?' Then he will show you an upstairs room, spacious, furnished, and all in order. That is the place you are to get ready for us." The disciples went off. When they reached the city they found it just as he had told them, and they prepared the Passover supper.

As it grew dark he arrived with the Twelve. They reclined at table, and in the course of the meal Jesus said, "I give you my word, one of you is about to betray me, yes, one who is eating with me." They began to say to him sorrowfully, one by one, "Surely not I!" He said, "It is one of the Twelve—a man who dips into the dish with me. The Son of Man is going the way the Scripture tells of him. Still, accursed be that man by whom the Son of Man is betrayed. It were better for him had he never been born."

During the meal he took bread, blessed and broke it, and gave it to them. "Take this," he said, "this is my body." He likewise took a cup, gave thanks and passed it to them, and they all drank from it. He said to them: "This is my blood, the blood of the covenant, to be poured out on behalf of many. I solemnly assure you, I will never again drink of the fruit of the vine until the day when I drink it in the reign of God."

After singing songs of praise, they walked out to the Mount of Olives.

Jesus then said to them: "Your faith in me shall be shaken, for Scripture has it,

'I will strike the shepherd
and the sheep will be dispersed.'

But after I am raised up, I will go to Galilee ahead of you." Peter said to him, "Even though all are shaken in faith, it will not be that way with me." Jesus answered, "I give you my assurance, this very night before the cock crows twice, you will deny me three times." But Peter kept reasserting vehemently, "Even if I have to die with you, I will not disown you." They all said the same.

They went then to a place named Gethsemani. "Sit down here while I pray," he said to his disciples; at the same time he took along with him Peter, James, and John. Then he began to be filled with fear and distress. He said to them, "My heart is filled with sorrow to the point of death. Remain here and stay awake." He advanced a little and fell to the ground, praying that if it were possible this hour might pass him by. He kept saying, "*Abba* (O Father), you have the power to do all things. Take this cup away from me. But let it be as you would have it, not as I." When he returned he found them asleep. He said to Peter, "Asleep, Simon? You could not stay awake for even an hour? Be on guard and pray that you may not be put to the test. The spirit is willing but nature is weak." Going back again he began to pray in the same words. Once again he found them asleep on his return. They could not keep their eyes open, nor did they know what to say to him. He returned a third time and said to them, "Still sleeping? Still taking your ease? It will have to do. The hour is on us. You will see that the Son of Man is to be handed over into the clutches of evil men. Rouse yourselves and come along. See! My betrayer is near."

Even while he was still speaking, Judas, one of the Twelve, made his appearance accompanied by a crowd with swords and clubs; these people had been sent by the chief priests, the scribes, and the elders. The betrayer had arranged a signal for them, saying, "The man I shall embrace is the one; arrest him and lead him away, taking every precaution." He then went directly over to him and said, "Rabbi!" and embraced him. At this, they laid hands on him and arrested him. One of the bystanders drew his sword and struck the high priest's slave, cutting off his ear. Addressing himself to them, Jesus said, "You have come out to arrest me armed with swords and clubs as if against a brigand. I was within your reach daily, teaching in the temple precincts, yet you never arrested me. But now, so that the Scriptures may be fulfilled..." With that, all deserted him and fled. There was a young man following him who was covered by nothing but a linen cloth. As they seized him he left the cloth behind and ran off naked.

Then they led Jesus off to the high priest, and all the chief priests, the elders and the scribes came together. Peter followed him at a distance right into the high priest's courtyard, where he found a seat with the temple guard and began to warm himself at the fire. The chief priests with the whole Sanhedrin were busy soliciting testimony against Jesus that would lead to his death, but they could not find any. Many spoke against him falsely under oath but their testimony did not agree. Some, for instance, on taking the stand, testified falsely by alleging, "We heard him declare, 'I will destroy this temple made by human hands,' and 'In three days I will construct another not made by human hands.'" Even so, their testimony did not agree.

The high priest rose to his feet before the court and began to interrogate Jesus: "Have you no answer to what these men testify against you?" But Jesus remained silent; he made no reply. Once again the high priest interrogated him: "Are you the Messiah, the Son of the Blessed One?" Then Jesus answered: "I am; and you will see the Son of Man seated at the right hand of the Power and coming with the clouds of heaven." At that the high priest tore his robes and said: "What further need do we have of witnesses? You have heard the blasphemy. What is your verdict?" They all concurred in the verdict "guilty," with its sentence of death. Some of them then began to spit on him. They blindfolded him and hit him, saying, "Play the prophet!" While the officers man-handled him.

While Peter was down in the courtyard, one of the servant girls of the high priest came along. When she noticed Peter warming himself, she looked more closely at him and said, "You too were with Jesus of Nazareth." But he denied it: "I don't know what you are talking about! What are you getting at?" Then he went out into the gateway. At that moment a rooster crowed. The servant girl, keeping an eye on him, started again to tell the bystanders, "This man is one of them." Once again he denied it. A little later the bystanders said to Peter once more, "You are certainly one of them! You're a Galilean, are you not?" He began to curse, and to swear, "I don't even know the man you are talking about!" Just then a second cockcrow was heard and Peter recalled the prediction Jesus had made to him, "Before the cock crows twice you will disown me three times." He broke down and began to cry.

As soon as it was daybreak the chief priests, with the elders and scribes (that is, the whole Sanhedrin), reached a decision. They bound Jesus, led him away, and handed him over to Pilate. Pilate interrogated him: "Are you the king of the Jews?" "You are the one who is saying it," Jesus replied. The chief priests, meanwhile, brought many accusations against him. Pilate interrogated him again: "Surely you have some answer? See how many accusations they are leveling against you." But greatly to Pilate's surprise, Jesus made no further response.

Now on the occasion of a festival he would release for them one prisoner—any man they asked for. There was a prisoner named Barabbas jailed along with the rebels who had committed murder in the uprising. When the crowd came up to press their demand that he honor the custom, Pilate rejoined, "Do you want me to release the king of the Jews for you?" He was aware, of course, that it was out of jealousy that the chief priests had handed him over. Meanwhile, the chief priests incited the crowd to have him release Barabbas instead. Pilate again asked them, "What am I to do with the man you call the king of the Jews?" They shouted back, "Crucify him!" Pilate protested, "Why? What crime has he committed?" They only shouted the louder, "Crucify him!" So Pilate, who wished to satisfy the crowd, released

Barabbas to them, and after he had had Jesus scourged, he handed him over to be crucified.

The soldiers now led Jesus away into the hall known as the praetorium; at the same time they assembled the whole cohort. They dressed him in royal purple, then wove a crown of thorns and put it on him, and began to salute him, "All hail! King of the Jews!" Continually striking Jesus on the head with a reed and spitting at him, they genuflected before him and pretended to pay him homage. When they had finished mocking him, they stripped him of the purple, dressed him in is own clothes, and led him out to crucify him.

A man named Simon of Cyrene, the father of Alexander and Rufus, was coming in from the fields and they pressed him into service to carry the cross. When they brought Jesus to the site of Golgotha (which means "Skull Place"), they tried to give him wine drugged with myrrh, but he would not take it. Then they crucified him and divided up his garments by rolling dice for them to see what each should take. It was about nine in the morning when they crucified him. The inscription proclaiming his offense read, "The King of the Jews."

With him they crucified two insurgents, one at his right and one at his left. People going by kept insulting him, tossing their heads and saying, "Ha, ha! So you were going to destroy the temple and rebuild it in three days! Save yourself now by coming down from that cross!" The chief priests and the scribes also joined in and jeered: "He saved others but he cannot save himself! Let the 'Messiah,' the 'king of Israel,' come down from that cross here and now so that we can see it and believe in him!" The men who had been crucified with him likewise kept taunting him.

When noon came, darkness fell on the whole countryside and lasted until mid afternoon. At that time Jesus cried in a loud voice, *"Eloi, Eloi, lama sabachthani?"* which means, "My God, my God, why have you forsaken me?" A few of the bystanders who heard it remarked, "Listen! He is calling on Elijah'" Someone ran off, and soaking a sponge in sour wine, stuck it on a reed to try to make him drink. The man said, "Now let's see whether Elijah comes to take him down."

Then Jesus, uttering a loud cry, breathed his last. At that moment the curtain in the sanctuary was torn in two from top to bottom. The centurion who stood guard over him, on seeing the manner of his death, declared, "Clearly this man was the Son of God!" There were also women present looking on from a distance. Among them were Mary Magdalene, Mary the mother of James the younger and Joses, and Salome. These women had followed Jesus when he was in Galilee and attended to his needs. There were also many others who had come up with him to Jerusalem.

As it grew dark (it was Preparation Day, that is, the eve of the sabbath), Joseph from Arimathea arrived—a distinguished member of the Sanhedrin. He was another who looked forward to the reign of God. He was bold enough to seek an audience with Pilate, and urgently requested the body of Jesus. Pilate was surprised that Jesus should have died so soon. He summoned the centurion and inquired whether Jesus was already dead. Learning from him that he was dead, Pilate released the corpse to Joseph. Then, having bought a linen shroud, Joseph took him down, wrapped him in the linen, and laid him in a tomb which had been cut out of rock. Finally he rolled a stone across the entrance of the tomb. Meanwhile, Mary Magdalene and Mary the mother of Joses observed where he had been laid.

The gospel of the Lord.

INTRODUCTORY PRAYER

One week separates us from Easter morning.
May the Lord help us to live in a holy way
during this "Holy Week"
in the remembrance of his holy Passion.

We bless you, Lord Jesus;
you loved us and offered yourself for us.
Give us the grace to take part in your Passion
by taking our part in the pain and suffering of the world.

And on the Day of your eternal Passover,
when you will come again in glory,
awaken us for the feast of your love.

We ask you this humbly, Lord,
you who suffered with us
and who reign with the Father and the Holy Spirit
in joy forever and ever. Amen.

HOMILY

Importance of the Death of Jesus

The accounts of the Passion have an important place in the gospels. Thus in Mark, the events that go from Palm Sunday to the death of Jesus on Good Friday comprise one-third of the gospel.[1] As for the Gospel of John, it is quite simply divided into two books: the book of the seven signs and the book of the Passion.[2] One could say that the gospels were "stories about the Passion with a detailed introduction."[3]

The community that chose to keep these texts about distress and extreme humiliation and to proclaim them to the world was nevertheless, the very one that Jesus had established as the witness of his resurrection. However, that community never wanted to exclude the mystery of the cross. They wanted to look death in the eye. Paul writes in his letter to the Galatians:

> O foolish Galatians! Before your eyes Christ was portrayed
> (*proegraphe*) crucified! Gal 3, 1

Thus the face of light of the risen Lord cannot erase the face of his agony. Magdalene's tears of joy on Easter morning will never allow us to forget the tears of blood on the night of his agony in Gethsemani or the somber grief of Good Friday. God does not evade death in the life of his Messiah. The Passion is not merely an .unfortunate interlude that, thanks to his powerful intervention, would terminate in the happy ending of the resurrection.

In other words, no proclamation of the gospel can either evade or short-circuit the scandal of Calvary. With Paul, we affirm:

> As for us, we preach Christ crucified, a scandal for the Jews and
> foolishness for the pagans. I Cor 1, 23

No homily can avoid speaking about the Passion or hide its bitterness in soothing words.

No homily can avoid speaking about our own death. I admit such a talk is not easy…Who, wanting to be heard today, dares to speak about death?

In the Gospel of Mark

In modern western societies, we often seek to dilute the anguish of death in the drugs of pleasure, power, money, or simply work. As for the dying, they are hidden in hospitals or they die, sometimes of a sweet euthanasia, in the shelter of human care. Our dead are made up in funeral parlors and appear more beautiful than the living mourners who, without make-up, come to cry over them.

In the Gospel of Mark there is no concealment of the anguish of death. It is Mark's gospel that reflects the humanity of Christ the most intensely and describes the Lord's sufferings of death most faithfully. We hear there the desolate groan of anguish in Gethsemani: "My soul is sad unto death." We witness the spittle, the slaps and all the mockings—a scene that Mark describes without caution. We see Peter warming himself before denying his Master shamelessly. We hear, in the Aramaic formula, the dreadful cry that Jesus uttered while dying:

> Eloi, Eloi, lama sabachtani?
> My God, my God, why have you forsaken me? Mk 15, 34

The Good News

The gospel is the Good News. The liturgy says to us today: All of you who are listening to Mark's account of the death of Jesus are hearing the Good News, you are welcoming joy, you are receiving peace. Like Jesus, you will die on the day God has chosen for you. Like Jesus, you will have the right to cry, to implore, to undergo anguish, to hope. Like Jesus, in your death, you will meet God your Father.

Do not be afraid to meet God. Do not be afraid to meet our Father, for no one loves us as much as he loves us. And no one waits for us in his home as he waits for us in heaven.

It is written in the psalm:

> From God, the Sovereign Lord,
> comes escape from death. Ps 68, 2

Yes, God invents an escape from death. Just as for Jesus, the escape from death is life. Just as the Father did for Jesus, the Father makes our death flow into the resurrection of the Lord.

The Word of the Cross

The Passion of Jesus remains a mystery for us.

We can contemplate it.

We cannot fully "understand" it. We cannot seize in our hearts the mystery of the Passion in its plenitude. All through the ages, Christian piety has fixed its eyes on the face of the crucified Lord to decipher from it the mystery of his tears.

Until the thirteenth century, Christian piety loved to portray the Lord as the living Christ in his royal and sacerdotal dignity.

In the fourteenth and fifteenth centuries, it was almost fascinated by a certain sorrowfulness. It would discover in the cross the perfect image of the suffering of the Just One. Often the cross was stripped of the light of Easter and only represented Christ tortured by agony, torn apart by anguish. A famous example is the crucifixion painted by Matthias Grunewald (c. 1460-1528) for the retable of Isenheim. It is clear that if we propose today an agonizing Christ to people whose ideal is the negation and the elimination of suffering—I am thinking about the people and the cultures of the far East marked by Buddhism—we have no chance to be heard.

In the nineteenth century, Christian piety loved to venerate in the cross the obedience and the resignation of Jesus to the will of his Father. This Christian resignation was a model to imitate. It was supposed to be opposed to a world in the process of paganizing itself and where the seeds of revolution were sprouting. One can regret that the goodness of Christ has sometimes been devaluated into affectation. We must not forget, in fact, that the obedience of Jesus was expressed in his strength in proclaiming his message of liberation in the face of death. The heart of Jesus is most certainly a meek and humble heart, but his meekness had a violence that overthrew the powers of hell; his humility conquered the world!

There is a diversity in the contemplation of the Passion of Jesus that goes back to the gospels themselves. Matthew, in fact, does not have the same perspective as Mark, and if he had his eyes on the writings of Mark, he was not afraid to present differences following his charism as an evangelist. And John, for his part, even if he happens to join Luke, is not anxious to copy him.

There is a fundamental lesson in these diverse and complementary readings of the Passion.

Each evangelist, each community, each epoch has had its particular contemplation of the Passion, its personalized reading of the death of Christ. This leads to the following conclusion: If we want to remain faithful to tradition, we cannot simply be content to repeat tradition. We also must have our personal reading of the Passion.

In saying this, I remember well the limits of my own ministry. Of course, I have my personal reading of the gospel. I cannot share it with you. I can simply present it to you. My ministry stops at the threshold of your heart. It is up to you to open your heart. Only he who created your heart and who placed in it the flame of the Spirit can go further.

In speaking about the Passion, Paul uses a marvelous expression. He is the only one who uses it. He says: *ho logos ho tou staµrou*, "the word of the cross."[4] The cross is the most formidable word that God ever spoke to the world.

Why Did Jesus Die?

In the last thirty years, the scriptural and theological landscape in which the cross of Jesus stands has changed a great deal. Texts have been dug up in the attempt to penetrate the secret of his death. There have been battles. Each side has counted its wounded…

Around 1960, the theologian Bultmann wrote that one could not know how Jesus himself had understood his own death. This observation was forceful. The question, nevertheless, remains valid, and exegetes and theologians have accepted it. Sometimes redemption has been simplified into the following popular outline:

- Adam sinned; men and women have sinned following him. God requires satisfaction for the offense.
- Since people cannot atone by themselves, Jesus did it in our place; he died for our sins.
- Then the Father, having obtained satisfaction, grants us forgiveness.

This outline, simplified to the extreme, still occupies the mentality of many Christians. It presents major improprieties.

What father would be so cruel as to satisfy himself with the death of his child? What animal would do it? And would God, who is love, want it? How can we suppose that he could be "satisfied" with the Passion of his Son?

The forgiveness of God is always a free gift. How then would God make the death of his Son a condition of forgiveness?

If, finally, nothing but the death of Jesus was capable of "appeasing" God's anger, as it is said, and of atoning for Adam's sin, who—as Abelard already asked—will be able to atone for the sin of those who condemned and killed Jesus?

The Answer of the Gospels

Let us go back to the gospels. Let us ask the question: What does the Gospel of Mark say about the death of Jesus?

Jesus was judged, condemned and then executed following a double trial, first before the Jewish authorities represented by the Sanhedrin, and then before the Roman authorities represented by Pontius Pilate.

The trial before the Sanhedrin involves many historical unknowns. We cannot be certain that the trial took place in good judicial form. And if it did, we cannot be certain that it resulted in a formal condemnation.[5]

The trial then traveled from the religious to the political realm. There were many deliberate deceptions and base actions on both sides. Jesus was finally condemned as a political agitator, which everyone knew he obviously was not. Therefore, he knew the ultimate depth of humiliation. His death was in some way stolen from him.[6] In reality, in Israel stoning was the noble form of death of martyrs who died for the sake of God. Crucifixion was the degrading punishment reserved for highway robbers and slaves. In crucifying Jesus, in degrading the man, they wanted to kill the prophet.

The fact is: Jesus died for the gospel, for the message that he proclaimed.[7] He was condemned because this message attacked the religious and political hope of the ruling classes and because its success was their defeat. Jesus, in fact, declared: Happy the poor, cursed be the rich.[8] He announced that the powerful were going to be brought down from their thrones—thrones of money, wisdom, power—and that the humble would be exalted.[9] He claimed that the sinners who welcomed the Kingdom were forgiven and that the righteous—at least those who considered themselves righteous, such as the Pharisees, professional fasters and sayers of prayers—remained in their sin.[10] Even worse, he willingly invited himself to the homes of publicans[11] and allowed himself to be surrounded by women with questionable pasts.[12] This new religion was intolerable, a religion that claimed in the face of the "justice" of the scribes and Pharisees that the publicans and the prostitutes would precede them into the Kingdom, a Kingdom that should come to them by right![13] This religion was intolerable, this religion that affirmed that the patience of God for the pagans was infinite, that if God had been impatient toward his people, Israel would not have survived its infidelities, while Tyre and Sidon, cities immersed in paganism, would have survived![14] This religion was intolerable, a religion that proclaimed that all the laws of Israel—tradition counted 613 of them![15]—could be summed up in two single laws: the love of God and the love of neighbor. And further, those two laws were so close to one another that they could be fused into a single one![16] Finally, this new religion was intolerable, this religion that taught that all the sacrifices which made up the glory of the Temple and upon which rested the very existence of Israel had to give precedence to mercy.[17]

Actually, it is the whole gospel that should be cited as intolerable. "This word is hard," they said. "Who can listen to it?[18]" The apostles themselves sometimes remained perplexed when faced with the newness of the gospel. "Who, then, can be saved?" they asked.

This is the Kingdom that Jesus announced, the love that he wanted to make triumph, the hope for which he died.

For Us, Today

What are the consequences of the death of Jesus in our lives? How is our religion, that is, our relationship with God, marked by that death?

"The word of the cross," as Paul says, is a homily of infinite power. It dominates the noise of the world. It is also the most intimate word that God speaks to our hearts.

Our lives, like the life of Christ, are inseparable from the gospel. Consequently, each time we live according to that gospel, each time we make the law of love triumph in our lives, we continue the battle of the Passion of Christ. By pushing back the frontiers of hate, we enlarge the frontiers of love. In uprooting the evil from our hearts, we embellish his Kingdom. In taking the part of the poor, the humble, the persecuted and all of those crippled by life, we place ourselves on the side of Christ. We are then on the path of that Passion. It is a path of resurrection.

Inversely, each time we neglect to love others, we place ourselves on the side of those who condemned the Messiah to death. We are not innocent. Through our sin, we are implicated in that Passion as we are implicated in the grace of Christ through the good that we do.

Thus, the cross dominates the history of the world. Nothing is more contemporary for us than those two pieces of wood raised up on Calvary. Nothing is more intimate to us than that sign of the Crucified One, which marked us at our baptism. Each one of us will be saved according to the position that we take in regard to that cross. We can, through the mediocrity of our lives, "crucify the Son of God again," as scripture says.[20] We can also, through the love we offer to our brothers and sisters, accept to be crucified with Christ, as Paul says,[21] in order to rise with him in glory.

The cross is our judgment. Let us pray that it may be our salvation. In seeing how we live, may the centurion of our day, like the centurion of the gospel, be able to say of Jesus: "Truly, this man was the Son of God!"[22]

The Time of Compassion

Jesus died almost two thousand years ago on the fifteenth of the month of Nissan, that is, on April 7 of the year 30.[23] Since that day, the time of the Passion is definitely closed. The time of compassion is open. It will be open until the end of time. Then, the Lord will change the time of compassion into the eternity of his glory.

To have compassion (*sym-paschein*) is to "suffer with." Compassion is "passion," suffering, with Christ. It has different faces.

There is first the compassion of Christ with our own sufferings. Jesus was incarnated in our pains and in our sins. The Book of Isaiah explains:

> Those were our sufferings that he took up
> and our pains with which he was burdened…
> He was pierced for our sins;
> he was crucified for our offenses.[24] Is 53, 4-5

There is, on the other hand, our compassion with Christ. We take part in his Passion. Paul explains:

> The Spirit attests with our spirit
> that we are children of God.
> Children, therefore, heirs.
> Heirs of God,
> therefore, co-heirs with Christ
> since we suffer with him
> to be also glorified with him. Rom 8,16-17

How can we suffer today with Christ?

All life one day meets the inevitable taste of tears. All life is a rendezvous with death. All suffering is thus a rendezvous with the cross of Christ.

It is the path of resurrection. Of course, it can also be a path of despair. But despair itself can be changed into a path of hope. The words "My God, my God, why have you forsaken me?" are very close to the words "Into your hands, I commend my spirit!"

All life also meets the sadness of those who surround us and who walk with us the path of our lives, the path of the cross. Every cross is an epiphany of Christ. Every passion is an invitation to compassion. "When one part suffers," said Paul, "all the parts suffer with it.[25]

The Girl of the Forest

The following story takes place in a Third World country where guerillas are still active. I will not name this country in order not to hurt anyone.

A contingent of soldiers progresses across the tropical forest on an expedition. They advance on a straight trail that winds across a deluge of foliage. At each step, the branches of the immense trees make triumphal arches for the soldiers.

Perhaps the trail is mined. What to do? How to know? The soldiers do as they usually do. They are neither better nor worse than other soldiers. As usual, at the first village, at the first hut, they requisition the first person. It is a very young woman, not yet an adolescent. Frail like a gazelle. Beautiful like a flower. She is forced to walk at a certain distance at the head of the column.

An immense flash of light. A thundering burst tears the silence that envelopes the forest and afterwards disperses into an infinite rumbling. Then, slowly, the waves of noise are diluted in the green darkness.

Poor child whose name no one will speak, of whom the only reminder will be the blood splattering the tall ferns, but whom God loves as if she were his only daughter in this world.

Is there a relationship between the girl of the forest blown up by a mine in the springtime of her life and the Crucified One of Calvary?

Yes, because each suffering is a face of Christ. Because, since Good Friday, we Christians cannot see a cross without seeing there at the same time the crucified Lord.

What then is religion? Let us relinquish all our books, all our certitudes, all our practices. Let us think about the problem of the girl in the forest, loved by God and killed by men.

When one person is down, all people should reach down to him, not to beat him down further but to raise him up. And when there is injustice or suffering, all should be there to defend the poor and to ease the pain. That is Christianity.

It is written in the Psalm:

> The Lord is at the right hand of the poor. Ps 109, 31

Each time you see a poor man or woman, look at the Lord. He is at their right hand. This is our faith.

When we take in our hands the branches of blessed palm, we remember that these branches represent the palms that the crowd carried when Jesus entered into the holy city. We signify in this way that we are welcoming Christ, that we want to walk with him, that our lives want to imitate his life.

When we carry this branch home and place it in our dwellings, we signify that spring, in this branch of greenery, has entered into our homes, and we signify that the springtime of God will come into our hearts.

May we be able to recognize the Lord Jesus in each suffering that comes to us. And on the day of the Passover for eternity, at the entrance into the eternal Jerusalem, it is the Lord who will come before us and will recognize each of us as his brothers and sisters. To him glory forever and ever. Amen.

PRAYER FOR THE TIME OF THE PASSION

Look, Lord, at the suffering of the world.
May your cross of light illumine our crosses
and become for us a path to heaven.

Remember us, O Lord,
remember us.

You humbled yourself unto death,
death on the cross,
you, the Lord of glory.

The weak who are crushed by the powerful of this world,

Remember us, O Lord,
remember us.

You were overwhelmed by sadness in Gethsemani,
you, the joy of the world.
Those who are overcome by sadness
and imprisoned in solitude,

Remember us, O Lord,
remember us.

You were betrayed by the kiss of Judas,
you, the faithful friend.
The poor who are sold by their brothers and sisters,

Remember us, O Lord,
remember us.

You were abandoned by all your Apostles,
you, the beloved Master.
The innocent who are unjustly imprisoned,

Remember us, O Lord,
remember us.

You were denied by your apostle Peter,
you, the blessed Son of God.
Those who are betrayed in his love,

Remember us, O Lord,
remember us.

You were condemned to death on the cross,
you, the life of the world.
Those who are unjustly accused and condemned,

Remember us, O Lord,
remember us.

You were helped by Simon of Cyrene,
you, the strength of the faithful.
The friend who helps us to carry our cross,

Remember us, O Lord,
remember us.

You were crucified in the midst of thieves,
you, the Sun of Justice.
Those who are persecuted for the sake of the Gospel,

Remember us, O Lord,
remember us.

You died on the cross, abandoned by all,
you, the Savior of the world.
The innocent who are tortured to death,

Remember us, O Lord,
remember us.

You were buried by Joseph of Arimathea,
you, the Resurrection of the world.
The friend who never forsakes his brother or sister,

Remember us, O Lord,
remember us.

We also commend to you, Lord,
all our personal intentions.

We want to bless you eternally,
Lord Jesus, who died for our sins
and rose for our life.
Give us the grace to take part in your Passion
by taking part in the suffering of our brothers and sisters.
To you be glory forever and ever. Amen.

NOTES TO PALM SUNDAY

1. Chapters 11 to 16, therefore six out of sixteen chapters.
2. The book of the seven signs, 2-13; the book of the Passion, 13-20.
3. M. Kähler, in *Der sogennante historische Jesus und der geschichtliche, Biblishce Christus* ("Passionsgeschichten mit ausfuhrlicher Einleitung"). Cited by B. Lzuret, "Christologie domatique," *Initiation à la pratique de la Théologie*, vol. 11 (Paris: Cerf, 1982): 310.
4. I Cor 1, 18.
5. The accusation relating to the Temple: "We have heard him say: 'I will destroy this Sanctuary made by the hand of man, and in three days, I will build another not made by the hand of man"' (Mk 14, 58), was not valid. Mark notes explicitly—he is the only one to do it—that the testimony of the false witnesses did not agree and that Jesus did not respond to it (14, 59. 61). As for the affirmation of the messianity of Jesus and of his divine sonship, it reveals fully the faith of the early community. But one would not know how to see it in the rough draft of a tribunal recorder. Analyzing the Jewish trial, H. Cousin concluded: "There was no Jewish trial, no condemnation to death carried out judicially against Jesus by the Jewish religious authorities." (*Le prophete assassine* [Paris: Editions Universitaries, 1976], p. 196.)
6. In the gospels, there is a tendency to accuse the Jewish authorities in order to exonerate the Roman authorities.
7. Cf. B. Lauret, "Christologie dogmatique." art. cit., pp. 357-363. R. Bultmann, *Die Geschichte der Synoptischen Tradition* (Gottingen, Vandenhoeck & Ruprecht), pp. 290-292 ("Jesus was condemned for his affirmation of being the Messiah," p. 292.)
8. Mt 5, 3; Lk 6, 20, 24.
9. Lk 1, 52; 14, 11; 18, 14 and Mt 23, 12.
10. Lk 18, 9-14.
11. Mt 9, 11; Mk 2, 16; Lk 5, 30.
12. Lk 8, 13.
13. Mt 21, 31.
14. Mt 13, 24-30; 11, 21 and Lk 10, 13.
15. Traditional figure attested to for the first time by Simeon ben Eleazar (c.190). See Strack-Billerbeck, *Kommentar zum Neuen Testament aus Talmund und Midrasch*, 3d ed., vol. I (Munich: C.H. Beck 1961), p. 900.
16. Compare Lk 10, 27 to Mt 22, 37-39 and Mk 12, 29-31. Paul writes: "A single precept contains the entire law: You shall love your neighbor as yourself" (Gal 5, 14).
17. Mt 9, 13 and 12, 7 citing Hos 6, 6.
18. Jn 6, 60.
19. Mt 19, 25.
20. Heb 6, 6.
21. Cf. Gal 2, 19.
22. Mk 15, 39.
23. See S. Dockx, *Chronologies néotestamentaires et Vie de l'Eglise primitive* (Paris-Gembloux: Ed. Duculot, 1976), pp. 3-29.
24. Is 53, 4-5. Mt 8, 17.
25. I Cor 12, 26.

EASTER SUNDAY

Reading I — Acts 10, 34, 37-43

A reading from the Acts of the Apostles

Peter addressed the people in these words: "I take it you know what has been reported all over Judea about Jesus of Nazareth, beginning in Galilee with the baptism John preached; of the way God anointed him with the Holy Spirit and power. He went about doing good works and healing all who were in the grip of the devil, and God was with him. We are witnesses to all that he did in the land of the Jews and in Jerusalem. They killed him finally, 'hanging him on a tree,' only to have God raise him up on the third day and grant that he be seen, not by all, but only by such witnesses as had been chosen beforehand by God—by us who ate and drank with him after he rose from the dead. He commissioned us to preach to the people and to bear witness that he is the one set apart by God as judge of the living and the dead. To him all the prophets testify, saying that everyone who believes in him has forgiveness of sins through his name."

The Word of the Lord.

Responsorial Psalm — Ps 118, 1-2. 16-17. 22-23

R/. (24) This is the day the Lord has made;
   let us rejoice and be glad.

Give thanks to the Lord, for he is good,
   for his mercy endures forever.
Let the house of Israel say,
   "His mercy endures forever."

R/. This is the day the Lord has made;
   let us rejoice and be glad.

"The right hand of the Lord has struck with power;
   the right hand of the Lord is exalted.
I shall not die, but live,
   and declare the works of the Lord.

R/. This is the day the Lord has made;
let us rejoice and be glad.

The stone which the builders rejected
has become the cornerstone.
By the Lord has this been done;
it is wonderful in our eyes.

R/. This is the day the Lord has made;
let us rejoice and be glad.

R/. Or: Alleluia.

Reading II — Col 3, 1-4

A reading from the letter of Paul to the Colossians

Since you have been raised up in company with Christ, set your heart on what pertains to higher realms where Christ is seated at God's right hand. Be intent on things above rather than on things of earth. After all, you have died! Your life is hidden now with Christ in God. When Christ our life appears, then you shall appear with him in glory.

The Word of the Lord.

OR

Reading II — I Cor 5, 6-8

A reading from the first letter of Paul to the Corinthians

Do you not know that a little yeast has its effect all through the dough? Get rid of the old yeast to make of yourselves fresh dough, unleavened loaves, as it were; Christ our Passover has been sacrificed. Let us celebrate the feast not with the old yeast, that of corruption and wickedness, but with the unleavened bread of sincerity and truth.

The Word of the Lord.

Gospel — Jn 20, 1-9

A reading from the holy gospel according to John

Early in the morning on the first day of the week, while it was still dark, Mary Magdalene came to the tomb. She saw that the stone had been moved away, so she ran off to Simon Peter and the other disciple (the one Jesus loved) and told them, "The Lord has been taken from the tomb! We don't know where they have put him!" At that, Peter and the other disciple started out on their way toward the tomb. They were running side by side, but then the other disciple outran Peter and reached the tomb first. He did not enter but bent down to peer in, and saw the wrappings lying on the ground. Presently, Simon Peter came along behind him and entered the tomb. He observed the wrappings on the ground and saw the piece of cloth which had covered the head not lying with the wrappings, but rolled up in a place by itself. Then the disciple who had arrived first at the tomb went in. He saw and believed. (Remember, as yet they did not understand the Scripture that Jesus had to rise from the dead.)

The gospel of the Lord.

INTRODUCTORY PRAYER

Alleluia! Christ is risen!
Love is stronger than death,
the cross has triumphed over sin,
the light of the Risen One has vanquished our darkness.
Let us give thanks to God our Father
through his risen Son, Jesus Christ,
in the joy of the Holy Spirit.

We pray to you, God our Father:
Renew our lives in the life of your risen Son.
Wherever we may go,
let him, the Risen One, do good through our hands.
Wherever we may love,
let him, the Living One, love through our hearts.
Wherever we may rejoice,
let him, eternal gladness, triumph in our hearts.
And lead us from the joy of this Passover
to the eternal Passover in your Kingdom
where we will sing "Alleluia"
forever and ever. Amen.

HOMILY

No homily can speak about the entire paschal faith, and all the homilies given on this Easter day cannot express the magnitude of the Paschal Mystery. Moreover, not any feast, nor any liturgy, nor all the feasts celebrated together and all the liturgies lived in the Church can celebrate the totality of the resurrection of the Lord.

Why? Because Jesus, born of Mary in Bethlehem of Judea during the reign of Caesar Augustus, "has been," as Paul tells us, "declared Son of God with power through his resurrection from the dead."[1] Thus "the man Christ Jesus"[2] today has entered into the world of glory, into the Kingdom of heaven. And there, in that world of heaven, our eyes of flesh cannot follow him. Only our faith can glimpse his mystery.

1. The Mystery of the Passover

Passover in Biblical Tradition

In order to understand the Christian Passover according to its original richness, one must place it again in the biblical tradition in which it was born. I will discuss principally the feast of light, the feast of creation, the feast of the Exodus and the feast of the Last Day.

The Feast of Light

Passover is the feast of light. At the time of Christ, it was said that Passover was the eternal Day. Indeed, on that vernal equinox, the sun shone twelve hours during the day, and the full moon twelve hours during the night. The risen Jesus appeared to the world and said: "I am the Light of the world."[3] He is the Light of life, eternal Day, symbolized by the new fire and the Easter candle.

That is why we dare to pray today: O risen Lord, make the dawn of your Day rise in our hearts. Be the sun of our lives for eternity.

The Feast of Creation

Passover is also the feast of creation. We call to mind that at the Easter Vigil the first reading is the account of creation. In the Mediterranean cosmic cycle, this feast had become the feast of spring. On that feast, one offered the first fruits of the harvest and the little lambs of the flock.

That is why we dare to pray thus: O risen Jesus, in your glorified body, a small part of our earth has become a new creation; a little of our dust has entered into the glory of heaven; in your risen body, our own bodies now touch the stars. We beg of you: make your springtime of grace come into our winter. Let jonquils of joy rise in our hearts! Let the new heavens and the new earth germinate in us, where justice will finally reside.[4]

The Feast of the Exodus

Passover is also the feast of the Exodus. On that day, the Israel of old threw off the Egyptian clothing of slavery, put on its garment of freedom, passed through the tumultuous waves of the Red Sea, and entered into the Promised Land. On that day, Jesus threw off his garment of mortality, put on the dazzle of glory and entered into the true Promised Land, the heaven of his Father.

If only I could lift a corner of the veil of heaven to see, Lord Jesus, how the Father welcomed you, the Beloved returning from the sojourn of the dead; to discover Abraham and his pretty Sarah; to see my friends Jeremiah, Amos, Micah and the saints of the Old Covenant feasting with you on Easter morning; to glimpse the angels—blessed angels who served you in the desert of temptation and who acclaimed your Resurrection!

That is why we pray to you: O risen Lord, help us to throw off the clothing of our sins; dress us in the garment of grace. Make us enter into the Kingdom of eternal joy.

The Feast of the Last Day

Passover is, finally, the feast of the awaiting of the Day of God at the end of time. At that time, he will close the book of history and will gather all the elect close to his heart. In Jerusalem, at the hour of midnight, the doors of the Temple would be opened as if to hasten and welcome the Lord or his Messiah. On that night, the risen Christ inaugurated "these last days"[5] and began to gather together those who love his Father.

That is why we dare to pray: O risen Lord, you who come in the middle of the night, count us among your wedding attendants with the faithful virgins. Fill the lamp of our path with the oil of your love; open for us doors in our night; remember us in your Kingdom!

The Radiance of Easter

In Christian antiquity, that is, from the first to the fourth century, the Church knew only one feast, that of the resurrection. Saint Athanasius (295-373) called it "the Great Sunday."[6] And every Sunday was considered as a *hebdomadal,* or weekly Passover.

This flamboyant irradiation of the paschal light upon the whole liturgical year, this domination of a single feast upon all the other Sundays, is signified in a superb way in the writing of Saint Paul. Have you noticed that in his letters he never cites the miracles in the life of Christ, that he almost seems to ignore the sermons or parables of Christ? Undoubtedly, Paul did not know Christ on the roads of Galilee. But he knew fully his mystery. That is why on almost each page he affirms the resurrection. For Paul, the great miracle in the life of Christ, the greatest teaching of his gospel, is his resurrection. In order to be saved, it is enough to believe that Jesus is Lord, that is, that he is risen.[7]

The "Universal Feast"

The Greek tradition has preserved for us a marvelous Easter homily.[8] It may date from the fourth century. Here is how one sang to the risen Christ at that time:

O mystical solemnity! O feast of the spirit!
O Passover of God that from heaven comes down to earth
and that from earth goes back to heaven!
O universal feast, assembly of all creation!

You destroy dark death,
you give life to all people,
you open the doors of heaven.
God manifests himself in flesh,
and flesh is glorified as God!

You fill the immense room of the wedding feast.
All wear the nuptial robe.
No one is thrown outside
for not having the wedding garment.

O Passover, light of new brightness,
splendor of the torches of the virginal attendants!
Through you, the lamps of our souls will never again go out,
for the divine and spiritual fire of charity
burns in all, in all spirits, in all bodies,
fed by the oil of Christ.

God, we pray to you, Lord of spirits and eternities,
Lord and King, O Christ:
Stretch out your great hands upon your sacred Church
and upon your holy people who belong to you forever.
You vanquished our enemies:
Today again raise up the trophies of our salvation.
Help us to sing with Moses the hymn of victory.
To you are the glory and the power
forever and ever! Amen.

2. The Earth of the Risen Lord

Children of Our Earth

We are children of our earth. "Heaven is the heaven of the Lord," the psalm tells us, "but the earth he has given to the children of Adam."[9] We live on our earth as in our kingdom. Our earth is our body; it is our blood. It is our daily bread and the wine of our feasts. It is everything that we cherish: our father, our mother, our wife or our husband, our children. Our earth is birth; it is love; it is marriage. It is song and laughter. It is urchins playing in the streets. It is all the grains of joy that we sow around us, whose ripening we await impatiently so that we may reap avidly. Our earth is also the hundred billion stars that we see tremble with joy at their posts[10] in the nights of spring. Our earth is the daisy crumpled by the morning cold, consenting to open its heart of petals only when it receives the kiss of the sun.

God gave this earth to us and we are so much children of this earth that we do not want to leave it. We say to the Lord: "If you want us to desire your heaven, your Kingdom, first you must save what we love on our earth, in our kingdom. An ethereal heaven where we would fly like angels with wings of light does not interest us who are the children of Adam!"

But this earth, our earth, our joy, is at the same time our anguish. A child is born: What a marvel! But it is born to die one day: What a grief! We dream of eternity, but the thread of our life is unraveling faster than a garment that is wearing out.[11] Our days slip away like the morning mist evaporates. Laughter is still on our lips when tears begin to cloud our eyes.

We love this earth, our earth, but we carry the desire for heaven like a wound in our hearts.

Our Earth, Dwelling of the Risen One

Today, angels from heaven tell us the news: A man who was dead has come out of his tomb alive! A man who was imprisoned in night for three days has risen again into the light of spring! In him, death was destroyed. In him, love was stronger than death. And this man is Jesus, our brother. He is firstborn of us all.

He came among us; he made our life his life; he made our death his death. He did not look down on us from on high, from the balcony of his eternity. He became one of us. "Son of Man" was the title that he loved to give himself, in Hebrew *Ben Adam*, son of the dust. Our earth became his dwelling. He loved a woman whom he called *Imma*, mama, because she had carried him near her heart as all the mothers of the earth carry their children. He ate the bread of Joseph the carpenter whom he called *Abba*, papa. Speaking about him and his family, people said:

> Is it not the carpenter, the son of Mary, the brother of James and Joses, and Judas and Simon? Are not his sisters among us?
>
> Mk 6, 3

And Peter, in the discourse that we read, affirms:

> We, his witnesses, ate and drank with him. Acts 10, 41

Such is the man who, by the power of God, came out of the tomb.

Now, the firstborn is inseparable from his brothers and sisters. He carries us along with him. Everything that is human—our body, our blood, all our tenderness and all our loves, all our desires and all our hopes—he places in God, in the glory of his resurrection, in his joy, in the light of God.

> He is seated at the right
> of the throne of Majesty in heaven, Heb 8, 1

the Letter to the Hebrews affirms emphatically, but he remains at the same time with us, in the midst of our dust, until the end of time.[12] The earth, our earth, became the dwelling of the risen Lord. And we, the children of this earth, are invited to follow him to heaven in his resurrection. He, the God of light, the Lord of eternities, dwells in us as in his own house. The Letter to the Hebrews affirms:

> Christ is faithful as a son
> at the head of God's house.
> And we are his house. Heb 3, 6

Through his resurrection, creation itself became closer to us. The billions of stars that mock us with their laughter in the infinity of the starry sky became our family, for Jesus became the "Firstborn of all creation;" therefore, he is also the firstborn of billions of stars.

His Resurrection is at the heart of our existence. It is in each spark of joy. It is in the hand that the beggar extends to us and in the hand that we extend to the beggar. It is in the forgiveness of our sins that we receive in his name.[13] It is in the eucharistic bread that we transform into his risen body; it is in the wine that is his glorified blood. It is even in the heart of our failures, for "when I am weak, then I am strong,"[14] said Paul. And that strength is the strength of the Lord's victory over death.

"What Must We Do?"

Like the Jews who were listening to Peter's first sermon on the resurrection of Jesus, we ask the question: "What must we do now?"

Paul answers in the second reading:

> Let us celebrate the feast
> not with old yeast:
> that of corruption and wickedness,
> but with bread without yeast,
> the bread of sincerity and truth. I Cor 5, 8

Paul alludes to an old rule of the paschal ritual that the Book of Exodus[16] preserves for us: in order to celebrate the new Passover, every trace of the old fermented bread must be removed. The Passover is celebrated on the night of the fourteenth to the fifteenth of Nissan. The father of the family, from the evening of the thirteenth would carefully inspect his whole house by the light of a lamp to search for remnants of the old fermented bread. For this inspection, which could be made until noon on the fourteenth, the ritual provided blessings, and the last blessing was supposed to annul the particles of bread that might have escaped the inspection. Paul tells us today: In order to celebrate the Passover of Jesus, cleanse the house of your heart. Get rid of the old yeast of corruption and wickedness. Celebrate the Passover with the new unleavened bread of sincerity and truth. Easter is new life. It is the best of your heart that is changed into the youth of the risen Christ.

In the first reading, Peter makes this extraordinary affirmation:

Wherever Jesus went,
he did good. Acts 10, 38

Do as Jesus did. Spend your life doing good and you will rise with him. Wherever you go, leave seeds of joy, plant grains of hope, sow flowers of light.

To live the resurrection is a certain new way of living on earth and of loving your brothers and sisters.

And then, everything that is beautiful in your heart, everything that is good in your life, will rise, on the day of your resurrection, like jonquils in the meadow of your heart, under the sun of Christ, for an eternal spring.

CONCLUDING PRAYER

Christ, our brother, is risen.
He intercedes for us next to his Father.
With confidence, let us then present our prayer to him.

Christ, you are risen from the dead;
have mercy on us.

Christ risen,
radiant Morning Star that rises in our night,
make the dawn of your eternal day
rise upon the darkness of our death.

Christ, you are risen from the dead;
have mercy on us.

Christ risen,
Springtime of God that appears in the winter of our world,
make the jonquils of an eternal spring
bloom again upon our desert wastelands.

Christ, you are risen from the dead;
have mercy on us.

Christ risen,
Exodus that frees us from slavery,
open for us the doors of freedom
and make us enter into the eternal homeland.

Christ, you are risen from the dead;
have mercy on us.

Christ risen,
Smile of God in our agonies,
open the graves of our despair
and give us eternal joy.

Christ, you are risen from the dead;
have mercy on us.

Christ risen,
Son of man, born of the Virgin Mary,
proclaimed Son of God in your resurrection,
make your brothers and sisters be born
in your eternal Kingdom.

Christ, you are risen from the dead;
have mercy on us.

Christ risen,
we also commend to you
all our personal intentions.

Lord Jesus, you who reign
in the joy of heaven, next to your Father,
do not forget your brothers and sisters on earth.
Are you not our Firstborn?
Fill our lives with your joy and your peace
so that we may announce to all people
that you are risen
and that you open for us the door of eternity.
To you our love forever and ever. Amen.

NOTES TO EASTER SUNDAY

1. Rom 1, 4.
2. I Tm 2, 5.
3. Jn 8, 12. The fundamental work on the meaning of Easter is the one by R. Ie D´éaut, *La Nuit Pascale* (Rome: Institut Biblique Pontifical, 1963). To the four themes mentioned, we must add the one of the sacrifice of Abraham (about which we spoke in the homily of the Second Sunday of Lent).
4. Cf. 2 Pt 3, 13.
5. Heb 1, 2.
6. Festal Letter, 1, 10. Cited by B. Lauret, "Christologie dogmatique" in I*nitiation à la pratique de la théologie*, vol. 11 (Paris: Cerf, 1982): 297.
7. Cf. Rom 10, 9.
8. *On the Holy Pasch.* 62-63. Trans. L. Deiss. Cf. SC 27,1 (1950), pp. 189-191.
9. Ps 115, 15.
10. Cf. Bar 3, 34.
11. Cf. Ps 102, 27.
12. Cf. Mt 28, 20.
13. Acts 10, 43.
14. 2 Cor 12, 10.
15. Acts 2, 37.
16. See Ex 12, 15; 13, 7.

SECOND SUNDAY OF EASTER

Reading I — Acts 4, 32-35

A reading from the Acts of the Apostles

The community of believers were of one heart and one mind. None of them ever claimed anything as his own; rather everything was held in common. With power the apostles bore witness to the resurrection of the Lord Jesus, and great respect was paid to them all; nor was there anyone needy among them, for all who owned property or houses sold them and donated the proceeds. They used to lay them at the feet of the apostles to be distributed to everyone according to his need.

The Word of the Lord.

Responsorial Psalm — Ps 118, 2-4. 13-15. 22-24

R. (1) Give thanks to the Lord for he is good,
his love is everlasting.

Let the house of Israel say,
"His mercy endures forever."
Let the house of Aaron say,
"His mercy endures forever."
Let those who fear the Lord say,
"His mercy endures forever."

R/. Give thanks to the Lord for he is good,
his love is everlasting.

I was hard pressed and was falling,
but the Lord helped me.
My strength and my courage is the Lord,
and he has been my savior.
The joyful shout of victory
in the tents of the just:

R/. Give thanks to the Lord for he is good,
his love is everlasting.

The stone which the builders rejected
has become the cornerstone.
By the Lord has this been done;
it is wonderful in our eyes.
This is the day the Lord has made;
let us be glad and rejoice in it.

R/. Give thanks to the Lord for he is good,
his love is everlasting.

R/. Or: Alleluia.

Reading II — 1 Jn 5, 1-6

A reading from the first letter of John

Everyone who believes that Jesus is the Christ
has been begotten by God.
Now, everyone who loves the father
loves the child he has begotten.
We can be sure that we love God's children
when we love God
and do what he has commanded.
The love of God consists in this:
that we keep his commandments—
and his commandments are not burdensome.
Everyone begotten of God conquers the world,
and the power that has conquered the world
is this faith of ours.
Who, then, is conqueror of the world?
The one who believes that Jesus is the Son of God.
Jesus Christ it is who came through water and blood—
not in water only,
but in water and in blood.
It is the Spirit who testifies to this,
and the Spirit is truth.

The Word of the Lord.

Gospel JN 20, 19-31

A reading from the holy gospel according to John

On the evening of that first day of the week, even though the disciples had locked the doors of the place where they were for fear of the Jews, Jesus came and stood before them. "Peace be with you," he said. When he had said this, he showed them his hands and his side. At the sight of the Lord the disciples rejoiced. "Peace be with you," he said again.

"As the Father has sent me,
so I send you."

Then he breathed on them and said:

"Receive the Holy Spirit.
If you forgive men's sins,
they are forgiven them;
if you hold them bound,
they are held bound."

It happened that one of the Twelve, Thomas (the name means "Twin"), was absent when Jesus came. The other disciples kept telling him: "We have seen the Lord!" His answer was, "I'll never believe it without probing the nail-prints in his hands, without putting my finger in the nail-marks and my hand into his side."

A week later, the disciples were once more in the room, and this time Thomas was with them. Despite the locked doors, Jesus came and stood before them. "Peace be with you," he said; then, to Thomas: "Take your finger and examine my hands. Put your hand into my side. Do not persist in your unbelief, but believe!" Thomas said in response, "My Lord and my God!" Jesus then said to him:

"You became a believer because you saw me.
Blest are they who have not seen and have believed."

Jesus performed many other signs as well—signs not recorded here—in the presence of his disciples. But these have been recorded to help you believe that Jesus is the Messiah, the Son of God, so that through this faith you may have life in his name.

The gospel of the Lord.

INTRODUCTORY PRAYER

We bless you, Lord Jesus.
All through this week
you have kept us in the joy of your Resurrection.

We pray to you:
Today again, come into the midst of our community
and say to us, as you did of old to your disciples:
"Peace be with you."
Then, with one heart and one soul
we will celebrate the power of your love
forever and ever. Amen.

HOMILY

One week ago the risen Christ left us and entered into the light of God. And yet, this Sunday is filled with his presence. As he was on the day of Easter, Jesus is still in the midst of our community and he says to us: "Peace be with you!"

Like the first disciples, we, too, are filled with joy in seeing the Lord. Our faith discovers him in the bread that we share and in the community, gathered together in his name.

Finally, like Thomas, we recognize him by the scars of his hands and by the wound in his pierced side and, with Thomas, we acclaim him: "My Lord and my God!"

1. The Risen Christ

The Peace and the Joy of the Risen One

Jesus appeared to his disciples—as the Gospel of John insists[1]—on the first day of the week, that is, Sunday. That is the day that the Book of Revelation majestically calls "the Lord's Day" (*kyriakè hèméra*),[2] the day of the Risen One.

Jesus greets his disciples with the traditional wish, "Peace be with you." In itself, the formula is banal. In the gospels, the people of the Semitic tongue greet each other with *Shalom*, while the people of the Greek tongue greet each other with *chairé*, "rejoice!"

But in the mouth of Jesus, peace possesses a savor, a light that the banal greeting does not have, because it is not banal that an executed person, expiring in the tortures of crucifixion, rises three days later and gives his peace to his disciples. Jesus indeed said:

> I leave you peace;
> I give you my peace. Jn 14, 27

And he really added then: "It is not as the world gives it that I give it to you." He lays claim to a particular peace which is not of this world. It is the peace of his resurrection.

Filled with that peace, the disciples are inundated with joy.[3] Like the peace, this joy is that of the risen Lord:

> May my joy be in you,
> and may your joy be complete: Jn 15, 11

Each Sunday, each "Lord's Day," we have a rendezvous with the Risen One. His presence brings us peace and joy. The light of that peace and the transparency of that joy are revealed in the quality of our Sunday celebrations.

If you see a community "lock the doors of the place where it is"[4] through fear of change, that is, if it barricades itself in rubricism, if it enchains itself in boredom, then one can say that this community has not yet opened the doors of its heart to the Lord. But if you see a congregation tremble with joy and radiate peace upon leaving Mass, then you can conclude: "This joyous and peaceful congregation has had a beautiful celebration; it has truly met the risen Christ."

This consideration should shed a light on what is called "the Sunday obligation." Clearly, sometimes people ask today: Is it still obligatory to go to Mass on Sunday? That is like asking the question: Are Christians obliged to be happy? Or even: Are they obliged to enjoy the peace of the risen Christ? One might as well ask: Is a starving person obliged to eat when the most succulent meal is presented to him? Or yet: When two lovers meet just once a week, are they truly obliged to embrace?

Are we not lovers of Christ? Desirous of his peace and his eternal joy? "Poor us" if we speak about Sunday obligation where Christ speaks about love, about peace, about joy!

Yes, Lord, give us your divine peace, the peace that the world cannot take from us. Fill us with your joy, the joy that satisfies infinitely.

Doubting Thomas

We can see and hear the apostles besiege Thomas: "If only you had been there! We saw the Lord. What joy he gave us! And suddenly, what peace rose up in our hearts!" And Thomas, calmly, obstinately: "If I do not see, no, I will not believe!"

I like the apostle Thomas.

First, because he is an apostle who has a lot of color. Some of the Twelve are pale. We only know their names. One would say that they buried their personalities in the apostolic whole. They make up the majority, as one says, like the rocks that fit in a wall to assure the solidity of the whole. Thomas shows up like a rock that makes itself noticed. He always has a nagging question. When Jesus declares that he is returning to the Father, Thomas inquires about the way. Might as well know where one is going:

> Lord, we do not know where you are going.
> How could we know the way there? Jn 14, 5

And when Jesus declares that Lazarus is dead and that he is returning to Judea in spite of the hostility of the Jews, Thomas says with a certain melancholy: "Let us go, too, and let us die with him."[5]

I also like the doubting Thomas.

He pleases me because I feel at least as doubting as he! I rather agree with him because I also want to see, to touch, to verify. That seems to me rather typical of a certain scientific, let us say even modern, mentality that always questions: "Proof, please!"

Faith will never be a resignation of intelligence, a subjugation of reason, a premium given to what is irrational.

There are people who believe themselves to be pious simply because they are credulous. They are not even Christians. They believe no matter what, no matter how, no matter when. They jump in the last boat, ready to abandon it at the first squall. They are seekers of revelations, of visions, of prodigies. Paul spoke about the health of faith. He uses nicely the verb *hygiainein*[6] which means "to have hygiene, health." A true faith can arise only if one practices a certain hygiene of the heart and of the spirit. Faith can grow only if it is healthy.

The Request for a Sign

Thomas will not believe without proof. He presents his conditions:

If I do not see
in his hands the mark of the nails,
if I do not put my finger in the nailprints,
if I do not put my hand in his side,
no, I will not believe! Jn 20, 25

In the Bible, the request for a sign seems rather complicated.

At the announcement of the birth of John the Baptist, Zechariah asks for a sign. He does not obtain one and becomes mute. At the Annunciation, Mary asks for a sign and obtains one.

The Pharisees ask for a sign "from heaven." No sign is given to them.[7] The apostles do not ask for a sign, and the sign of the Transfiguration, a sign from heaven par excellence, is given to them.

The subject of signs is more complicated. King Ahaz is invited by the prophet Isaiah to ask for a sign "springing from the depths of Sheol or in the heights of heaven." Fearing to obtain it, therefore being forced to believe and being obliged to change his conduct, he refuses pharisaically under the pretext of not tempting the Lord. Isaiah gives him the sign of Immanuel.[8]

Everything depends, it seems, on the quality of the faith that asks for a sign. If it is a righteous heart that asks for a sign to believe better and to follow the Lord on the road that he lays out, the sign is given.

Everything depends also on the quality of the sign that is requested. If it is a sign made of wonders and spectacles to amuse our curiosity, the sign is refused. Jesus says to the Pharisees: "If you do not see signs and wonders, you will by no means believe!"[9] But if it is a sign that opens our hearts to a better knowledge of God, then one can say that the whole earth, from the red poppy in the fields of wheat to the white galaxies in the fields of heaven, is filled to the brim with signs of God; and the whole Bible is like a dictionary that allows us to decipher the signs of God; and the Gospel of John itself is the gospel of the seven signs that reveal Jesus to us.

As for me, I think this: if we ask for a sign from God, a word from God, a smile from God, that sign will be given to us on the condition that we ask for it with a sincere and upright heart.

And if we do not ask for it, it will be given to us just the same if we serve God with a sincere and upright heart. For our God is not a mute God—it is the idols that are mute!—but a God who speaks, a God who loves, a God who communicates with those who love him.

The sign that is the most humble and also the most marvelous, the most hidden in the mystery of your heart and also the most evident to the eyes of the world, is the peace and joy of your heart.

To you also, as he said to the apostles, the Lord says: "Peace be with you!" And you also, like the apostles, will be filled with a great joy. When you feel that peace and that joy rise in your heart, then your account is good; you are on the road to resurrection.

Condescension of the Risen Lord

Wonderful and marvelous condescension[10] of the risen Christ!

"To condescend" is to "descend with," "to descend to the same level." Here, it is to descend to the level of Thomas' needs, to answer his demands, to show him his pierced hands and his open side.

This same amazing condescension is found in the Gospel of Luke: to conquer the terror and fear of the disciples, Jesus allows himself to be touched by them and eats a piece of broiled fish.[11]

In Thomas' case, there is, moreover, a symbolic lesson. The sufferings of the Passion are the sign of Jesus to Thomas. They are also the sign of Jesus to our community today.

Our world is filled with crucified hands that stretch out to us. Will we know how to recognize in them the hands of Christ? Our earth is reddened by the blood of hearts pierced by suffering. Will we know how to discover in them the heart of the risen Lord?

"Happy Are Those Who Believe Without Having Seen"

This is the last of the Beatitudes about which the gospels tell us. After this beatitude, there is nothing more except the eternal vision. This is the beatitude that Jesus said especially for us.

This last beatitude joins the first beatitude, the one that was proclaimed at the dawn of salvation, when Jesus was still near the heart of his mother:

> Happy the one who believed
> that what had been said to her by the Lord
> would be accomplished. Lk 1, 45

Yes, happy is she, the one who said: "May it be done to me according to your Word."[12]

The whole gospel—from the birth of Jesus to his resurrection—is placed between these two beatitudes, two beatitudes of faith: They are like two pillars planted in the rock of God from which is suspended the arch of the bridge that allows us to go from birth to resurrection.

Our whole life also is placed between these two beatitudes of faith. Our life is full of the beauty of the Risen One if it is illuminated by the joy of faith. "Happy are those who have believed," it is said. May we be happy with our faith! Do we believe enough in our happiness? May our faith be radiant enough to lead unbelievers "into temptation" of believing!

2. The Community of the Risen One

"One Heart and One Soul"

I would not like to end this homily without picking up a sentence from the first reading. In this passage taken from the Acts of the Apostles, Luke writes:

> The multitude of those who had adhered to the faith had one heart and one soul. Acts 4, 32

"One heart, one soul." This is the image of what the Church must be. A community of love, a communion of thought.

Luke insists upon the sharing of goods in the early community. He writes:

> They put everything in common…
> No one among them was in need. Acts 4, 32. 34

Behind the text of Acts is a regulation from Deuteronomy concerning the sabbatical year: every seven years, the solidarity among believers and the generosity toward the poor required the remission of debts. And that rule of the sabbatical year ended precisely with the affirmation:

> There will not be any poor among you. Dt 15, 14

With the beautiful elegance of a biblist, Luke then affirms this: this sabbatical year wanted by Deuteronomy, this year creating a community without poor, is already realized here in the early Church through the resurrection of Christ. Here is the messianic community. Here is a community without poor, for it is a community of sharing and of love.

This consideration—better yet, this reality—touches us today directly.

The Christian ideal of "one heart, one soul" can only be realized if each believer accepts, in a certain way, to share with his brother and sister. To share, of course, material riches — to share also intellectual riches and to share especially the riches of love. There is no Christian community without this sharing.

May the Lord make each community "one heart and one soul!" And may he dwell in our midst!

To him alone be glory forever and ever.

CONCLUDING PRAYER

With one heart and one soul
let us implore the risen Christ:

My Lord and my God!

Reveal to us your presence,
O risen Christ,
in the word that is proclaimed to us.
May it resound in our hearts
like a song of spring.
Then, with Thomas, we will be able to acclaim you:

My Lord and my God!

Reveal to us your presence,
O risen Christ,
in the bread that we share.
May it satisfy our hunger for eternity
like a festive meal.
Then, with Thomas, we will be able to acclaim you:

My Lord and my God!

Reveal to us your presence,
O risen Christ,
in the community that we form in your name.
May it fill us with joy and peace
like a smile of love.
Then, with Thomas, we will be able to acclaim you:

My Lord and my God!

Reveal to us also your presence,
O risen Christ,
in the depths of our heart.
May its silence speak to us of you.
May your remembrance make us sing
like the song of the robin in the morning.
Then, with Thomas, we will be able to acclaim you:

My Lord and my God!

Let us also pray for all our personal intentions.

May your divine peace, O risen Lord,
warm our hearts
like a springtime sun.
May your heavenly joy invade our souls
like the dawn of a new day.
With Thomas, with one heart and one soul,
may we be able to acclaim you eternally:

My Lord and my God!

NOTES TO SECOND SUNDAY OF EASTER

1. Jn 20, 19 and 26.
2. Rv 1, 10.
3. Cf. Jn 20, 20.
4. Cf. Jn 20, 19.
5. Jn 11, 16.
6. Cf. Ti 1, 13: "May they be healthy in the faith." And Ti 2, 2: "May the aged be healthy in the faith."
7. Mk 8, 12. According to Mt 12, 39 and 16, 4, only the sign of Jonah is given to them. According to Lk 11, 29-32, this sign is the conversion of the Ninevites. This diversity of evangelic traditions shows the hesitations of the early community before the question of "signs."
8. Cf. Is 7, 14: "The virgin will be with child and will give birth to a son whom she will call Immanuel."
9. Jn 4, 48.
10. Greek tradition spoke about "condescension" (*sygkatabasis*) to signify the Incarnation of the Word, that is, the descent of the Word into the midst of humanity.
11. Lk 24, 39-42.
12. Lk 1, 38.

THIRD SUNDAY OF EASTER

Reading I — Acts 3, 13-15. 17-19

A reading from the Acts of the Apostles

Peter said to the people: "The 'God of Abraham, of Isaac, and of Jacob, the God of our fathers,' has glorified his servant Jesus, whom you handed over and disowned in Pilate's presence when Pilate was ready to release him. You disowned the Holy and Just One and preferred instead to be granted the release of a murderer. You put to death the Author of life. But God raised him from the dead, and we are his witnesses.

"Yet I know, my brothers, that you acted out of ignorance, just as your leaders did. God has brought to fulfillment by this means what he announced long ago through all the prophets: that his Messiah would suffer. Therefore, reform your lives! Turn to God, that your sins may be wiped away!"

The Word of the Lord.

Responsorial Psalm — Ps 4, 2. 4. 7-8. 9

R/. (7) Lord, let your face shine on us.

When I call, answer me, O my just God,
you who relieve me when I am in distress;
Have pity on me, and hear my prayer!

R/. Lord, let your face shine on us.

Know that the Lord does wonders for his faithful one;
the Lord will hear me when I call upon him.

R/. Lord, let your face shine on us.

O Lord, let the light of your countenance shine upon us!
You put gladness into my heart.

R/. Lord, let your face shine on us.

As soon as I lie down, I fall peacefully asleep,
for you alone, O Lord,
bring security to my dwelling.

R/. Lord, let your face shine on us.

READING II — 1 JN 2, 1-5

A reading from the first letter of John

My little ones,
  I am writing this to keep you from sin.
But if anyone should sin,
  we have, in the presence of the Father,
Jesus Christ, an intercessor who is just.
  He is an offering for our sins,
  and not for our sins only,
  but for those of the whole world.
The way we can be sure of our knowledge of him
  is to keep his commandments.
The man who claims, "I have known him,"
  without keeping his commandments,
  is a liar; in such a one there is no truth.
But whoever keeps his word
  truly has the love of God made perfect in him.

The Word of the Lord.

GOSPEL — LK 24, 35-48

A reading from the holy gospel according to Luke.

The disciples recounted what had happened on the road to Emmaus and how they had come to know Jesus in the breaking of the bread.

While they were still speaking about all this, he himself stood in their midst [and said to them, "Peace to you."]. In their panic and fright they thought they were seeing a ghost. He said to them, "Why are you disturbed? Why do such ideas cross your mind? Look at my hands and my feet; it is really I. Touch me, and see that a ghost does not have flesh and bones as I do." [As he said this he showed them his hands and feet.] They were still incredulous for sheer joy and wonder, so he said to them, "Have you anything here to eat?" They gave him a piece of cooked fish, which he took and ate in their presence. Then he said to them, "Recall those words I spoke to you when I was still with you: everything written about me in the law of Moses and the prophets and psalms had to be fulfilled." Then he opened their minds to the understanding of the Scriptures.

He said to them: "Thus it is likewise written that the Messiah must suffer and rise from the dead on the third day. In his name, penance for the remission of sins is to be preached to all the nations, beginning at Jerusalem. You are witnesses of this."

The gospel of the Lord.

INTRODUCTORY PRAYER

We bless you, risen Lord Jesus,
Today, as on the day of the first Easter,
you are in the midst of your disciples
and you say to us:
"Do not fear! It is I!"

And we pray to you:
Help us to recognize your living presence
in the word that you proclaim to us,
in the bread that you share with us,
and in the community of all the brothers and sisters
that you gather together with us
to celebrate your Father, in the joy of the Holy Spirit,
forever and ever. Amen.

HOMILY

1. The Responsorial Psalm

"In Peace I Lie Down"

Saint Benedict (+ c.547) in his rule for his monks provided that one should say this psalm every evening as a prayer of Compline.[1] The psalm says, in fact:

In peace I lie down,
soon I am asleep. Ps 4, 9

This is not always true. For one can have a conscience perfectly at peace and still suffer from insomnia. But what is always true is what that psalm affirms:

When I cry, you answer…
You ease my anguish. Ps 4, 2

Happy is the one whose sleep at night is a confident offering to the Lord! Happy is the one whose rest is a prayer! Gregory Nazianzen (329/339-390) prayed in this way:

> Grant to my eyes a light sleep
> so that my voice, which sings to you,
> does not remain mute too long.
> Your creation will awaken
> to sing praises with the angels.
> May my sleep, in your presence,
> make my prayer rise to you.[2]

And if the Lord, nevertheless, wants us to think of him in our insomnia or in long nights of illness, blessed be he! It is written in another psalm:

> When upon my bed I dream of you,
> all through the night I meditate on you. Ps 63, 7

Happy is the one whose rest in the grave is an awaiting of the love of God, who watches over him and prepares for him a morning of resurrection!

Happy is Jesus!

In peace he lay down in the tomb on the evening of Good Friday, and the Father, "who does wonders,"[3] awakened him on the morning of Easter.

"Make the Light of Your Face Shine Upon Us"

I imagine the child Jesus praying this psalm with Joseph and Mary. He was from a pious family, as one knows. One can also think that he was an intelligent and bright child. I then imagine him asking his father Joseph the question: "Tell me, Abba, when will the light of His face shine upon us?"

And Joseph, who did not know—how could he have been able to foretell?—that his son, a carpenter like himself, was one day going to rise from the dead, satisfied him by answering: "God knows, for it is written in the psalm, 'For his friend, that is, for the one whom he loves, the Lord does wonders.'"

In his commentary on the Gospel of Luke, Origen explains admirably how the light of God shines on our faces:

> If you want to, you can, beginning now, fix your eyes on the Savior.
>
> Indeed, when you direct the most profound look of your heart toward Wisdom, toward Truth, toward the contemplation of the

> only Son of God, your eyes are fixed on Jesus. Happy is the assembly about which scripture attests that all had their eyes fixed on him! I would like our assembly to receive a similar witness, that the eyes of all—catechumens and faithful, men, women and children—had their eyes, not those of the body, but those of the soul, fixed on Jesus!
>
> For when you look at him, his light and his contemplation will make your faces radiant with light. You will be able to say then: "The light of your face, Lord, has risen upon us!"[4]

Marvels upon marvels for the one who marvels at God! For the light of God, that radiance of his splendor, is not first in the things that we see; it is first in our hearts! It is there that it shines; it is there that it transfigures everything!

Marvels upon marvels for the one who marvels at the resurrection of Jesus. For the light of the resurrection illuminates our whole earth with splendor. The smallest suffering, like the darkest distress, can become, in the resurrection, dawns of joy.

2. The First Letter of Saint John

The Christian ideal is never to sin. John bears witness to that ideal when he affirms:

> Whoever is born of God does not sin,
> for the seed (divine) remains in him.
> He cannot sin,
> for he is born of God.[5]

We are walking toward that ideal; that is to say that we are on the path of holiness but have not yet arrived. It is wisdom to accept the delays of progress. It is humility and truth to recognize oneself as a sinner. For against all pride, especially Christian pride, John affirms:

> If we say we have not sinned,
> we are making God a liar
> and truth is not in us. I Jn 1, 10

The life of a Christian is situated between these two affirmations: the Christian, on the one hand, does not sin; the Christian, on the other hand, cannot pretend that he does not sin without making God a liar. In short, the ideal is holiness. This holiness is utopia.

This ideal of holiness and this experience of sin, this perpetual tension between what we should be and what we really are, opens in our heart the wound of sadness toward ourselves, the bruise of dissatisfaction before our own life.

Rites of Purification

In order to forget our sin, if not to erase it, we are skillful at inventing for ourselves rites of purification in which we can dissolve our anguish and recover our purity.

If you are a pilgrim of Hinduism, you can plunge yourself into the waters of the Ganges and hope to come out purified.

If you belong to the Moslem faith, you scrupulously observe the fast of Ramadan and you add to it, at least once in your life, the pilgrimage to Mecca: then there is good hope for you for forgiveness.

The old religions of the Fertile Crescent counted on the blood of goats and bulls[6] to recover the virginity of the soul. Poor beasts, who only asked to live for the glory of God and found themselves immolated for sacrificial ideology!

And Christians? Easy! It was enough—it is still enough today—to confess, that is, to tell a priest one's foolish acts, to do "penance" (usually a prayer) and to come out of the confessional with one's head erect and one's soul clean as new snow.

We must render this justice to the human conscience: No religion—unless in total error—has ever thought that the exterior rite could erase sin without the conversion of the heart. We must even say that this search for purity, in all the religions of the world, glorifies the holiness of God. The most humble, the most awkward rite is like a hand held out to the mercy of God. God reigns so high in his heaven and we crawl so low on earth that we explain ourselves to the ineffable God as well as we can. Is it our fault that God created us so fragile, so vulnerable, so miserable?

But the danger is great in degrading interior conversion into an exterior rite. Then, the ablution of the body in the waters of the Ganges replaces the purification of the heart; the walk to Mecca replaces the spiritual walk with God; the life of goats replaces our lives, which we do not want to offer; and exterior confession replaces interior conversion.

Jesus, Sufferer for Our Sins

John proposes to us today another attitude, the only attitude that is fully Christian: to recognize oneself simultaneously as a sinner and as one forgiven.

Jesus Christ, the Righteous,
is the victim offered for our sins,
and not only for ours
but also for those of the whole world. 1 Jn 2, 1-2

The Good News of Christian salvation is the following: We no longer depend on a "securing" rite but on the goodness of Jesus alone. We can no longer cleanse ourselves, but we accept being forgiven through his mercy. We truly recognize what we are — sinners and forgiven, forgiven, because we recognize ourselves as sinners!

Sin, then, no longer opens an ulcer of despair in our souls. It becomes the opportunity to meet the mercy of Christ; it is at the source of our thanksgiving. "Confession" is what it should always be: "confession," that is, proclamation of the mercy of God.

3. The Gospel

There is in this Sunday's gospel, which gives the last instructions of Jesus to his apostles just before the ascension, a great insistence on the Word of God. According to Luke, Jesus in fact declares:

It was necessary that everything be fulfilled
that was written about me
in the Law of Moses, the Prophets and the Psalms. Lk 24, 44

"The Law of Moses, the Prophets and the Psalms"

Jesus cites the Scriptures according to the classification that was in circulation in his epoch and that is still valid today. One distinguishes in the Bible:

The Law or Torah

By "Law," one meant the Pentateuch, that is, the first five books of the Bible. These books were attributed to Moses, hence the expression "The

Law of Moses." They were considered the heart of the Word of God. They are still the only books that the Samaritans recognize as the Word of God.

The Prophets or Nebiim

In the prophetic books, one distinguishes between the first prophets or former prophets (the books that we count among the historical books)[7] and the latter prophets (Isaiah, Jeremiah, Ezekiel and Daniel,[8] and the twelve minor prophets).

The Hagiographies or *Ketubim* make up the rest of the Bible. The Book of Psalms is the most important. It is by metonymy that Jesus speaks of the psalms to designate the whole of the *Ketubim*.

"Everything That Was Written about Me..."

Jesus explains to his apostles everything that was written about him "in the Law of Moses, the Prophets and the Psalms."

There is, therefore, a story about Jesus in the Law or Pentateuch, a story about Jesus in the Prophets, and a story about Jesus in the psalms! And we are invited, just like the apostles, to discover on each page of the Law, of the Prophets and of the psalms the face of Christ Jesus. Who among us would not like to know that story of the Messiah? Who among us would not like to hear his voice? Here we can discover the features of his face in the Law, the Prophets and the psalms. "The writings of Moses," said Saint Irenaeus, "are the words of Christ."[9]

Even more, those are the only writings whose authenticity—divine origin—is guaranteed by the Holy Spirit. All other books, all other "prophecies" or "revelations," can disappear—and will disappear—like "the grass withers and the flower wilts:" those words alone are eternal.[10]

Happy is the community about which it might be said what was said about the apostles:

> Then he opened their minds
> to the understanding of the Scriptures. Lk 24, 45

Happy is the priest, happy is the minister who knows how to open for his community a door of light upon the treasure of the scriptures, upon the face of Christ!

"Not to Know the Scriptures is Not to Know Christ"

The words of Jesus are always messengers of joy; but sometimes they also weigh upon our hearts, for they are also judgment. But this judgment is also for our joy. Today the words of Jesus ask the question that no one can avoid: Do we know the story of Jesus written in the Law of Moses?

Let us be precise: How does Deuteronomy, for example, speak to us about Jesus? Do we know the story of Jesus in the Prophets? Even more precisely: Do you know Jeremiah, the prophet of God's tenderness? What do you know about Isaiah, the prophet of the seraphim and the singer of God's holiness? Ezekiel, the prophet of the new heart? Daniel, the spokesman for the Son of Man? Do you know the "minor" prophets, who are minor in name only, but whose message is more infinite than the azure of heaven? Do you hear Amos, running through the mountains of Samaria, crying at the top of his voice: "Prepare yourself, Israel, to meet your God"? Do you know Micah, who assures you that God takes pleasure in forgiving? And Zephaniah, who was so dear to Mary because he speaks of the "Daughter of Zion"? What do you know about Hosea, who, in his bruised love for his wife Gomer, discovers that a sin is an omission not first of the Law but first of love? What do the psalms say? Do you know the story of Jesus in the psalms? Each Sunday, the responsorial psalm offers us a portrait of Jesus. Do we contemplate it? Or do we simply read a text to satisfy a rubric? Saint Augustine, speaking about the prayer of Jesus, said admirably:

> Let us recognize our words in him
> and his words in us.

Do we recognize the words and the prayer of Jesus in the psalm?

Saint Jerome (c. 347-419/420) consecrated his whole life to the study of God's word. He recommends to us:

> Let us obey the precept of Christ, who says: "Search the scriptures" (Jn 5, 39). Whoever does not know the scriptures does not know the power of God and his wisdom. Not to know the scriptures is not to know Christ.[12]

We Know the Scriptures?

You will perhaps answer me: You priests and you ministers, you surely have the opportunity to know the scriptures; you swim like fish in the biblical waters; you walk morning and evening in the garden scented with scriptures...

I will answer: We know the scriptures? First, it is not as certain as that. You know as well as I do that there are priests and ministers who, through no fault of their own, are underdeveloped on the biblical level. Nevertheless, I will say: You also can, you must, know the Word of God. What is asked of each of you is to honestly make every effort within your power. Good books exist. All of you know how to read. Make the effort of which you are capable. Nothing more, but nothing less.

We know the scriptures. But who of us would dare to pretend that he knows them enough? In other words: Who would be able to affirm that he has sufficiently scrutinized, admired and blessed the face of Christ Jesus? that he has sufficiently listened to his Word?

And finally: One can very well master the techniques of biblical knowledge without approaching Christ. Paul affirms that one can even read the Word with a veil over one's heart...[13] It is not necessarily the scholars of Holy Scripture who are the closest to Christ. They can be close to Greek, to Hebrew, to Aramaic, but far from the Lord. But woe to us if we are men of knowledge without being men of love...

Kierkegaard speaks very nicely about the fiancé who receives a letter from his beloved and who, in order to read it, arms himself with dictionaries and grammar books.[14] Of course, reading with the help of a dictionary can be very useful. Sometimes it is even necessary. But it does not replace reading with the heart, with that which the Spirit inspires in us. All knowledge, biblical and other, is only crutches; they serve us very usefully to go before Christ. But crutches to go before the beloved have never replaced the joy of seeing his face.

Finally, there are those who have neither Bible nor psalter, nor gospel, who do not even know how to read. What must they do? Are they, therefore, condemned to perish in darkness?

They must read the Word that God has written in their hearts. Paul affirms: "For we have the mind of Christ."[15] Yes, there are faithful who have nothing except the essential: the mind of Christ and the light of the Spirit of God.

I often think about a little old lady, a grandmother in the African bush, who had no book and who did not know how to read or write but had a heart full of Christ. I also think about a little pygmy boy who, with his family, followed the game trail in the equatorial forest, was without equal in getting the wild honey at the summit of trees scaling heaven or in trapping the fish hidden under the rock in the river, and who had no idea of what a school could be but had eyes full of heaven... When one spoke to him about God, it was like a song that he already knew by heart.

Three Lessons of Holy Scripture

At the end of his gospel, Luke mentions three lessons of scripture:

- The angels teach a lesson to the holy women. They say to them:

  "Remember how he had spoken to you...when he was still in
  Galilee..." And they remembered his words. Lk 24, 6. 8

- Jesus gives a course in scripture to the pilgrims of Emmaus.

He says to them:

"Minds without intelligence, slow to believe everything
that the Prophets announced..."
And beginning with Moses
and running though all the Prophets,
he interpreted for them in all the Scriptures
what concerned him. Lk 24, 25, 27

"All the prophets...In all the Scriptures..." Even in the most "minor" prophets, like Obadiah and Haggai, whose message takes up two pages of the Bible? Carried away by his enthusiasm, here Luke has undoubtedly simplified. He went to the essential: all of Scripture speaks of Jesus.

- Finally, Jesus gives a course in exegesis to his apostles on "the Law of Moses, the Prophets, and the psalms."

Would the ideal of the Christian community then be to become a Church of biblists, an assembly of learned exegetes?

The ideal is not a Church of biblists but a biblical Church, a Church rooted in the Word and that identifies ourselves, by what we are, with the Gospel that we proclaim. For the important thing is not what we say but what we are.

One must, undoubtedly, always make the effort to better understand the Word. Never, since the Church existed, has it been so easy to approach the Word of God. Never, since the Church existed, has it been so easy to obtain a book of value on the Word: At the entrance of our Churches and smallest chapels, one finds excellent ones. And never, since the Church existed, has it been so urgent to know our faith better.

What is the effort that each one of us brings personally to a better understanding of the Word?

A Fourth Lesson

To the three lessons of scripture that Luke mentions one must add a fourth. It is the most important, the one that our own life gives to us, the one that we give in our own life.

Each husband is a word of God for his wife. Each wife is a gospel for her husband. And parents, through the witness of their lives, give the lesson of scripture to their children and the children to their parents. Each one of us is a lesson of scripture for our brothers and sisters.

It is about this lesson that Jesus spoke when he said: "You will be my witness."[16]

It is the most living lesson, never boring, always a bubbling source of joy. Who would be able to refuse to give it in the name of Christ Jesus?

To him be glory forever and ever.

CONCLUDING PRAYER

The risen Christ says to us today:
"You will be my witnesses."
Let us pray to him so that our witness may be faithful.

Christ, you are risen from the dead; have mercy on us.

How could we witness,
O risen Lord,
that you are the Holy One, the Righteous One,
if your holiness does not appear through our own lives?
Make us faithful witnesses of your holiness.

Christ, you are risen from the dead; have mercy on us.

How could we witness,
O risen Lord,
that you are living, firstborn from the dead,
if your Resurrection does not transfigure our lives?
Make us faithful witnesses of your Resurrection.

Christ, you are risen from the dead; have mercy on us.

How could we witness,
O risen Lord,
that you are the sun of joy on the sadness of the world
if your light does not shine first on our faces?
Make us faithful witnesses of your light.

Christ, you are risen from the dead; have mercy on us.

How could we witness,
O risen Lord,
that you are the reconciliation offered for our sins
if your forgiveness does not occur first in our hearts?
Make us faithful witnesses of your forgiveness.

Christ, you are risen from the dead; have mercy on us.

How could we witness,
O risen Lord,
that you are present in all the scriptures
if we do not discover your face of glory
on each page of the Law of Moses,
in each oracle of the Prophets,
in each prayer of the psalms?
Make us faithful witnesses of your Word.

Christ, you are risen from the dead; have mercy on us.

We also commend to you, O risen Lord,
all our personal intentions.

In spite of the poverty of our witness,
you make of us, Lord, witnesses of your Resurrection.
We thank you for counting us worthy to serve you.
Keep us in your love
forever and ever. Amen.

NOTES TO THIRD SUNDAY OF EASTER

1. *Rule of Saint Benedict*, 18, 19. Cf. SC 182 (1972), p. 532. *Carminum liber* 1, 1, 32. PG 37, Sll A—514 A.
2. Ps 4, 4.
3. *Homilies on Saint Luke*, XXXII. This commentary dates from 248/249.
4. I Jn 3, 9. "The divine seed," literally, "the sperm (*sperma*) of him," that is to say, either Christ (as in 1 Jn 5, 18) or the principle of divine life that we hold from our birth of God.
5. Cf. SC 87 (1962).
6. Cf. Heb 9, 13.
7. The Books of Joshua, Judges, Samuel, and Kings. In classifying these books among the prophetic books, Israel was affirming that history itself can be a prophecy. History was effectively a prophecy of Jesus, the Messiah, who was going to "fulfill" that history.
8. Daniel figures in the Hebrew Bible among the *Ketubîm* between Esther and Esdra-Nehemiah. In the Greek Bible, the Book of Daniel is placed after Ezekiel.
9. *Against Heresies*, IV, 2,3. Cf. SC 100 (1965), p. 400.
10. Cf. Is 40, 8.
11. *Enarratio in Psalm*. 85, 1. CCL 239, 1176.
12. *In Isaiam, Prologus*. CCL 73,1.
13. Cf. 2 Cor 3, 15.
14. *Complete Works of S. Kierkegaard*, vol. 18 (Paris, 1966), pp. 85-86. Quoted by R. Refoulé, art. "D'une naïveté premiere a une naïveté seconde," in *La Vie Spirituelle*, 591, July-August, 1972, pp. 523-524.
15. I Cor 2, 16. Cf. also 7, 40.
16. Cf. Lk 24, 48. Acts 1, 8.

FOURTH SUNDAY OF EASTER

Reading I — Acts 4, 8-12

A reading from the Acts of the Apostles

Peter, filled with the Holy Spirit, spoke up: "Leaders of the people! Elders! If we must answer today for a good deed done to a cripple and explain how he was restored to health, then you and all the people of Israel must realize that it was done in the name of Jesus Christ the Nazorean whom you crucified and whom God raised from the dead. In the power of that name this man stands before you perfectly sound. This Jesus is 'the stone rejected by you the builders which has become the cornerstone.' There is no salvation in anyone else, for there is no other name in the whole world given to men by which we are to be saved."

The Word of the Lord.

Responsorial Psalm — Ps 118, 1. 8-9. 21-23. 26. 28. 29

R/. (22) The stone rejected by the builders has become the cornerstone.

Give thanks to the Lord, for he is good,
  for his mercy endures forever.
It is better to take refuge in the Lord
  than to trust in man.
It is better to take refuge in the Lord
  than to trust in princes.

R/. The stone rejected by the builders has become the cornerstone.

I will give thanks to you, for you have answered me
  and have been my savior.
The stone which the builders rejected
  has become the cornerstone.
By the Lord has this been done;
  it is wonderful in our eyes.

R/. The stone rejected by the builders has become the cornerstone.

Blessed is he who comes in the name of the Lord;
we bless you from the house of the Lord.

I will give thanks to you, for you have answered me
and have been my savior.

Give thanks to the Lord, for he is good;
for his kindness endures forever.

R/. The stone rejected by the builders has become the cornerstone.

R/. Or: Alleluia.

Reading II — 1 Jn 3, 1-2

A reading from the first letter of John

See what love the Father has bestowed on us
in letting us be called children of God!

Yet that is what we are.
The reason the world does not recognize us
is that it never recognized the Son.

Dearly beloved,
we are God's children now;
what we shall later be has not yet come to light.

We know that when it comes to light
we shall be like him,
for we shall see him as he is.

The Word of the Lord.

Gospel — Jn 10, 11-18

A reading from the holy Gospel according to John

Jesus said:
"I am the good shepherd;
the good shepherd lays down his life for the sheep.
The hired hand, who is no shepherd
nor owner of the sheep,
catches sight of the wolf coming
and runs away, leaving the sheep
to be snatched and scattered by the wolf.
That is because he works for pay;
he has no concern for the sheep.

"I am the good shepherd.
I know my sheep
and my sheep know me

in the same way that the Father knows me
and I know the Father;
for these sheep I will give my life.
I have other sheep
that do not belong to this fold.
I must lead them, too,
and they shall hear my voice.
There shall be one flock then, one shepherd.
The Father loves me for this:
that I lay down my life
to take it up again.
No one takes it from me;
I lay it down freely.
I have power to lay it down,
and I have power to take it up again.
This command I received from my Father."

The gospel of the Lord.

INTRODUCTORY PRAYER

We bless you, God our Father.
In your risen Son Jesus
and in the love of your Holy Spirit,
you make us your children.

Also we pray to you:
Let our life be beautiful with your splendor
so that the whole world may glorify you.
Let our love for our brothers and sisters
imitate your love for all people.
And let our joy, a reflection of your joy,
bear witness to the resurrection of your Son Jesus.
He lives and reigns with you in heaven,
and remains with us
forever and ever. Amen.

HOMILY

Jesus, the Good Shepherd

At each moment during this paschal time, the Church meets the risen Christ.

At each moment on the path of our life, we meet in the same way the smile of the risen Lord, and each Sunday reveals to us new riches of his Kingdom.

Today, this face is the one of the Good Shepherd.

The "Good" Shepherd

The image of the shepherd, we sometimes notice, is less expressive in our urban and Western civilization than it was in the agricultural and Eastern civilization in the time of Jesus.

This is true. One can still encounter shepherds and flocks of sheep at the bend of a path in Palestine, but one does not encounter any in our modern cities and villages except in re-enactments of folklore.

The image of the Good Shepherd nevertheless keeps all its power. It is not necessary to have lived with shepherds to understand the image of the Good Shepherd any more than it is necessary, for example, to have lived with lions to understand the expression "strong and brave as a lion."

Personally, I would say in passing, that the images used by the Bible are always the best, better in any case, than those that we would be able to substitute for them. To say it quite clearly, I believe that Jesus is always right.

The image of the shepherd possesses in fact the power of the Word of God. It actualizes precisely the numerous texts of the Old Testament where God presents himself as the Shepherd of Israel. Here, as elsewhere, one can understand the New Testament only in the light of the Old.

"I am the Good Shepherd:" the affirmation is full of splendor and of tenderness. John's text says literally: "I am the Shepherd, the beautiful."[2]

Yes, Lord, you are our Beautiful and Good Shepherd, but an absolutely unique shepherd, a shepherd resplendent with the splendor of God and a shepherd transfiguring the ugliness of the sheep that we are, smelling of hay and milk, into the beauty of the children of God.

Fourth Sunday of Easter

"I Know My Sheep"

In the immenseness of the universe, we can sometimes have the impression of being only a pawn that chance moves about on the chessboard of the world at the pleasure of its fancy.

I was thinking about that while remembering the superb pictures that the Apollo mission had taken of the world. Seen from the moon, the earth appears only like a minuscule moon lost in the darkness of the universe. Where is my city, my village, my home situated in this limitless universe?

And in comparison with those billions of galaxies, each one of which includes millions of stars that dance farandoles of joy for God, what is the real grandeur of man or woman? What is the weight of my presence in the galaxies?

There are equally billions of years of light that take my breath away. The cosmos existed for fifteen to seventeen billion years. To say it poetically, with the Book of Job:

> God placed the cornerstone of the world
> among the joyous concerts of the morning stars
> and the unanimous acclamation of the sons of God. Job 38, 6-7

What is the duration of my life worth? The breath of an instant? Does God know me in these nameless durations? Does God know my name?

There are also what one calls general laws. Of course, laws are necessary and we know that laws are general, that they are valid for the whole world, except perhaps for a particular case, except precisely for my particular case. Does God know my particular case? What is the value of a general law for a man whose wife has left him or for a woman whose husband has abandoned her without being at fault? Who will persuade them that this general law is good for them? Does God have only an idea of these particular cases?

Very near to me there is a hospital that has a whole section dedicated to children with disabilities, children whose bodies are twisted with malformations or whose intelligence is dimmed. It is a pity to see them move around—or sometimes even play ball—lying on their stomachs on little carts. It is even a greater pity to see their minds crawl, so to speak, before God. From time to time, go to a hospital to see these children. You will leave there looking with joy at your two hands that can move and your two feet that can walk, and you will thank God.

Transcendence of G
Cosmos
Danger ? Power > Judgement
Rejected by so many
Immanance of G
G very close to me
Classic spirituality
Danger – just G + me – Romanticism
N.Y. Times ~~study~~
Connection to both
The G who cares
We who care because
G does
* Lucien Deiss p269

Those are extreme, unique cases. But is not each one of us a unique case? Today, Jesus says to us: "I know my sheep." Today, the Good Shepherd reveals to us:

> "I call my sheep '*Kat' onoma*', that is to say, each one by name.[3] It is I who invented your name for you and gave it to you.
>
> "I know you in the particular joy that makes you dance on the road of your life.
>
> "I know you also in the burden of pain that you carry like a chain of slavery, within a thick darkness that envelopes you like a cloak.
>
> "I know your heart in its most secret places because it is I who formed your heart for you; I held it in my hands before giving it to you.
>
> "And I, who am a millionaire of stars and who know each star by its name,[4] say that this universe weighs less in my hand than a beat of your heart. And I, who am a millionaire of the centuries, affirm that this immensity of time is worth less to me than an instant of your life. Because for me to know someone is to love him, to create him while loving him!"

God knows me in this way: What a marvel! He knows me as he loves me. His knowledge is love.

In other words, we exist under the look of God because his love has called us into existence, not to a vague, undetermined existence but to my particular, personal existence. God loves me just as I am. He alone loves me in this way!

The general rule is precisely that for God there is not any undetermined love, or, said better: each general tenderness is also a particular tenderness. In the same way that God created each rose with its particular perfume, each star with the laughter of its scintillation, each wave of the sea with the crest of its light, each robin with its personal melody, thus did he create each sheep with its particular name and thus did he love each one of us in our personal riches.

Of course, he remains the shepherd of the whole flock. But also remains "my" shepherd, mine, the one who guides me. We may well say:

> The Lord is my shepherd,
> I shall not want. Ps 23, 1

It is as though each one possessed God completely for himself all alone.

And each one of us possesses completely that solicitude of the shepherd, that look that rests upon him, that providence that leads him.

The prophet Ezekiel marvelously described the particular care of God for each one of his sheep:

> Oracle of the Lord God:
> It is I who will pasture my sheep;
> it is I who will make them rest.
> The one who is lost, I will seek;
> the one who is astray, I will lead back.
> The one who is wounded, I will tend;
> the one who is sick, I will heal.
> The one who is fat and in good health,
> I will watch over.
> I will shepherd with justice. Ez 34, 15-16

"My Sheep Know Me"

To this personal call of God, we must make a personal response. Jesus says:

> The sheep follow the shepherd
> for they know his voice...
> My sheep know me. Jn 10, 4. 14

Do you know the voice of Christ? More precisely: Do you recognize his voice in the innumerable calls that he sends to you on the path of your life?

The call is personal. The answer must likewise be personal. One cannot say: "See, I answer the Lord like everyone else. I do exactly like the other Christians." But what if God would ask something else of you? What if God would ask more of you? What if God would ask everything of you?

"The good shepherd gives his life for his sheep."[5] Jesus did not intend to describe thus the behavior of Palestinian shepherds but really the behavior of the Messiah of God: He offered his life for his sheep. In this way, he gave witness of the greatest love."

See the quality of his call. See the quality of your answer. Answer him with your personal voice. Do not seek to imitate your brother or sister: They must answer for themselves. They cannot answer for you. They do their best to sing their melody. You do your best to sing your own melody. Go toward God with your own face. Why borrow a mask? Go toward him with your face of eternity, that face that his love, day after day, wants to fashion for you.

The Authentic Image of the Shepherd and the Sheep

How regrettable it is that the allegory of the Good Shepherd has sometimes been devaluated by a pious and watered-down imagery. Of course, they intended to do well. One represented Jesus in a rose robe and with blond curls next to a bleating sheep. It is touching on good will but quite far from the gospel!

For Jesus the Good Shepherd is the one who vanquished death; he is the Lion of Judah who triumphed over all the hostile powers of the Kingdom and over all the devils!

How regrettable it also is that Christians have sometimes been represented as an amorphous flock of sheep! It is quite precisely the contrary! One can enter into the flock of Christ only if one possesses a vigorous personality, a personality that one receives through baptism. The sheep of Christ are all sheep, personalized through their faith, stubborn in their hope, rooted in their love, who answer only if one calls them personally by their name, who recognize only one shepherd, their Master, Jesus.

"One Flock, One Shepherd"

This unity of the flock and this uniqueness of the Shepherd are so important that they constitute the existence of the Church. In other words, the Church stakes its existence on this unity. The Church is "one," or we do not exist. A community divided into factions would be a conglomerate of sects but not the flock of Jesus Christ.

This unity of the Church is also a sign of our messianity. The Church of messianic times, announced by the prophet Micah, is a Church gathered together in unity:

> I will reunite the remnant of Israel.
> I will gather them like sheep in the enclosure,
> like a flock in the middle of your pasture.
> God will be at their head. Mi 2, 12-13

This unity is the criterion for the Shepherd as well as for the sheep.

Jesus prayed:

That all be one,
as you, Father, are in me
and I am in you,
that they also be one in us
so that the world may believe
that you sent me. Jn 17, 21

One Flock

One sometimes confuses the image of the flock with that of the sheepfold or the enclosure. One thinks then about fat and plump sheep on eternal vacations, spending peaceful days in the shelter of high enclosures that no thief can scale, under the cover of dense thickets that no fox can jump.

But Jesus speaks not about one enclosure but about one flock (*mia poimnè*). Belonging to the Church has never been a rest sheltered from thieves and foxes. It is a flock exposed to the full wind of the tempest. A flock open to all the straying sheep who want to join it through faith. A flock open to those who, unfortunately, want to leave it at their loss.

It is a flock that the one voice of Christ unites: "They listen to my voice!"

One Shepherd

Sometimes the allegory of the Good Shepherd has been used to apply to priests, to bishops or to the pope. Actually, in the evangelic text, nothing allows this slippage in interpretation. The gospel, rather, affirms the contrary: There is only one shepherd. And he is Christ.

This reality keeps in the peace of humility all those who engage in a pastoral ministry in the name of Christ. Our joy is to be the face of Christ. Our sadness is not to represent the face of Christ well enough. Our hope is to become the face of Christ more each day.

And this joy, this sadness, this hope, we share with all Christians. For all of us, each one according to his vocation, must be the transparency of Christ, the reflection of his face.

"They Will Listen to My Voice"

For his sheep, Jesus gave his life. For them, he rose. The author of the Letter to the Hebrews explains:

> The God of peace brought back from the dead our Lord Jesus.
> Through the blood of an eternal covenant,
> he became the Great Shepherd of the sheep. Heb 13, 20

He created in this way the flock of sheep gathered together after his resurrection around Peter and the Twelve. And he entrusts them to Peter:

> Shepherd my lambs. Shepherd my sheep. Jn 21, 15. 17

What are Peter and all those whom Christ established "overseers to shepherd the Church of God"[7] going to do to call the sheep who are not yet a part of the flock, to make them hear the voice of Christ? "They will listen to my voice," says Jesus.

Peter's voice does not count — nor Paul's, nor mine, nor any other. Only the voice of Christ is capable of gathering together the stray sheep into a single flock. Or rather, all our voices are speaking, attracting, only if they repeat, like an echo, the voice of Jesus.

Pray for your priests, for your ministers, for all the servants of the Word. Pray that they will make you hear the voice of Christ. Pray that you will listen to the voice of Christ.

Indeed, you have the right to criticize us. But you also have the duty to pray for us. Through your critiques, you can be our conscience. Through your prayers, you must be our support. And through your friendship, you are our brothers and sisters.

Shepherd and Lamb

In a vision radiant with glory, John evokes in the heavenly liturgy of Revelation the immense crowd of the redeemed "from every tongue, race, people and nation." "They come," he says, "from the great trial." At their head walks Christ, the risen Lamb. But this Lamb is at the same time their Shepherd: "The Lamb will be their Shepherd. He will lead them to the springs of the waters of life."

> Blessed be you, Lord Jesus,
> Shepherd and Lamb!
>
> When you are slain, you are Lamb.
> When you die, you are Shepherd.
> When you rise, you are God.
>
> And when you reign in heaven,
> you remain our brother forever and ever!

CONCLUDING PRAYER

You are, Lord Jesus, our Good Shepherd,
messenger of the beauty of God on earth
and servant of his goodness for us.
Listen to our prayer.

Guide us, O Lord,
on your paths of light.

You are, O Lord, our Good Shepherd;
you call us each by name.
Help us to recognize your voice
in the calls of your gospel
and to respond to it by name.

Guide us, O Lord,
on your paths of light.

You are, O Lord, our Good Shepherd;
you walk at the head of your flock.
Help us to follow you day after day
on the path of your cross and of your resurrection.

Guide us, O Lord,
on your paths of light.

You are, O Lord, our Good Shepherd;
you know each one of your sheep.
Help us to recognize your presence
at the heart of our joys and our pains.

Guide us, O Lord,
on your paths of light.

You are, O Lord, our Good Shepherd;
you offer your life for your sheep.
Help us to receive it in abundance
and to offer our own life
for the service of the Gospel.

Guide us, O Lord,
on your paths of light.

You are, O Lord, our Good Shepherd;
you gather us into one flock.
You, the only Shepherd,
keep us in the unity of your sheepfold.

Guide us, O Lord,
on your paths of light.

You are, O Lord, our Good Shepherd.
We commend to you also the sheep
who are still outside of your sheepfold.

Guide us, O Lord, on the paths of life
and lead us to your Father,
in the joy of the love of your Spirit,
for you are our Good Shepherd
forever and ever. Amen.

NOTES TO FOURTH SUNDAY OF EASTER

1. The principal references are Jer 23, 1-8, Ez 34, 1-31, Zec 11, 4-17 and Ps 23.
2. Jn 10, 11.
3. Jn 10, 3.
4. Cf. Ps 147, 4.
5. Jn 10, 11.
6. Cf. Jn 10, 15 and 15, 13.
7. Acts 20, 28.

FIFTH SUNDAY OF EASTER

Reading I

Reading I — **Acts 9, 26-31**

A reading from the Acts of the Apostles

When Saul arrived back in Jerusalem he tried to join the disciples there; but it turned out that they were all afraid of him. They even refused to believe that he was a disciple. Then Barnabas took him in charge and introduced him to the apostles. He explained to them how on his journey Saul had seen the Lord, who had conversed with him, and how Saul had been speaking out fearlessly in the name of Jesus at Damascus. Saul stayed on with them, moving freely about Jerusalem and expressing himself quite openly in the name of the Lord. He even addressed the Greek-speaking Jews and debated with them. They for their part responded by trying to kill him. When the brothers learned of this, some of them took him down to Caesarea and sent him off to Tarsus.

Meanwhile throughout all Judea, Galilee and Samaria the church was at peace. It was being built up and was making steady progress in the fear of the Lord; at the same time it enjoyed the increased consolation of the Holy Spirit.

The Word of the Lord.

Responsorial Psalm — Ps 22, 26-27. 28. 30. 31-32

R/. (26) I will praise you, Lord, in the assembly of your people.

I will fulfill my vows before those who fear the Lord.
  The lowly shall eat their fill;
They who seek the Lord shall praise him:
  "May your hearts be ever merry!"

R/. I will praise you, Lord, in the assembly of your people.

All ends of the earth
  shall remember and turn to the Lord;
All the families of the nations
  shall bow down before him.

To him alone shall bow down
  all who sleep in the earth;
Before him shall bend
  all who go down into the dust.

R/. I will praise you, Lord, in the assembly of your people.

And to him my soul shall live;
  my descendants shall serve him.
Let the coming generation be told of the Lord
  that they may proclaim to a people yet to be born
  the justice he has shown.

R/. I will praise you, Lord, in the assembly of your people.

R/. Or: Alleluia.

Reading II — 1 Jn 3, 18-24

A reading from the first letter of John

Little children,
  let us love in deed and in truth
  and not merely talk about it.
This is our way of knowing we are committed to the truth
  and are at peace before him
  no matter what our consciences may charge us with;
  for God is greater than our hearts
  and all is known to him.
Beloved,
  if our consciences have nothing to charge us with,
  we can be sure that God is with us
  and that we will receive at his hands
  whatever we ask.
Why? Because we are keeping his commandments
  and doing what is pleasing in his sight.
His commandment is this:
  we are to believe in the name of his Son, Jesus Christ,
  and are to love one another as he commanded us.

Those who keep his commandments remain in him
and he in them.
and this is how we know that he remains in us:
from the Spirit that he gave us.

The Word of the Lord.

Gospel — Jn 15, 1-8

A reading from the holy gospel according to John

Jesus said to his disciples:

"I am the true vine
and my Father is the vinegrower.
He prunes away
every barren branch,
but the fruitful ones
he trims clean
to increase their yield.
You are clean already,
thanks to the word I have spoken to you.
Live on in me, as I do in you.
No more than a branch can bear fruit of itself
apart from the vine,
can you bear fruit
apart from me.
I am the vine, you are the branches.
He who lives in me and I in him,
will produce abundantly,
for apart from me you can do nothing.
A man who does not live in me
is like a withered, rejected branch,
picked up to be thrown in the fire and burnt.
If you live in me,
and my words stay part of you,
you may ask what you will—
it will be done for you.
My Father has been glorified
in your bearing much fruit
and becoming my disciples."

The gospel of the Lord.

INTRODUCTORY PRAYER

We bless you, Lord Jesus.
You gather us together today
to celebrate your holy Resurrection.

And we pray to you:
You are the Word of the Father:
Make us silent in your presence.
You are the living bread that comes to us from heaven:
Make us hunger for eternity.
You are the Vine; we are your branches:
make us bear much fruit
to the glory of your Father,
in the joy of your Holy Spirit,
forever and ever. Amen.

HOMILY

I. Paul's First Visit to Jerusalem After His Conversion

Paul's conversion on the road to Damascus had resounded like a clap of thunder in the serene heaven of the early Christian community. His first official visit to Jerusalem after his conversion was also full of lightning. It is told to us in two accounts:

- The first account is that of Luke in the Acts of the Apostles (9, 26-31). It is the text of the first reading.
- The other account is by Paul himself in the Letter to the Galatians (1, 17-21).

These two accounts complete each other and reveal two complementary theologies.

According to Luke, when Paul arrived in Jerusalem, "all were afraid of him"—how understandable!—and it was only thanks to the intervention of Barnabas that he was able to meet the apostles. This meeting, according to Luke, was cordial and open on the part of the apostolate: "Paul came and went in Jerusalem with the apostles, preaching with confidence in the name of the Lord."[1]

According to Paul, the scope of his meetings with the Twelve was reduced. He notes well that he visited Cephas, but then adds: "I did not see the other apostles except James, the brother of the Lord." He minimizes, therefore, his contacts with the Twelve. Besides, he only stayed in Jerusalem for two weeks.[2]

Those two weeks were undoubtedly troubled. Paul was not an easy-going man. His listeners were hardly any more so. To avoid allowing him to be massacred by his opponents, the Christian community took him to Caesarea and sent him to Tarsus, his country of origin.[3]

Without outlining here a theology of vocation or of mission, I would like to present three brief remarks concerning mission, conversion and the time of God.

Two Complementary Visions of Mission

There is, on the one hand, in Paul's account a clear desire to claim the specific feature of his missionary vocation. He writes, not without some solemnity:

> He who, from the maternal womb, set me apart and called me through his grace, has deigned to reveal in me his Son so that I may preach him to the Gentiles. Gal 1, 15-16

Indeed, from his conversion on the road to Damascus, Paul began immediately to preach Jesus in the synagogues, proclaiming that Jesus is "the Son of God."[4] He notes explicitly that he engaged in his mission "without consulting flesh and blood, without going up to Jerusalem to find the apostles, his predecessors."[5]

There is, on the other hand, in Luke's account, a clear desire to unite Paul with the apostles, witnesses of the resurrection. Thus, the subsequent missions will be in some way rooted in Jerusalem, the Mother-Church, authenticated by the authority of the Twelve.[6] Thus, the missionary vocation to the nations proceeds from a particular charisma, but it is rooted in the Christian community.

A community is fully Christian only if it is missionary, that is, if it takes charge, in a general way, of the conversion of the whole world and, in a particular and privileged way, through the ministry of some of its members who have the charisma for it, of a pagan community. To say it another way:

A light is a light only if it shines in the darkness. There is no self-service for individual salvation any more than there is any light to enlighten itself.

Question: Is our community Christian, that is, a "light of the world?"[7]

Conversion and Mission

For Paul, mission is directly tied to conversion. As soon as he met the risen Lord, Paul began to preach him with confidence, with an audacity that sometimes bordered upon provocation, first in Damascus and then in Jerusalem. There is no true conversion without mission. Likewise, there is no true mission without the conversion of the missionary. Conversion is at the center of paschal preaching.[8] We can thus measure the quality of our paschal conversion by the quality of the mission that it creates.

The Time of God

Seen from the balcony of our twentieth century, the events of the beginning of the Christian era crowd together and flatten in time.

Replaced in the depth of time, they create questions.

Here is the chronology of Paul's life, as the best studies allow us to establish it.[9]

• Death of Jesus	14 Nissan 30
• Paul's conversion	Spring 35
• Arrival in Jerusalem	Summer 37
• Return to Tarsus	2 weeks later
• Barnabas seeks Paul in Tarsus	Spring 47
• They teach one year at Antioch	Spring 47 Spring 48
• First mission	Around 48-49
• Martyrdom of Paul	Around 68

Clearly, Paul is converted in 35, does not begin his mission until 48, thirteen years later, and dedicates to it some twenty years, from 48 to 68.

Here, then, is the greatest missionary of the apostolic age, the "Doctor of nations," as he is called — and he did nothing for thirteen years! Thirteen years lost for missionary work. Supremely casual is the attitude of God with regard to time. Truly, God is rarely for ideal solutions, those that we call such in our foolishness and which are only those of our myopia about the ways of God.

You will think perhaps that Paul is a particular case. For the Twelve, it was not that way. And you will picture the apostles after Pentecost, leaving their homes, wives and children in tears and setting out for far countries that Providence had assigned to them.

Reality is more prosaic. After the resurrection, the apostles returned again...to fishing (according to Jn 21). We then find them in Jerusalem. Tradition believed that they remained there for twelve years upon orders from the Lord.[10] That is possible. It is not certain. We simply know in a sure way that Peter will leave Jerusalem only after the martyrdom of James, the Lord's brother.[11] That took place around the years 43-44, some fourteen years after the resurrection.

Time is money, we say.

God values time just as he values money. That is to say that he counts it for nothing. What a lesson for us who do not want to waste a minute and are eager for work! God thinks that all life, even the fullest, can have its "obscure years," its "time of Nazareth;" that is, those thirty years that the Lord spent "doing nothing" except the trade of a carpenter. Thirty years "lost" for the proclamation of the Kingdom. Thirty years offered to the worship and the praise of the will of the Father.

That which counts finally is our presence before God in the simplicity of love. It is there, in his presence, that our lives mature. To stand in silence before God in love is as important as preaching while traveling around the world.

But both the one and the other are necessary for the Kingdom.

2. The First Letter of John

Faith and Love

This passage from the First Letter of John presents traditional Johannine themes. The author sums up the will of God for us in this way:

> Here is his commandment:
> to have faith in his Son Jesus Christ
> and to love one another. 1 Jn 3, 23

Faith secures the vertical relationship with God; love for one another, the horizontal dimension. The two relationships overlap. To believe in God, in reality, is also to believe that our brothers and sisters are signs of God and consequently to love them. And to love our brothers and sisters is also to believe that the image of God dwells in them.

God Is Greater Than Our Hearts

There is another trait that I would like to underline in this passage, a trait that hits us like an arrow, penetrates our hearts and attaches itself forever in our minds. If we love, in truth, writes John,

> before God we will have our hearts in peace.
> Our hearts will have much to condemn us:
> God is greater than our hearts. 1 Jn 3, 19-20

Superb words: God is greater than our hearts!

Sometimes we seek God as if we could catch him inside of things, discover him in the infinite blue of the waves of the sea or in the insolent splendor of the mountain, see him in the smile of a child or find him in the peaceful face of an old person.

God is everywhere, of course. The whole earth is the reflection of his splendor. But he is not first in things; he is first in our hearts.

It is there that the new heavens, inaugurated by the Lord's resurrection, begin. Change your heart, and you will have the new heavens in you.

It is there that the new earth begins. Change your heart, and you will have the new earth in you!

As we advance on the path of our life, we see better what counts in us. Not first the work that we have realized but the way in which our hearts has been transfigured, specifically the quality of that transfiguration. It is the quality of God's presence in us.

Indeed, our hearts would always like to accuse us and to preach anguish to us. Are we not all mediocre, all sinners? But we shall be able to say to our hearts: "Rest in peace, my heart. God who is in you is greater than your anguish. And he loves you."

3. The Allegory of the Vine

It is almost unnecessary to mention the importance of the vine in the Mediterranean basin and especially in Israel. For the sake of curiosity, the word vine appears 139 times in the Old Testament and 32 times in the New;

the word wine appears 203 times in the Old and 38 times in the New Testament.

The vine is the traditional symbol of the Chosen People. In the restoration of the Temple, Herod, who was a construction genius, had installed an immense vine in gold above the entrance which led from the vestibule into the Holy of Holies. According to Josephus, its branches were the height of a man.[12] This vine grew unceasingly thanks to the grapes of gold that the faithful offered and that the priest hung there as time went on.[13]

The most moving text on the vine is the lament that the Book of Isaiah has preserved for us:

> Let me sing to my friends
> the song of the beloved for his vineyard!
>
> My beloved had a vineyard
> on a fertile hillside.
> He spaded it; he cleared it of stone;
> he planted there a choice vine.
> In the middle he built a tower;
> he even dug a wine press there.
>
> He hoped for beautiful grapes from it,
> but it gave him sour grapes. Is 5, 1-2

The True Vine

Jesus affirms: "I am the Vine, the true" (*hè ampélos, hè alethine*).[14]

All through the centuries, God had tried to plant a vine that would give choice grapes. Without respite, he sent prophets and saints to dig in the hardness of the heart of Israel, to clear away the stones of its idols, to plant there his words of life. All through the centuries, the vine had given sour grapes. Most certainly, there had been choice grapes—there have always been saints who were foolish with love for God—but the whole of the vintage turned to sour grapes.

Jesus, is finally the true Vine, the one that will give fruit that responds to the expectation of God. Here is realized the prophecy of messianic times:

> That day, one will say:
> the delicious vine, sing about it!
> I, the Lord, am its keeper…
> Night and day I guard it. Is 27, 2-3

Jesus also signifies that there may be numerous ways to enter the Temple to sing the praises of God. But a single way is true: One must enter by the portico that bears the True Vine. He alone is the way to go to the Father.

To Bear Fruit

The allegory of the Vine is almost covered by a veil of sadness. Jesus is facing the betrayal of Judas, who left in the night,[15] the defection of his disciples, and his agony and death. The tone remains peaceful, however, but expresses well the seriousness of the Christian life. The accent is placed on the absolute necessity of bearing fruit. The expression to bear fruit comes back, like an antiphon, six times in the allegory.

Two possibilities are envisioned:

- We are cut off when we do not bear fruit.
- We are purified when we bear fruit.

These two possibilities are the only ones. They are underlined by a play on words in the Greek text: He cuts it off, *airéi*; he purifies it, *kathairéi.*[16]

The act of remaining grafted onto the divine vine without producing fruit, of drinking the lifegiving sap without blooming, simply allowing oneself to be carried by the vine, is not envisioned. Or rather, it is envisioned as an impossibility. In clear terms, one cannot be a part of the Church if one does not bear fruit. A Christian life that is a parasite on the gospel is not possible.

No one can avoid the following questions: Where are our flowers? Where are our grapes? Where is the vintage for heaven? It is to the glory of the Father that our lives bear much fruit[17]: do our lives celebrate the glory of the Father?

Let each one look again into his heart.

To Allow Oneself To Be Pruned

Let us suppose that we bear fruit. Not much perhaps, but just some pretty flowers and some ruddy grapes. We are tempted to tell ourselves then: "Our account is good. Here we are on the highway to the Kingdom; here we are on the list for paradise. There is nothing more than to wait..." Who among us has not dreamed of a tranquil life without trouble, of an upright Christian life, of course, but without religious excess, of a life where one bears fruit quite simply like an apple tree gives its crop of apples each fall?

And one thinks secretly: "Lord, leave me in peace with my wife (pretty and sweet, preferably!), with my two lovely children, with my work without unemployment. I go to mass every Sunday." How reasonable seems the invitation of the psalm:

> Trust in the Lord and do good,
> dwell in the land and live tranquilly! Ps 37, 3

And how threatening is the story of Job, who says: "I was living peacefully when the Lord shook me, seized me by the neck."[18]

But here exactly is the problem: this ideal of Christian tranquility does not harmonize at all with the text of the allegory of the Vine. For the shoot that bears fruit is precisely the one that interests the Father-vinedresser. That is the one that he cuts, prunes, purifies.

The verb to prune, purify (*katharein*), is very pretty. It means to clean, whence "to prune" but also "to purify" (the word "cathari" that designated the heretic Albigenses, who in the twelfth and thirteenth centuries claimed to be "pure," comes from the same root).

As an expert vinedresser, the Father wields the pruning shears of the Word. Jesus says to his disciples:

> You are already clean
> thanks to the Word that I spoke to you. Jn 15, 3

Day after day, this Word wounds us like a sword, burns us like a sun, upsets and turns our hearts upside down like a hurricane or pacifies our souls like the calm of evening after a day of great wind. Whoever has opened his heart to it is never again tranquil. Or rather, his tranquility will be to allow himself to be pruned at each moment.

Other prunings are possible. The Father is very skillful at handling the pruning shears to cut into the heart of our tendernesses and into the tranquility of our lives! He also uses the pruning shears of great sufferings that purify us by humbling us to the extreme, or simply the pruning shears of our own mediocrity in the banality of daily life. Everything is for him a pretext to cut. But it is in order to make us produce more fruit. It is in order to make us advance in the joy of his love.

How many marvelous vines, full of promises, became undergrowth because they refused to be cut! And how many lives, scattered into a thousand leaves and shoots, became marvelous vines and were loaded with grapes for having accepted the purifications of love!

To Remain in Christ

Another privileged theme in the allegory of the Vine is the one of remaining in Christ.

John loves the verb to remain (*menein*). This verb is a part of his literary habits. He uses it eleven times in the allegory of the Vine (15, 1-10), forty times in the gospel and twenty-eight times in the letters. (By comparison, Mark uses it two times and Matthew three times.)

Remaining in Christ could be treated on a mystical level. John gives it an eminently practical aspect. He proposes in the allegory of the Vine a very beautiful progression:

• To remain in Christ is to bear fruit. One is the condition of the other:

> Remain in me and I in you.
> Just as the branch cannot bear fruit by itself,
> if it does not remain in the vine,
> the same way you neither
> if you do not remain in me. Jn 15, 4

• But how can we remain in Christ? By remaining in his love:

> Just as the Father loved me,
> so have I loved you.
> Remain in my love…

• How can we remain in love? By practicing the commandments. Far from being just an attitude, love expresses itself in obedience:

> If you keep my commandments,
> you remain in my love,
> as I have kept the commandments of my Father
> and remain in his love. Jn 15, 10

John, the most mystical of the evangelists, reveals himself the most incarnated in the daily realities of the Christian life: There is not any true love without works.

The necessity of remaining in Christ is affirmed again further in a negative way:

> Apart from me, you can do nothing Jn 15, 5

Instead of "apart from me" (*chôris emou*), one could also translate "without me." The general meaning remains the same.

Paul had to meditate on this word of Christ, he whose ideal was precisely the life "in Christ." To the affirmation "apart from me you can do nothing," Paul answers triumphantly: "I can do everything in the One who strengthens me."[19]

Augustine has a very beautiful page on the primacy of the love in which we must remain.

> It is love alone that distinguishes the sons of God from the sons of the devil.
>
> They can very well all sign themselves with the sign of the cross of Christ, all answer "Amen," all sing "Alleluia," all be baptized, all enter into churches and all build the walls of basilicas: The sons of God are distinguished from the sons of the devil only through love. Those who have love are born of God. Those who do not have it are not born of God. There is the great sign, the great discernment. You can have everything that you want; if you lack that alone, the rest is good for nothing. But if you lack all the rest and you have love, you have fulfilled the Law.[20]

Each eucharist makes us advance in the celebration of the Holy Vine and offers us to drink, in the cup of blessing, the wine of the Promised Land, the blood of Christ Jesus.

In return, may our lives produce fruits in abundance and thus give glory to our Father in heaven forever and ever.

The Song of the Vineyard

Let me sing for my friend
the song of the Beloved and his vineyard.

Like a heavenly vine,
like a cutting from heaven,
you were planted in Nazareth
in the garden of the Virgin Mary.
Blessed are you, O Lord!

Like a perfume of springtime,
you spread the Good News,
and your shoots extended
into the immense field of the world.

Like a wall, you encompassed the Church
with the rampart of your Word.
You built there, like a tower,
the truth of your gospel.

Like the grapes of harvest,
you were crushed
on the winepress of Calvary,
and your holy blood
reddened the tree of the cross.

Like a festive wine,
you intoxicated your disciples
on the day of Pentecost.
Filled with the Holy Spirit,
they began to sing
the marvels of your Father.

Like a beloved brother,
you call all your people
to work in your vineyard.
Each day spent with you
sings like a holiday.

And in the evening of our lives, you give us
the joy of an eternal feast.

We bless you, God our Father,
for the marvelous vine
that your love planted
in the womb of our earth.
We thank you for counting us worthy
to be your branches
despite the dry wood of our lives.
Help us to remain in the love of Jesus
and, day after day, to bear fruit
that the sun of your Spirit will ripen
for the vintage of your glory.

NOTES TO FIFTH SUNDAY OF EASTER

1. Acts 9, 26. 28.
2. Gal 1, 18-19.
3. Cf. Acts 9, 29-30.
4. Acts 9, 20.
5. Gal 1, 17.
6. One finds a similar tie with the Church of Antioch: They are the ones who sends Barnabas and Paul out as missionaries (Acts 13, 1-3), and it is to them that the missionaries render an account of their mission on their return (14, 27-28).
7. Mt. 5, 14.
8. Cf. Acts 2, 38; 3, 26; 10, 43.
9. We are using the givens of S. Dockx, *Chronologies néotestamentaires et Vie de l'Eglise primitive* (Paris-Gemblous: Ed. Duculot, 1976).
10. See L. Deiss, *God s Word and God s People* (Collegeville, MN: The Liturgical Press, 1976), pp. 317-318.
11. Cf. Acts 12, 17.
12. F. Josephe, De Bello Judaico, V, 4. See Michel-Bauernfeind, Falvius Josephus, De Bello Judaico, II, 1 (Munich: Kosel-Verlag, 1963), p. 138.
13. We know that this restoration at the beginning of Jesus' public ministry, around the year 27, had already lasted 46 years (according to Jn 2, 20) and that it ended only around 64-66, six years before the taking of Jerusalem and the destruction of the Temple. Practically all through his life, Jesus saw the Temple under construction. See J. Jeremias, *Jerusalem au temps de Jesus* (Paris: Cerf, 1967), pp. 39-43.
14. Jn 15, 1.
15. Cf. Jn 13, 21-31.
16. Jn 16, 2.
17. Cf. Jn 15, 8.
18. Job 16, 12.
19. Phil 4, 13.
20. *In Epistolam lohannis ad Parthos*, Treatise V,7. Cf. SC 75 (1961), p. 260.

SIXTH SUNDAY OF EASTER

READING I — ACTS 10, 25-26. 34-35. 44-48

A reading from the Acts of the Apostles

Peter entered the house of Cornelius who met him, dropped to his knees before Peter and bowed low. Peter said as he helped him to his feet, "Get up! I am only a man myself."

Peter proceeded to address [the relatives and friends of Cornelius] in these words: "I begin to see how true it is that God shows no partiality. Rather, the man of any nation who fears God and acts uprightly is acceptable to him."

Peter had not finished these words when the Holy Spirit descended upon all who were listening to Peter's message. The circumcised believers who had accompanied Peter were surprised that the gift of the Holy Spirit should have been poured out on the Gentiles also, whom they could hear speaking in tongues and glorifying God. Peter put the question at that point: "What can stop these people who have received the Holy Spirit, even as we have, from being baptized with water?" So he gave orders that they be baptized in the name of Jesus Christ. After this was done, they asked him to stay with them for a few days.

The Word of the Lord.

RESPONSORIAL PSALM — Ps 98 1. 2-3. 3-4

R/. (2) The Lord has revealed to the nations his saving power.

Sing to the Lord a new song,
for he has done wondrous deeds;
His right hand has won victory for him,
his holy arm.

R/. The Lord has revealed to the nations his saving power.

The Lord has made his salvation known:
in the sight of the nations he has revealed his justice.
He has remembered his kindness and his faithfulness
toward the house of Israel.

R/. The Lord has revealed to the nation his saving power.

All the ends of the earth have seen
  the salvation by our God.
Sing joyfully to the Lord, all you lands:
  break into song; sing praise.

R/. The Lord has revealed to the nation his saving power.

R/. Or: Alleluia

Reading II — I Jn 4, 7-10

A reading from the first letter of John

Beloved,
  let us love one another
  because love is of God;
  everyone who loves is begotten of God
  and has knowledge of God.
The man without love has known nothing of God,
  for God is love.
God's love was revealed in our midst in this way:
  he sent his only Son to the world
  that we might have life through him.
Love, then, consists in this:
  not that we have loved God,
  but that he has loved us
  and has sent his Son as an offering for our sins.

The Word of the Lord.

Gospel — Jn 15, 9-17

A reading from the holy gospel according to John

Jesus said to his disciples:
"As the Father has loved me,
so I have loved you.
Live on in my love.
You will live in my love
if you keep my commandments,
even as I have kept my Father's commandments,
and live in his love.

All this I tell you
that my joy may be yours
and your joy may be complete.
This is my commandment:
love one another
as I have loved you.
There is no greater love than this:
to lay down one's life for one's friends.
You are my friends
if you do what I command you.
I no longer speak of you as slaves,
for a slave does not know what his master is about.
Instead, I call you friends
since I have made known to you
all that I heard from my Father.
It was not you who chose me,
it was I who chose you
to go forth and bear fruit.
Your fruit must endure,
so that all you ask the Father in my name
he will give you.
The command I give you is this:
that you love one another."

The gospel of the Lord.

INTRODUCTORY PRAYER

We praise you and we bless you, God our Father,
because you manifested yourself to us
as the God of love
and you reveal this love to us
in the face of your Son Jesus Christ.

And we pray to you:
Help us to discover more clearly each day
this face of love of your Son Jesus
in each of our joys and pains,

in the face of all of those who travel with us,
until the Day when we will see you face to face,
you, our Father in heaven,
your Son Jesus, who became our brother,
and the Spirit who lives in our hearts
forever and ever. Amen.

HOMILY

1. The Announcement of the Good News

The first reading tells us about the conversion of the centurion Cornelius. He was a Gentile, an officer of the Roman army of occupation. This conversion illustrates the victory that the responsorial psalm sings:

> The Lord has made his victory known
> and revealed his justice in the eyes
> of the nations. Ps 98, 2

Importance and Significance of the Conversion of the Centurion Cornelius

In the Book of the Acts of the Apostles, Luke gives primary importance to the conversion of the centurion Cornelius. This conversion is indeed the shining illustration of the principle proclaimed by Paul:

> The nations are admitted to the same heritage,
> members of the same body,
> sharing in the same promise
> in Christ Jesus,
> through the Gospel. Eph 3, 6

Luke lived this principle with jubilation when he accompanied Paul on his missionary travels. He also underlined it intensely in his gospel.[1] The centurion Cornelius of Caesarea in Acts gives his hand to the centurion of Capernaum in the gospel. With the widow of Sarepta, with Naiman the Syrian, with the Samaritans and with all the "strangers" who populate the third Gospel, he bears witness that Jesus is truly the "light of the nations,"[2] that is, of the Gentiles.

This importance is already underlined by the size of the account. (This Sunday's reading only gives the most significant excerpts.) In reality, the account covers all of chapter 10 and goes to 11,18: sixty-six verses.

By comparison, the important account of Pentecost only covers forty-one verses, and that of Paul's conversion, thirty verses.

It also seems that Luke antedated the account. Clearly, exegetes have good reason to think that the first conversion of the "Greeks," that is, the Gentiles and their entrance into the Church—said better, their welcome into the Christian community—took place at Antioch[3] before the conversion of the centurion Cornelius. But Luke managed to place this conversion, realized under the ministry of Peter, before the conversion at Antioch. He thus gave Peter—nicely elegant on his part—"the honor of having opened the doors of the Church to the Gentiles: Once these doors are opened, Paul will be able to do the rest."[4]

This conversion furnishes finally an excellent introduction to the reunion of the apostles in Jerusalem. The assembly, rather reticent to admit Gentiles, was conquered, according to Luke, by the account of Peter, and stated: "Thus then, even to the nations God has given the repentance that leads to life."[5]

Today, as in apostolic times, mission is important in the life of the Church. Important for us not as a condition of our survival and, by calculation, of proselytism, but first as a sign and expression of our life.

Said clearly: A community peacefully installed in its Sunday habits and positively assured of its salvation thanks to its sacramental practice but having no apostolic care, no opening onto the suffering of the world, no prayer for the conversion of all the nations, no sacrifice for missions, that community, I say, is a community in the act of dying in its faith. Faith is a light: it is living only if it shines. Love is a fire: it is burning only if it warms.

God of all People with Upright Hearts

Luke insists on the religious quality of Cornelius' life:

> He was pious and God-fearing...He gave large alms to the Jewish people and prayed to God unceasingly. Acts 10, 2

When the angel of God appeared to him, he said to him:

> Your prayers and your alms have gone up for a memorial (*eis mnèosynon*) before God. Acts 10, 4

The expression for a memorial has a precise meaning in biblical vocabulary. It is understood to mean: "Your prayers and your alms went up before God and he has remembered you."

The fact of belonging to those whom God remembers is a privilege reserved for the chosen people. It is the people of the promise who fill the memory of the God of love. This is why, in its prayers, Israel takes refuge unceasingly in that remembrance: "Remember! Do not break your Covenant with us!"

Here, the angel of God, through the account of Luke, affirms that all people with upright hearts live in the memory of God. Peter explains:

> God does not show partiality,
> but whatever their race,
> he welcomes people who worship him
> and do what is just. Acts 10, 34. 35

Who belongs to the heart of God? Whom does he remember with love? All men and women with upright hearts who do what is just.

How many modern centurions, today still, belong to the heart of God, but do not belong to the Church!

And how many Christians, who belong to the Church, do not belong to the heart of God!

The "Acts of the Holy Spirit"

A small Pentecost shines in the house of Cornelius. Luke says:

> Peter spoke again when the Holy Spirit
> seized all of those who were listening to the Word.
> One heard them say mysterious words
> and sing the grandeur of God. Acts 10, 46

The Spirit is at work all through the account: it is he who speaks to Peter, and it is in him that Cornelius and those in his house are baptized.[7] He is so much at work all through the Acts of the Apostles that one could call them "The Acts of the Holy Spirit."

Today, every mission is still the fruit of obedience to the Spirit. Just as the Spirit rested upon Jesus and consecrated him for the announcement of the Good News to the poor,[8] in the same way today it must rest upon whoever proposes to be a messenger of Christ. Otherwise the mission of the messenger is only propaganda, and the ministry is useless agitation.

Community Dimension of the Mission

It is suitable to underline the communal dimension of apostolic work, inasmuch as it concerns the missionaries and those who welcome them.

Peter, indeed, is not alone in his work: he is accompanied "by the brothers from Joppa." And Cornelius, at Peter's arrival, assembles "all his family and his close friends." Then he receives baptism with all those of his house.[9]

I would like to underline here the particular force that the smallest cell of the Church—the family—represented for the mission. One imagines the apostles willingly leaving on missionary paths while abandoning wives and children at home. Poor wives of the apostles, whose eyes were full of tears for their husbands kidnapped by the Holy Spirit! But such a vision of the mission — so piously romantic — does not do justice to the texts...or to the Holy Spirit! The apostles, in fact—some at least—took their wives with them for their apostolic work. Paul explicitly claims this right while, personally, he does not use it:

> Do we not have the right to take with us a believing woman[10] (*adélphèn gynaika*) like the other apostles and the brothers of the Lord and Cephas? I Cor 9, 5

We learn then that Cephas, that is, Peter, the other apostles and the brothers of Jesus (that is to say, his cousins) took their wives with them in their apostolate. Without doubt we are not accustomed to imagining the first pope devoting himself to the apostolate aided by his wife. As for Paul himself, he liked to be helped by the couple Prisca and Aquila, whom he called his "collaborators in Jesus Christ."[11]

The forms in which missionary activity was exercised were therefore very rich, more diversified in any case than those we know today. Do not our customs of apostolate seem hardened, on the one hand through lack of imagination and through intellectual laziness but also on the other hand through lack of reference to the practice of the early Church?[12]

Paul presents an excellent principle when he affirms:

> In the Lord, man does not go without woman nor woman without man...And all come from God. I Cor 11, 12

This principle is equally valid for the apostolate.

What a marvel if each family, as in the time of the Acts of the Apostles, could become a Church where the announcement of the Good News resounds!

What a marvel if each catechumen, like the centurion Cornelius, could bring together "his family and his close friends" and invite them to welcome with him the Word of God!

What a marvel if each missionary, like Peter returning to Caesarea, could be accompanied by "brothers from Joppa!"

What a marvel if each apostle, like Paul, could have the friendship of a Prisca and an Aquila who would be his "collaborators in Jesus Christ!"

Finally, what a marvel if each announcement of the resurrection of Jesus could be accompanied by an effusion of the Spirit, another Pentecost that would make all sing the marvels of God!

2. He Loved us First

There are, in the second reading, these words of infinite tenderness:

> Love consists of this:
> it is not we who loved God
> but it is he who loved us. I Jn 4, 10

The Vulgate really seizes the meaning of the text by translating: *Prior dilexit nos*, he loved us first.[13]

There is this fundamental revelation: The love of God dominates our life; our existence in God begins in that eternity where God pronounced our names, where he smiled at us, where he said to us: "It is you that I want. I am making you exist because I love you. And I am clothing you in the splendor of my Son, Jesus."

The days of our life are only the realization, in time and in space, of this name of love that he gave to us, of the accomplishment of his will in us. He loved us first!

In truth, it is not sufficient to say that the love of God exists in our life. One must say rather: The love of God makes our life exist. It is not sufficient to say: The love of God is revealed in our life. One must say further: The love of God reveals our life and explains its meaning to us.

This total anteriority of the love of God, this fundamental, existential obligingness of his love, signifies also that we, beggars of God, can offer to him only what he has first given to us. We offer to the Lord only what we have received. In the wonderful prayer that David makes in the evening of his life, he says:

> Blessed be you. Lord, God of Israel our father,
> always and forever!
> Everything comes from you and we offer to you
> what your hand has given to us. I Chr 29, 10. 14

Yes, blessed be God who allows us to offer to him what his love has given to us! May he be blessed for accepting the offering of this life that he himself invented for us! He loved us first.

We say that we love the Lord, that we have discovered his face. But it is he who has kindled his love in our hearts; it is he who has revealed to us the light of his face! He loved us first.

We say that we believe in him. But it is he who tore away the darkness, who enlightened the eyes of our hearts, who called us "from the darkness to his marvelous light!"[14] He loved us first.

We say that we have cast our hope in God, as one casts a sure and solid anchor.[15] But it is the breath of his Spirit that billowed our sails and guided our boat to the shores of eternity! He loved us first.

That also means that God created us just as we are. It is he who placed upon you that weight of pain that burdens your heart so that you may place it in him and remain in his peace: "Cast your burden upon the Lord, and he will help you with [illegible]"[17] It is he who invented the melody of the joy that sings in your heart. It is he who also modeled your face. Perhaps you think: He could have succeeded better. He answers you that he would not have been able to love you better. Is he not the potter? Are we not the clay in his hands?[17] Who loves first? Who loves the most? The potter or the clay?

It is said sometimes that some coffins carried on earth are too heavy, heavy with all the tears that one could not cry, heavy with all the sobs that one could not sob, heavy with all the joys that one could not sing or share, with all the loves that one could not love. But God knows you. He molded you. He loved you first, exactly as the potter loves the vase that he is fashioning: He dreams about it like a work of art while it still exists only in his desire. But for God, we are all works of art, not in a dream but in reality. We are, says Paul, "vases filled with mercy: He has prepared them for his glory."[18]

But why struggle to search for comparisons when no image can ever say more than this: God loves you as nobody else can love you. Because he loved you first. That is why he created you. Søren Kierkegaard (1813-1855) comments:

> You who loved us first, O God—alas! We speak of it as if you had loved us first only one time, in a historic way, whereas, unceasingly, many times throughout our days and life, you have loved us first.
>
> When we get up in the morning and we turn our soul toward you, you are first, you loved us first: If I get up at dawn and at the same moment turn my soul and my prayer toward you, you precede me. You loved me first.
>
> When I withdraw from distraction and gather my soul to think of you, you are first.[19]

God loved us first. In return, may he be the first in our love.

3. It Is I Who Chose You

The words of John, "He loved us first," join these words of Jesus that the Gospel presents to us today:

> It is not you who chose me:
> it is I who chose you. Jn 15, 16

It is good to understand this about the apostolic vocation itself: it was not the disciples who chose to create the call of Jesus and to follow him; on the contrary, it was he who called them to the apostolate. One can also understand this sentence not only about the call to apostolic work but, more profoundly, about the call to existence itself. It was not we who chose to exist; it was God who took the initiative in that call.

This life, this fact of "being," is the most fabulous gift that God has given us. The temptation will be to regard oneself as proprietor of one's life, to possess it like a treasure that one manages, a property that one administers. Grace will be to allow God to manage it for us and, therefore, to have confidence in the love of God, who invades our life and fills it with his joy.

This confidence rests in and is rooted in God. But not first in God "Father almighty, creator of heaven and earth," as we affirm in the Creed, whose words we invented, but in the God who loves us according to the words that Jesus invented for us:

As the Father loved me,
I too have loved you.
Remain in my love. Jn 15, 9

At the root of God's existence—if I dare use these words, but how can we speak about God without stammering in human words?—there is love: God is love, Jesus is "the Son of his love,"[20] the Spirit is the bond of their mutual tenderness. It is this love of the Father that rests on the Son, in the bond of the Spirit, which is given to us.

The Psalm affirms:

The whole earth is filled with his love. Ps 33, 5

Therefore, our whole life also is filled with this love. And each moment of our life is called to be lived in and transfigured by this love.

What can we offer in response to God? We hardly dare to raise our eyes toward him...God is a consuming fire: Who would dare to take that fire in hand? God is an abyss of wisdom[21]: Who would dare to scrutinize the depths of that abyss?

Lord, your love is infinite, eternal. And yet, it does not crush us with its splendor. It even fills us with sweetness and confidence. I will answer you while hiding behind these words that your servant Augustine invented for you:

Too late I have loved you, O beauty so ancient
and so new, too late I have loved you!
And here you were in my heart,
and I, outside, that is where I searched for you,
and in the grace of those things that you created,
and I, poor, disfigured, was rushing around.
You were with me, and with you I was not.
They kept me far from you, these marvels
that, if they were not in you, would not exist!
You called, cried, broke my deafness.
You shone, illuminated, chased away my blindness.
You smelled sweet, I inhaled your perfume, I aspired.
I tasted, I am still hungry, I am still thirsty.
You touched me, I burned with desire for your peace![22]

Yes, blessed be the Lord who burned us with the desire of his peace! To him glory, to him our love forever and ever!

CONCLUDING PRAYER

You are resplendent beauty
more dazzling than a thousand springs.
Who would not admire you?
But your beauty, O our Father,
is first the beauty of your love.
Seduce us.

Remember us, O Lord, in your great love.

You are a furnace of holiness
burning hotter than the sun.
Who would not adore you?
But your holiness, O our Father,
is first the holiness of your love.
Purify us.

Remember us, O Lord, in your great love.

You are steadfast peace,
sweeter than the smile of a child.
Who would not bless you?
But your peace, O Father,
is first the peace of your love.
Pacify us.

Remember us, O Lord, in your great love.

You are infinite almightiness
more powerful than a storm.
Who would not venerate you?
But your almightiness, O our Father,
is first the almightiness of your love.
Strengthen us.

Remember us, O Lord, in your great love.

You are a fountain of eternal mercy
deeper than the ocean.
Who would not love you?
But your mercy, O our Father,
is first the mercy of your love.
Have mercy on us.

Remember us, O Lord, in your great love.

You are resplendent light
more inaccessible than the stars.
Who can contemplate your brilliance?
But your light, O our Father,
is first the light of your love.
Illuminate us.

Remember us, O Lord, in your great love.

You are immeasurable immensity;
the infinity of the sea sings your praise.
Who would not exalt you?
But your immensity, O our Father,
is first the immensity of your love.
Fill us with your presence.

Remember us, O Lord, in your great love.

You are supreme majesty;
you imprison the stars
in the palms of your hands.
Who would not glorify you?
But your majesty, O our Father,
is first the majesty of your love.
Reign in us.

Remember us, O Lord, in your great love.

You are endless music in our lives,
more melodious than a song of love.
Who would not praise you?
But your music, O our Father,
is first the music of your love.
Sing in our hearts.

Remember us, O Lord, in your great love.

You are, O our Father,
splendor beyond everything that one can imagine,
happiness beyond everything that one can desire,
tenderness beyond everything that one can love.

Sixth Sunday of Easter

You are everything, for you are Love,
and you give us everything
in giving us your Son Jesus
with the joy of the Holy Spirit.
What can we say to you, Father, except:
Thank you for your love,
eternally, thank you!

NOTES TO SIXTH SUNDAY OF EASTER

1. Cf. Lk 4, 25-27; 7, 1-10; 10, 29-37; 17, 11-19. See L. Deiss, *Synopse* (Paris: Desclee de Brouwer, 1991), p. 348.
2. Lk 2, 32.
3. Cf. Acts 11, 19-29
4. J. Dupont, *Etudes sur les Actes des Apotres*, Coll. Lectio Divina, 45 (1967), p. 411.
5. Acts 11, 18.
6. Jer 14, 21.
7. Cf. Acts 10, 19 and 11, 16.
8. Cf. Lk 4, 18-19 (=Is 61, 1-2), and here in Peter's discourse Acts 10, 38.
9. Cf. Acts 10, 23-24 and 10, 44-48.
10. I Cor 9, 5. Literally "a woman-sister." "Sister" through communion in the faith (cf. Rom 16, 1). "Woman," be it no matter what woman, be it wife. The presence of a woman who would not have been the wife would have presented not an aid, but a complication in the apostolic work.
11. Rom 16, 3.
12. See J.P. Audet, *Mariage et Celibat dans le Service pastoral de l'Eglise* (Paris: Ed. de l'Orante, 1967).
13. The Vulgate is the Latin version of the Bible, established by Jerome (+419/420) upon the invitation of Pope Damas 1 (366-384). This version was made from the original biblical languages but took into account the old Latin versions that already existed in the churches.
14. I Pt 2, 9.
15. Cf. Heb 6, 18-19: "In the hope which is offered to us we have a sure and solid anchor."
16. Ps 55, 23.
17. Cf. Jer 18, 1-6.
18. Rom 9, 23.
19. Quoted in *Devant Dieu* (Le Puy-Lyon: Ed. Mappus, 1954), p. 163.
20. Col 1, 13. One ordinarily translates this "beloved Son." The translation "Son of his love" is the literal translation of the Greek.
21. Cf. Dt 4, 24 and Rom 11, 33.
22. *Confessions*, Book X, 26,30. Oeuvres de Saint Augustine, Coll. Bibliothèque Augustinienne, 14 (Paris: Desclée de Brouwer. 1962), p. 208.

ASCENSION

Reading I — Acts 1, 1-11

The beginning of the Acts of the Apostles

In my first account, Theophilus, I dealt with all that Jesus did and taught until the day he was taken up to heaven, having first instructed the apostles he had chosen through the Holy Spirit. In the time after his suffering he showed them in many convincing ways that he was alive, appearing to them over the course of forty days and speaking to them about the reign of God. On one occasion when he met with them, he told them not to leave Jerusalem: "Wait, rather, for the fulfillment of my Father's promise, of which you have heard me speak. John baptized with water, but within a few days you will be baptized with the Holy Spirit."

While they were with him they asked, "Lord, are you going to restore the rule to Israel now?" His answer was: "The exact time it is not yours to know. The Father has reserved that to himself. You will receive power when the Holy Spirit comes down on you; then you are to be my witnesses in Jerusalem, throughout Judea and Samaria, yes, even to the ends of the earth." No sooner had he said this than he was lifted up before their eyes in a cloud which took him from their sight.

They were still gazing up into the heavens when two men dressed in white stood beside them. "Men of Galilee," they said, "why do you stand here looking up at the skies? This Jesus who has been taken from you will return, just as you saw him go up into the heavens."

The Word of the Lord.

Responsorial Psalm — Ps 47, 2-3. 6-7. 8-9

R/. (6) God mounts his throne to shouts of joy;
a blare of trumpets for the Lord.

All you peoples, clap your hands,
shout to God with cries of gladness,
For the Lord, the Most High, the awesome,
is the great king over all the earth.

R/. God mounts his throne to shouts of joy;
a blare of trumpets for the Lord.

God mounts his throne amid shouts of joy;
  the Lord, amid trumpet blasts.
Sing praise to God, sing praise;
  sing praise to our king, sing praise.

R/. God mounts his throne to shouts of joy;
  a blare of trumpets for the Lord.

For king of all the earth is God;
  sing hymns of praise.
God reigns over the nations,
  God sits upon his holy throne.

R/. God mounts his throne to shouts of joy;
  a blare of trumpets for the Lord.

R/. Or: Alleluia.

Reading II — Eph 1, 17-23

A reading from the letter of Paul to the Ephesians

May the God of our Lord Jesus Christ, the Father of glory, grant you a spirit of wisdom and insight to know him clearly. May he enlighten your innermost vision that you may know the great hope to which he has called you, the wealth of his glorious heritage to be distributed among the members of the church, and the immeasurable scope of his power in us who believe. It is like the strength he showed in raising Christ from the dead and seating him at his right hand in heaven, high above every principality, power, virtue and domination, and every name that can be given in this age or the age to come.

He has put all things under Christ's feet and has made him thus exalted, head of the church, which is his body: the fullness of him who fills the universe in all its parts.

The Word of the Lord.

Gospel — Mk 16, 15-20

The conclusion of the holy gospel according to Mark

[Jesus appeared to the Eleven and] said to them:
"Go into the whole world and proclaim the good news to all creation. The man who believes in it and accepts baptism will be saved; the man

who refuses to believe in it will be condemned. Signs like these will accompany those who have professed their faith: they will use my name to expel demons, they will speak entirely new languages, they will be able to handle serpents, they will be able to drink deadly poison without harm, and the sick upon whom they lay their hands will recover." Then, after speaking to them, the Lord Jesus was taken up into heaven and took his seat at God's right hand. The Eleven went forth and preached everywhere. The Lord continued to work with them throughout and confirm the message through the signs which accompanied them.

The gospel of the Lord.

INTRODUCTORY PRAYER

We bless you, Lord Jesus,
on this day of your Ascension.
You are the Lord of infinite glory
and you remain our brother for eternity.
You reign next to your Father in the heavens
and you remain in our midst until the end of time.

We pray to you:
You gave us this earth
to make your glory dwell in it.
May the love of the beauty of this world
be for us a path to the splendor of heaven.
May the desire for the good things of the earth
teach us to prefer celestial realities.
And may the humble work of each day
in the service of your Kingdom
reveal your presence and your love
to all our brothers and sisters.
To you be glory
forever and ever. Amen.

HOMILY

1. Exegetic Explanations

Luke presents to us two accounts of the Lord's ascension. Each account has scriptural and theological profundity.

The first account is found at the end of Luke's gospel.[1] The ascension appears like the immediate crowning of the passion and resurrection. It seems to take place on the very day of Easter, for no temporal distance separates the mystery of the resurrection from the mystery of the ascension. Here Luke reflects the theology of John. In John's gospel, the crucifixion and glorification are deeply united: The crucifixion of Jesus is an elevation, an exaltation.[2] For us, this theology signifies that cross and resurrection are intimately bound in our lives. Each cross accepted with love is an entrance into the resurrection of Christ.

The second account of the ascension is found at the beginning of the Book of the Acts of the Apostles.[3] There the ascension marks the beginning of the mission of the Church.[4] Therefore the ascension is a beginning more than a departure. Luke signifies in this way that each ascension of our soul, each elevation to God, is also a mission to our brothers and sisters. Our death itself is not a departure but a beginning of eternity.

One might say that the ascension is really the most spectacular mystery in the life of Jesus. In order to describe this mystery, Luke utilizes the vocabulary and images common to his day, the only ones that his readers could understand. But, as elsewhere in the Bible, it is always advisable to distinguish between the conceptual material that is used (the vocabulary and the images) and the spiritual message that is signified.

Forty Days

Forty days: That is the length of time that Christ lived with his own people after his resurrection:

> Forty days he appeared to them and spoke to them about the Kingdom of God. Acts 1, 3

It is, therefore, the time that the apostles used to "wean themselves" from Christ according to the flesh and to accustom themselves to the risen Christ according to the Spirit. Those forty days are to be considered a round number, having a theological value. They bring to mind the forty days of

Christ's fasting, which prepared him for public life. One can also think about the forty years of Exodus: just as God accompanied the people of the Exodus for forty years to prepare them to enter into the Promised Land, Jesus walked with his disciples for forty days to speak to them about the Kingdom of God.

The Ascent into Heaven

The ascent into heaven is clearly a matter of a symbolic image. We could say that Jesus did not "ascend" into heaven if by that we mean a local ascent into the interstellar heaven (as we ascend into the clouds when we are in an airplane). The heaven of Jesus is not the starry firmament in which the sun and the moon dance with the stars and billions of galaxies. That heaven is an immense desert. It is interesting only for the space telescope.

We must add that the body of Jesus is a glorified body. We cannot, therefore, recognize him with the eyes of our flesh. We must contemplate him in faith.

Perhaps it is also time to rid ourselves of other ideas of heaven that fill our minds and encumber us like a heavy chain around our neck.

The idea that heaven is a future compensation is one example. This idea is represented in this way: In heaven, we will revel in proportion to all the bitterness of the present life that we will have endured with patience. This compensatory-heaven is built on trivial bookkeeping that seeks to balance the sufferings here below with the pleasures up above. It pleases us because, unfortunately, we have a mercenary mentality. Of course there will be a compensation. But it will be one of love. The love of God surpasses all our poor human calculations; the measure of joy that he will give to us is a joy beyond measure. Paul speaks of this "compensation" when he says:

> I consider that our present sufferings are without comparison
> with the glory that is to be revealed in us. Rom 8, 18

Yes, God is greater than the hope of humanity. He is infinitely better than what our heart can desire or even imagine.

In our unconscious mind, there is also the idea of a movie-heaven. It is rooted in the idea that we have about the beatific vision. We imagine that we will be in a movie-heaven where we will gaze upon divine immensity in boring immobility, or further, dressed in white robes and holding palms in our hands,[5] we will be out of breath singing canticles to fill eternity while hoping secretly that the eternal movie will sometimes become funnier and our canticle more stirring. What poor limited creatures we are!

But then, you will say, tell us what heaven is! I will not tell you. Not because I do not want to, but because I cannot. I simply know that God is greater than my heart and that his immense joy fills all creation.

The Cloud

Luke writes that Jesus disappeared from the eyes of his apostles "into a cloud."[6] The cloud of the ascension calls to mind the cloud that led the people of the Exodus across the desert or even the cloud that covered Mount Sinai when God spoke to his people.[7] As at the Transfiguration, the entrance of Jesus into the cloud signifies his belonging to the sphere of God. This cloud is the radiance of God: it seizes like light, encompasses like perfume, warms like love.

The Triumph of Humanity in Jesus

The most obvious mystery of the ascension is the triumph of humanity in the risen Jesus.

What are we? Fragile flesh. Our life is only a puff of wind; we find ourselves threatened at each moment. A tiny artery ruptures in our head, and we are on the edge of death!

What are we? A darkened spirit that has no credible explanation when faced with the least suffering and is thrown into full disarray when faced with death.

What are we? We are each a heart moved by fear, a heart desiring to love and be loved, even before loving heaven. And when we love, we are like prisoners who cannot fully reach each other, who tap against the partition of their cells in order to forget their bars. A prison cell where a thousand riddles run around without finding escape.

Well, that is exactly what Jesus carried to heaven: our humanity. That is what he saved.

Our hands, like his hands, one day will hold in heaven what they have held here on earth.

Our eyes, like his eyes, will be saved, for one day I will see God face to face, in the same way that a man sees the woman he loves and a woman sees the man she loves!

Our heart, as it loves: That is what is saved. The heart of a mother who loves her child: that is the love that is saved, saved and transfigured, not simply saved in the way that an antique dealer keeps and preserves an old thing but transfigured by the resurrection, rejuvenated with a thousand splendors. Saved like a child who falls into the arms of its father! For God is our Father.

Saint Catherine Labouré tells about the time when the Virgin appeared to her at the chapel of the Rue du Bac in Paris:

> I made only one move toward her (putting myself) on my knees on the steps of the altar, my hands leaning on the knees of the Holy Virgin.[9]

I dream of that day when I, too, like Catherine, will be able to place my wrinkled brow on Mary's knees and say to her: "It is you, the Mother of Jesus, the woman clothed with the sun and crowned with stars! How I have longed to see your face!"

A day will come, the day of my ascension, when I will meet Joseph, and with eyes full of joy, I will say to him, "It is you, the carpenter of Nazareth who loved little Miriam! What good fortune you had! All men do not have a Miriam to love, a Miriam to marry! It is surely of you that the Holy Spirit said in the Book of Proverbs: 'To find a wife is to find happiness.'"[10]

A day will come, the day of my ascension, when I will be able to say: It is you, my good angel, my guardian angel! How busy you were sometimes trying to protect me! Thank you for having accompanied me on all the paths of my life."

A day will come, the day of my ascension, the Day of joy, when my eyes will meet the eyes of my Lord Jesus. I will see him face to face, as I see you, better than I see you. And then I will say to him...What will I say to him? Probably nothing. For I will see everything in his eyes. I will see in them my own joy. I will see the place that his love has prepared for me from all eternity...

And if a single one of these words that I have just said were not true, then the whole Christian faith would fall into ruin. Then there would be nothing more to love, nothing more to believe.[11]

Jesus presents the mystery of his ascension in this way:

I leave to prepare a place for you…
I will come back to take you with me
so that where I am,
you will be also. Jn 14, 2-3

In the prayer after communion, the liturgy prays in this way: "God, put in our hearts a great desire to live with Christ, in whom our human nature is already near to you."

2. The Mystery of the Ascension

The Prayer of the Ascension

On this feast of the ascension, the liturgy puts on our lips the prayer of the letter to the Ephesians. A wonderful prayer, but in a difficult and labored text. For often, when Paul wants to say everything, when he wants to say too much, he beats the words to bend them to what he wants to say. I am translating this prayer literally:

May the God of our Lord Jesus Christ,
the Father of glory,
give you a spirit of wisdom and revelation,
so that the eyes of your heart being enlightened,
you may know the hope
to which he calls you,
which is the riches of the glory
of his inheritance among the saints. Eph 1, 17-18

Yes, the Father who gives us the glory of heaven must enlighten the eyes of our hearts!

Then we will be able to recognize what our inheritance is: it is found in heaven. We will live there with Christ, our brother, and with our friends, the saints.

The Grace of the Ascension

The grace of the ascension is twofold.

It is, on the one hand, to live, beginning now, in heaven, in the house of the Father.

> There where your treasure is,
> there is your heart also. Mt 6, 21

May our hearts live then with our treasure! The Father who waits for you is there, as the father of the prodigal son waited for the return of the one who was lost. Even more, not only was he waiting for him, but "while the son was still far away," says Jesus, "the father ran to throw himself on his neck and embraced him."[12] Marvelous God! It is not you who is first going to take the initiative to go before him; it is he who is coming to meet you!

The Holy Spirit, who burns in your heart with love and makes you sing all along your way, is there.

And Jesus is there, since he is your Way.

The grace of the ascension was lived with magnificence by two men who, so to speak, ascended into heaven before Jesus!

The first was the patriarch Enoch. Genesis says of him: "He disappeared, for God took him away." In speaking of him, Genesis gives one of the most beautiful definitions of a faithful person according to God's heart: "Enoch walked with God."[13] Happy are they who have made of their lives, day by day, a walk with God! Happy are they, for they are on the path of the ascension. They are walking across death, beyond death, for they are always living with God.

The second faithful to ascend was the prophet Elijah. It is said of him: "Elijah was taken up to heaven in a whirlwind."[14] Elijah was the prophet who fought all his life to maintain, against the naturistic cults of the Canaanites, the faith of God present in the midst of his people. Now, the vocation of Elijah was characterized by this superb cry: "Yahweh lives, before whom I stand!"[15] Happy are they who stand before Yahweh, for they are on the path of the ascension. They also, like Enoch, walk across death, beyond death, for they stand before God, the source of life.

The second grace of the ascension is to dwell now on this earth while preparing it for heaven. It is to render the earth more habitable by filling it with the joy of the Good News. It is to make the beauty of heaven shine on earth, to save the earth by loving it. Only sin is hateful. But sin is ugliness, boredom, sadness.

The Church will make people believe that there is a heaven when we will agree to speak with love about the earth. We will make people believe in God if we testify that we ourselves believe in humanity. We will be taken seriously when we will speak seriously about human joy, about laughter, about dance... There may be a certain search for heaven that actually hides a flight from the tasks of this world. Such an attitude is not Christian. It makes the gospel a lie.

We know well that one saves only what one loves. God himself saved the world only by loving it: "He so loved the world that he gave his only Son."[16]

The Christian most desirous of heaven is the one who works the most diligently to fill the earth with the splendor of heaven.

"You Will Be My Witness..."

While ascending into heaven, Jesus asks us to be his witnesses on earth:

> You will be my witnesses in Jerusalem,
> in all of Judea and Samaria
> and unto the ends of the earth. Acts 1, 8

We are the witnesses of Jesus. Witnesses of his mystery. Witnesses, today, of his ascension. We are witnesses of the desire for heaven that we must carry within us. About the quality of that desire, Paul explains:

> Since you are risen with Christ,
> seek the realities above,
> there where Christ is,
> seated at the right hand of God. Col 3, 1

And Saint Augustine comments: "Today our Lord Jesus Christ ascends into heaven. May our heart ascend there with him."[17]

Yes, our hearts must be sufficiently beautiful so that they may be witnesses of Christ in heaven. That is to say, they must reflect a little of heaven in the gray tones of our earth. May our souls be like bursts of heaven. May they seduce our brothers and sisters to look higher, to look where we ourselves are looking.

What I am saying now is foolish: We must carry a little bit of heaven in us for others. The light of Christ must shine on our faces so that they may enlighten the night of our brothers and sisters. Who can accomplish this marvel while we ourselves are threatened by night, except the One alone who can enlighten the eyes of our heart, Jesus Christ.[18]

To Christ who is ascended into heaven and who remains in our midst until the end of time, our love and glory forever and ever.

PRAYER OF THE ASCENSION

Christ Jesus,
ascended into heaven next to your Father,
do not forget your brothers and sisters on earth,
and intercede for us!

Christ, you are risen from the dead;
have mercy on us.

Christ risen,
see our darkened eyes
fascinated by the beauty of the earth.
Illuminate them with your light,
fill them with the beauty of heaven.

Christ, you are risen from the dead;
have mercy on us.

Christ risen,
see our enslaved hands
attached to the vanity of this world.
Free them from servitude,
that they may rise toward heaven as signs of prayer.

Christ, you are risen from the dead;
have mercy on us.

Christ risen,
see our mouths filled with bitterness,
full of songs of the earth.
Fill them with your smile,
put on our lips the songs of heaven.

Christ, you are risen from the dead;
have mercy on us.

Ascension

Christ risen,
see our bruised feet
worn out on the paths of the earth.
Show us the way of the Kingdom,
make us run on the path of heaven.

Christ, you are risen from the dead;
have mercy on us.

Christ risen,
see our hearts of stone;
they are heavy with the desires of earth.
Save all our human loves,
enrich them with the love of heaven.

Christ, you are risen from the dead;
have mercy on us.

Christ risen,
we also entrust to you all our other intentions.

You are marvelous, Lord Jesus,
for your Ascension has filled our earth
with the peace and the joy of your heaven.
Keep us in that peace;
make us grow in that joy
forever and ever. Amen.

NOTES TO ASCENSION

1. Lk 24, 50-53.
2. Cf. Jn 3, 14.
3. Acts 1, 6-11.
4. Acts 1, 18.
5. Cf. Rv 7, 9-12.
6. Acts 1, 8.
7. Ex 13, 21 and 19, 16.
8. Cf. Lk 9, 34.
9. R. Laurentin, *Vie de Catherine Labouré* (Paris: Desclée de Brouwer, 1980), p. 84.
10. Prv 18, 22.
11. After having made a similar supposition, Paul continued in this way: "But no, Christ is risen from the dead, firstfruits of those who have fallen asleep" (I Cor 15, 20).
12. Lk 15, 20.
13. Gn 5, 24.
14. Luke describes the ascension of Jesus by utilizing the account of the "carrying off" of the prophet Elijah. Luke writes: He (Jesus) was carried up (*ánelèmphthe*, Acts 1, 2) and having been carried up (*ánalèmphtheis*) to heaven (Acts 1, 11). The text of 2 Kgs 2, 11, according to the Greek version (LXX), declares: Elijah was carried up (*ánélèmphthè*)... to heaven.
15. 2 Kgs 3, 14.
16. Jn 3, 16.
17. Serm. "Mai" 98,1. PLS 2, 494.
18. Cf. Eph 1, 18.

SEVENTH SUNDAY OF EASTER

READING I — ACTS 1, 15-17. 20-26

A reading from the Acts of the Apostles

In those days Peter stood up in the midst of the brothers—there must have been a hundred and twenty gathered together. "Brothers," he said, "the saying in scripture uttered long ago by the Holy Spirit through the mouth of David was destined to be fulfilled in Judas, the one that guided those who arrested Jesus. He was one of our number and he had been given a share in this ministry of ours.

"It is written in the Book of Psalms,
'May another take his office.'

"It is entirely fitting, therefore, that one of those who was of our company while the Lord Jesus moved among us, from the baptism of John until the day he was taken up from us, should be named as witness with us to his resurrection." At that they nominated two, Joseph (called Barsabbas, also known as Justus) and Matthias. Then they prayed: "O Lord, you read the hearts of men. Make known to us which of these two you choose for this apostolic ministry, replacing Judas, who deserted the cause and went the way he was destined to go." They then drew lots between the two men. The choice fell to Matthias, who was added to the eleven apostles.

The gospel of the Lord.

RESPONSORIAL PSALM — Ps 103, 1-2. 11-12. 19-20

R/. (19) The Lord has set his throne in heaven.

Bless the Lord, O my soul;
and all my being, bless his holy name.
Bless the Lord, O my soul;
and forget not all his benefits.

R/. The Lord has set his throne in heaven.

For as the heavens are high above the earth,
so surpassing is his kindness toward those who fear him.
As far as the east is from the west,
so far has he put our transgressions from us.

R/. The Lord has set his throne in heaven.

The Lord has established his throne in heaven,
  and his kingdom rules over all.
Bless the Lord, all you his angels,
  you mighty in strength, who do his bidding.

R/. The Lord has set his throne in heaven.

R/. Or: Alleluia.

Reading II — 1 Jn 4, 11-16

A reading from the first letter of John

Beloved,
  if God has loved us so,
  we must have the same love for one another.
No one has ever seen God.
Yet if we love one another
  God dwells in us,
  and his love is brought to perfection in us.
The way we know we remain in him
  and he in us
  is that he has given us of his Spirit.
We have seen for ourselves, and can testify,
  that the Father has sent the Son as savior of the world.
When anyone acknowledges that Jesus is the Son of God,
  God dwells in him
  and he in God.
We have come to know and to believe
  in the love God has for us.
God is love,
  and he who abides in love
  abides in God,
  and God in him.

The Word of the Lord.

Gospel Jn 17, 11-19

A reading from the holy gospel according to John

Jesus looked up to heaven and prayed:

"O Father most holy,
protect them with your name
which you have given me,
[that they may be one, even as we are one.]
As long as I was with them,
I guarded them with your name
which you gave me.
I kept careful watch,
and not one of them was lost,
none but him who was destined to be lost—
in fulfillment of Scripture.
Now, however, I come to you;
I say all this while I am still in the world
that they may share my joy completely.
I gave them your word,
and the world has hated them for it;
they do not belong to the world,
[any more than I belong to the world]
I do not ask you to take them out of the world,
but to guard them from the evil one.
They are not of the world,
any more than I am of the world.
Consecrate them by means of truth—
'Your word is truth.'
As you have sent me into the world,
so I have sent them into the world;
I consecrate myself for their sakes now,
that they may be consecrated in truth."

INTRODUCTORY PRAYER

Lord, we want to bless you endlessly
because you revealed yourself to us
as the God of Love.

And we pray to you, in union with your Son Jesus:
Keep us faithful in your name,
fill us unceasingly with your joy,
and sanctify us by the truth.
your Son Jesus Christ,
in the love of the Holy Spirit
forever and ever. Amen.

HOMILY

1. Election of Matthias to Replace Judas

The Church is preparing herself to receive the Holy Spirit. She repairs her unity wounded by the defection of Judas and chooses Matthias to replace him. Such is the meaning of the first reading of today's Mass.

Literary Unity

Luke succeeded in presenting his account in a beautiful literary style. It flows naturally, like water from a spring. A finer analysis, however, reveals that he used two different sources:

- A source that relates the end of Judas.
- Another source that tells of the election of Matthias.

In speaking about the end of Judas, Luke writes:

> (His end) was so known by all the residents of Jerusalem that this field was called in their language *Hakeldema*, that is, "Field of Blood."[1] Acts 1, 19

It is curious that Luke places in the mouth of Peter explanations on Hakeldama that the residents knew very well. He has an equally nice distraction when he makes Peter, who was speaking in Aramaic to Arameans, say that Hakeldama "in their language" means "Field of Blood." One notes finally that Peter, who quotes two psalms and who is supposed to speak Aramaic, quotes them (partially) according to the Greek translation of the Bible.

One is therefore led to think that Luke is writing, for the sake of Theophilus, a biblical account on the basis of old oral traditions. To give it a biblical character, he prefaces it in the way used for old stories or legends by beginning with "in those days."

2. The End of Judas

The end of Judas is told to us according to a double tradition: that of Matthew in his Gospel and that of Luke in the Acts of the Apostles.

According to the tradition of Matthew, on the very day of Jesus' death, Judas takes his money to the Temple, throws the pieces in the sanctuary, then goes to hang himself. The priests gather the money and buy with it the "Potter's Field" for the grave of strangers.

Matthew's account alludes to the death of the traitor Ahitophel. This was the epoch when Absalom was rebelling against his father David. The traitor Ahitophel proposes to Absalom to make David die, as Judas proposes to the priests to deliver Jesus to them. Ahitophel does not succeed in his plan and returns home to hang himself.

In the Bible, this is the only case of suicide by hanging. The suicide of Judas is similar to it. Judas appears as the traitor par excellence. Jesus, on the contrary, is the new David, persecuted and betrayed by one of his own. Through his resurrection, he affirms his royalty over the new house of Israel, the Church of the risen ones.

The end of Judas in Luke's account recalls rather the frightful end of the persecutor Antiochus Epiphanes who was struck with a horrible suffering in his body.[4] Now Antiochus Epiphanes is the very type of the persecutor, and his death is the example of the end that awaits the impious.

Judas is then considered not only a traitor, but also a persecutor of Jesus and of his Church.

In his discourse, Peter explains:

> This Judas was, however, one of us
> and had received his portion of our ministry. Acts 1, 17

In his betrayal he abandoned the service of Christ. He became, like Antiochus Epiphanes, persecutor of the people of God. Luke's accounts are ordinarily of great delicacy and omit details that could offend the sensibilities of his Greek readers. But he does not hesitate here to relate in horror:

> This man fell head first,
> burst open in the middle,
> and his intestines spilled out. Acts 1, 18

The death of Judas is consistent with the description of the death of the impious according to the Book of Wisdom:

> The Lord will strike them down first. Ws 4, 19

This description also presents a theological point. The intestines, in biblical vocabulary, are actually the seat, the center, of pity and mercy. In affirming that "his intestines spilled out," Luke affirms that Judas was a man without intestines, without heart as we would say today. Here is a man who betrayed and persecuted Jesus, because that man was without heart!

The Destiny of Judas

The destiny of Judas has something mysterious about it that fascinates the Christian conscience. Of course, Judas had his faults. But Peter also had his, and John, Thomas, and all the others had theirs. Judas could have become Saint Judas—there really is a Saint Jude—but Judas became the symbol of all betrayals.

We do not know how God exercised on his behalf the infinite riches of his forgiveness. Judgment belongs to God alone. And this judgment is always one of his mercy.

Romano Guardini presents the following remarks which always seem topical:

> Judas was called to become an apostle and could have been one. But one day the will of conversion must have been paralyzed.
>
> It is foolish to think that it is pleasant, without restriction, to live next to a saint, indeed next to the Son of God; to imagine that one cannot become good at this contact. One can there become a demon! The Lord himself says: "Is it not I who chose you Twelve? And one of you is a demon." Judas was not one from the beginning, as people believe; he became one, and next to the Savior.[5]

Even today, it is foolish to think that just by living in the Church in the midst of "saints" we would become saints ourselves.

3. The Ministry of the Twelve

Why did the Twelve want to replace Judas? Indeed, around the year 44 when James, the Lord's brother, underwent martyrdom, one did not think to replace him when one had a very suitable candidate at hand who was already well-known — Paul. It is noteworthy that Paul himself never claimed such a place.

In reality, the problem of replacement is not raised by the death of Judas but by his desertion. It is his betrayal that rendered his place vacant. When James disappeared, no one thought that his place was vacant.

Witnesses of the Resurrection

What is the function of the Twelve? Luke presents it in this way:

> It is necessary that, among the men who accompanied us the whole time the Lord Jesus went and came among us, beginning with John's baptism up to the day when he was taken up from our midst, one of them become with us a witness of his resurrection.
> Acts 1, 21-22

The text is as confused as one would have it. The message to be passed seemed so important that one sacrificed the literary form. I would like to present three remarks.

"It is necessary:" Here is a phrase dear to Luke.[6] It expresses the will of God without other justification. Thus we find "it is necessary that the Scriptures be fulfilled," "everything that has been written (about Jesus) in the Law of Moses, in the Prophets and the psalms," "what the Holy Spirit had announced in the scriptures."[7] It is in this divine necessity, which does not need to be supported by any human justification, that the election of a new apostle is written.

It is necessary that the elect must have accompanied Jesus and the Twelve from the baptism by John to the time of the ascension. A continuity then "is necessary" between the Jesus of history, the one who walked in the midst of the crowds in the dust of Galilean roads, and the Christ of faith, the Lord who opened a path of glory on the road to heaven, escorted by angels. In other words, one wants firsthand witnesses. Peter will say in a superb way that the Father revealed his risen Christ to witnesses chosen in advance, "to us who ate with him and drank with him after his resurrection."[8] One measures the distance of the requirements: to have eaten and drunk with Jesus and to have contemplated the Lord resplendent with glory.

Finally, and this is the essential, this witness bears upon the resurrection of Jesus: witnesses are necessary, and it is necessary that they witness the resurrection.

> It is you who are my witnesses, oracle of the Lord,
> and my servants whom I have chosen. Is 43, 10

This prophecy, "you are my witnesses," appears many times in the Book of Isaiah.[4] It is taken up by Jesus:

> You will be my witnesses
> in Jerusalem, in all of Judea and Samaria
> and unto the ends of the earth. Acts 1, 8

In the book of Isaiah, the witness bore upon the oneness of God and his suzerainty over the world. In the Book of Acts, it bears upon the suzerainty of Jesus, established by his resurrection.

Today, as in the time of Acts, witnesses are still necessary. And it is necessary that they witness the resurrection of Jesus. The Christian is the one who witnesses and proclaims to the world: "The Lord is risen!" He proclaims it not necessarily by what he says, but first by what he is. He lives in such a way that one who does not know Christ concludes on seeing him: "Someone living dwells in him. He is transfigured by a new life. His life is unified by a love."

When the world will say of each Christian, alluding to Paul, "It is no longer he who lives; it is the risen Christ who lives in him,"[10] then it will be ready to believe in the resurrection.

4. The Election of Matthias

Here are a few remarks that I would like to submit for your meditation.

The most venerable institution in the early community is that of the Twelve. In the oldest gospel source, Mark presents it in this way, not without solemnity:

> Jesus calls to him those whom he wished.
> And they went to him.
> And he established the Twelve
> so that they might be with him
> and he might send them to proclaim the message. Mk 3, 13-14

The Twelve are a typically Jewish institution. They proclaim the message to the twelves tribes of the house of Israel.

It is necessary to note the extreme flexibility of the institution in its early times. Indeed, after the death of James (around the years 43-44), one does not think about replacing him. And the group of the Twelve, that is, the most venerable group of the early community, the group-witness of the resurrection, quite simply broke up: the Church, in reality, no longer addressed herself at that time only to the tribes of Israel, but to all the tribes of the earth. Of course, the Church is forever built on the foundation of the Twelve—they are the twelve foundations on which is built the New Jerusalem, each of which bears the name of one of the apostles[11]—but it is built consequently on all the "apostles" (that is, all those who, like Paul and Barnabas, are "sent" into the mission), on the "prophets" (that is, those who speak in the name of Christ), on the "teachers" (that is, those who teach in the name of Christ) and on all the other charisms that together edify a community that is renewed unceasingly in a thousand splendors.[12]

What can we conclude? That in the Church, no institution exists for itself: it exists for the announcement of the Kingdom. An institution can be born, then disappear normally in the world without slowing the progress of the Church but simply serving it. Such was the case, for example, of the deaconesses who existed in the early Church, who disappeared in the Roman rite, who can again be established. It is not necessary to make any institution absolute, however venerable it may be. The Church itself, as an institution, exists only for our salvation, for the edification of the Kingdom. And Christ himself, as we sing in the Creed, came *propter nos homines et propter nostram salutem*, for us and for our salvation.

A Community of Brothers and Sisters

Luke affirms without question the precedence of Peter in the heart of the early community.[13] He attributes to him the initiative of the election of Matthias.

But he also affirms without question that the believing community is a community of brothers and sisters.

The word brother is a part of his favorite vocabulary.[14] He underlines it here in the source that he uses, even at the price of making his text dull:

> Peter rose in the midst of the brothers... and he said: "Brothers..."
>
> Acts 1, 15-16

The use of this appellation so frequently in the early community goes back to Jesus himself. The Church in the early times was living to the letter the recommendation of her Lord:

> For you, do not call yourselves "Rabbi,"
> for you have only one Teacher.
> In reality, you are all brothers and sisters,
> And do not call anyone among you "Father" on earth,
> for you have only one Father,
> the (Father) in heaven. Mt 23, 8-9

These words burn us. Is it necessary to take them truly literally, or to consider them simply as an impossible ideal? What should we do when our beloved Church is overflowing with "Fathers," "Reverend Fathers," even "Most Reverend Fathers,"—there are also "Reverend Mothers"—without counting Monsignors, and all the rest? There is no question, of course, about the respect due to authority. The principle of Paul is always valid:

> Give everyone what you owe him…
> if honor, give him honor. Rom 13, 7

This principle, which is valid for those in authority, is valid also for the most humble brother and sister in the Church.

This having been said, I think that we can distinguish two levels.

There are on the one hand titles. Let us suppose that we cannot change them. There are such heavy traditions in the Church...And we cannot change peoples' hearts overnight by magic. There are also different sensibilities concerning the gospel. What seems important to one community may seem secondary to another. We look then at these titles like wounds in the heart of the Church, hoping that time—and the grace of the Lord—will soon heal these wounds.

There are on the other hand realities. They are not always expressed by the words. For one can be called "Father" and act like a very loving brother. One can also make himself be called "brother" and act like a tyrant.

May our beloved Church be a community of brothers and sisters, gathered around Peter, whom tradition called "the servant of the servants of God!"

And since it is not asked of us to realize the reform the Church but simply to reform ourselves, let us be, each one on his part, a brother for his brother, a sister for her sister! Let us be it in the name of love for the One who, being universal Lord, appeared in our midst as a brother!

A Service and a Gift

Vocation is presented as "a part of the ministry" (literally, of the diaconate).[15] The term diaconate means service ministry. (The word deacon means servant). Luke speaks in this way of the diaconate of the Word which is insured by the Twelve, of the daily diaconate that the Seven insure for the widows, of the diaconate that Paul received to "bear witness to the Gospel of the grace of God."[16] At the source of every diaconate or ministry in the believing community is the Lord Jesus himself:

> I am in the midst of you
> as one who serves (*diakoni*). Lk 22, 27.

Following the example of Jesus, every Christian vocation is a service of Christ in the service of his brothers and sisters.[17] This service is at the same time a gift, a portion that one receives *(kleros)*. The word designates what one obtains by fate, whence the portion, the lot, the inheritance. Behind the word stands out the affirmation of the psalm:

> The Lord is the portion
> of my inheritance and my cup. Ps 16, 5 (LXX)

Every vocation appears like a call: one receives it like a service, one keeps it like a love.

Marvelous is the Lord! He gives to each one a portion of the ministry in his Church.

He gave this portion to Judas: He received it like a service, but did not keep it like a love. And he betrayed.

He gave this portion to Matthias: He received it like a service, kept it like a love. And remained faithful.

He gives this portion to each one of us. May we be able to always keep it like a love! This portion, it is not "fate"—which is blind chance—that gives it to us, but it is Providence, which is the clearsighted love of God, that gives it to us.

Like all love, vocation—that of Matthias and our own—is a secret garden. No one can enter into the dialogue that binds me to God. No one can answer to it in my place.

For Matthias, one would have been able to think of a democratic election where the voters—about 120—would have designated the candidate of their choice. One prefers the drawing of lots. One then abandons the choice to God. Matthias alone will answer in his ministry to the love that chose him.

Happy are those who, like Matthias, welcome the choice of God and keep it like a love! Happy are those who realize not necessarily the marvelous things that change the face of the earth, but who accomplish marvelously the daily tasks, those that change the face of our heart. The Church does not have a Matthias to elect every day, but every day she has need of the ministry of our love.

CONCLUDING PRAYER

One can use the prayer of the Sixth Sunday, which develops the theme "God is love" (1 John, 4, 8), a theme that we find this Sunday in the second reading (I Jn 4, 16).

NOTES TO SEVENTH SUNDAY OF EASTER

1. The *Lectionary* has abridged the text a little in order not to make the liturgy of the word too long.
2. It is hardly possible to determine which account is closest to the events themselves.
3. 2 Sm 17, 23. The verb *apagchesthai* (to hang oneself), used to describe the suicide of Ahitophel, is used in the New Testament only for the suicide of Judas.
4. See 2 Mac 9.
5. *Le Seigneur*, Vol. 2 (Paris: Alsatia, 1945), pp. 55-56.
6. The phrase "it is necessary" appears 40 times in Luke (18 times in the Gospel and 22 times in Acts) compared with 6 times in Mark and 8 times in Matthew.
7. Cf. Lk 22, 37; 24, 44: Acts 1, 16.
8. Acts 10, 41.
9. Cf. Is 43, 12; 44, 8.
10. Cf. Gal 2, 20.
11. Cf. Rv 21, 14.
12. Apostles and prophets: cf. Eph 2, 20. Apostles, prophets, teachers and other charisms: Eph 4, 11-12; I Cor 12, 28-30.
13. Cf. Acts 1, 15; 2, 14, 37; 3, 1-7, 12; 4, 8, 13; 5, 3, 8-9, 15, 29; 10-11.
14. It appears 81 times in Luke (24 times in the Gospel and 57 times in Acts compared with 20 times in Mark, 39 times in Matthew, and 14 times in John.)
15. Acts 1, 17.
16. Cf. Acts 6, 1-2, 4; 20, 24
17. Cf. Lk 22, 24-27; Jn 13, 4-15.

PENTECOST SUNDAY

Reading I — Acts 2, 1-11

A reading from the Acts of the Apostles

When the day of Pentecost came it found the brethren gathered in one place. Suddenly from up in the sky there came a noise like a strong, driving wind which was heard all through the house where they were seated. Tongues as of fire appeared which parted and came to rest on each of them. All were filled with the Holy Spirit. They began to express themselves in foreign tongues and make bold proclamation as the Spirit prompted them.

Staying in Jerusalem at the time were devout Jews of every nation under heaven. These heard the sound, and assembled in a large crowd. They were much confused because each one heard these men speaking his own language. The whole occurrence astonished them. They asked in utter amazement, "Are not all of these men who are speaking Galileans? How is it that each of us hears them in his native tongue? We are Parthians, Medes, and Elamites. We live in Mesopotamia, Judea and Cappadocia, Pontus, the province of Asia, Phrygia and Pamphylia, Egypt, and the regions of Libya around Cyrene. There are even visitors from Rome—all Jews, or those who have come over to Judaism; Cretans and Arabs too. Yet each of us hears them speaking in his own tongue about the marvels God has accomplished."

The Word of the Lord.

Responsorial Psalm — Ps 104, 1. 24. 29-30. 31. 34

R/. (30) Lord, send out your Spirit,
and renew the face of the earth.

Bless the Lord, O my soul!
O Lord, my God, you are great indeed!
How manifold are your works, O Lord!
the earth is full of your creatures.

R/. Lord, send out your Spirit
and renew the face of the earth.

If you take away their breath, they perish
 and return to their dust.
When you send forth your spirit, they are created,
 and you renew the face of the earth.

R/. Lord, send out your Spirit
 and renew the face of the earth.

May the glory of the Lord endure forever;
 may the Lord be glad in his works!
Pleasing to him be my theme;
 I will be glad in the Lord.

R/. Lord, send out your Spirit
 and renew the face of the earth.

R/. Or: Alleluia.

Reading II
I Cor 12, 3-7. 12-13

A reading from the first letter of Paul to the Corinthians

No one can say: "Jesus is Lord," except in the Holy Spirit.

There are different gifts but the same Spirit: there are different ministries but the same Lord; there are different works but the same God who accomplishes all of them in every one. To each person the manifestation of the Spirit is given for the common good.

The body is one and has many members, but all the members, many though they are, are one body; and so it is with Christ. It was in one Spirit that all of us, whether Jew or Greek, slave or free, were baptized into one body. All of us have been given to drink of the one Spirit.

The Word of the Lord.

Gospel
Jn 20, 19-23

A reading from the holy gospel according to John

On the evening of that first day of the week, even though the disciples had locked the doors of the place where they were for fear of the Jews,

Jesus came and stood before them. "Peace be with you," he said. When he had said this, he showed them his hands and his side. At the sight of the Lord the disciples rejoiced. "Peace be with you," he said again.

"As the Father has sent me,
so I send you."

Then he breathed on them and said:

"Receive the Holy Spirit.
If you forgive mens' sins,
they are forgiven them;
if you hold them bound,
they are held bound."

The gospel of the Lord.

INTRODUCTORY PRAYER

Father of our Lord Jesus Christ
and Source of the Holy Spirit:
We praise you and we bless you for your Church
that you assembled on the day of Pentecost.

Today again, send your Spirit upon us:
May he loosen our lips for your praise,
may he burn our hearts in the fire of your love,
and through the voice of the risen Jesus, our brother,
may he help us to sing
the marvels of your love
in all the languages of the earth.
To you be glory
forever and ever. Amen.

HOMILY

1. The Feast of the Covenant and of the Law

Pentecost in Jewish Tradition

Originally Pentecost was an agrarian feast of Canaanite origin. It was celebrated fifty days after Passover, from which it gets its name "Pentecost," which is the transliteration of the Greek *pentecoste* meaning "fiftieth." During this feast, one celebrated the end of harvest. It was a joyous feast: "You will rejoice in the presence of the Lord your God," enjoins the ritual of the feast.[1]

Like the Feast of Passover, Pentecost was attached to the history of Israel, more precisely to the Exodus. Two traditions are to be considered.

According to the Book of Jubilees—an apocryphal book that dates from the second century before the Christian era and represents the ideas of the Priestly tradition—Pentecost celebrates the gift of the Law at Sinai. At Qumran, on that day they celebrated what was called "the entrance into the Covenant."

According to the second tradition, which represents the ideas of official Pharisaism, Pentecost celebrates the gift of the Law that was given, we thought, fifty days after the escape from Egypt. The Talmud of Babylon affirms: "Pentecost is the day when the Law was given."[2]

To summarize: At the time of Christ, Pentecost was a joyous agricultural feast when one celebrated the Covenant and the gift of the Law, or, to say it concisely: The gift of the Law of the New Covenant.

The Christian Pentecost

Is there an interest for us Christians to know these Jewish antiquities? Yes, there is more than an interest, there is a necessity. If we were not familiar with them, we would not possess the key to unlock the meaning of Luke's text. We would understand an account, but not the one that Luke wanted to write. In fact, this text reveals some peculiar, almost bizarre traits. It is through them that the evangelist wants to present the Christian Pentecost as a new Sinai.

Luke writes:

> Suddenly there came from heaven a sound
> like that of a violent gust of wind. Acts 2, 2

And later he writes (I am translating literally):

> When this voice was heard Acts 2, 6

One can ask: Why so much noise to invoke the Spirit of Jesus? It is that the revelation of Sinai is realized in the noise of thunder and that the thunder was presented afterwards as the voice of God.[3]

Luke writes further:

> And there appeared to them
> tongues as of fire. Acts 2, 3

Now, at Sinai, it is also written, "All the people saw voices and flames."[4] It is undoubtedly difficult to see voices, except if they are symbolized by tongues of fire. Luke insists finally on the unity of the community of Pentecost:

> And when the day of Pentecost was completed,
> they were all united together. Acts 2, 1

Now, according to tradition, the community of Sinai was also "together, with a perfect heart."[5]

All of these allusions were perfectly clear to those familiar with the Greek Bible in the time of Luke. In perceiving them, the community must have blushed with pleasure. It could conclude with Luke — and we, who labor to follow them on the paths of biblical vocabulary, follow them in this conclusion: Just as the people of the Exodus, fifty days after coming out of Egypt, received the Law at Sinai and entered into the Covenant, in the same way the community of Jesus, fifty days after the Lord's Resurrection—which was his Exodus from the world—received his law, which is the Spirit of Jesus, and entered into the New Covenant.

And it is here that fundamental questions rise to the surface of the heart. No one can avoid them.

First question: Do I live in the grace of Pentecost? Have I made a covenant with the risen Christ? Is my personal relationship with him a relationship of servant to master or an authentic relationship of Covenant, a relationship of love? Or, transforming the question into a prayer: Lord, give us the grace of Pentecost. Help us to live day by day more faithfully in your Covenant of love!

Second question: Is the law that rules my life the Decalogue of Sinai or is it the Spirit of the risen Christ? Lord, give us the grace of Pentecost. At each moment of our lives, let your Spirit of love be the law of our hearts!

The True Children of God

Paul has some astounding words:

Those who are led by the Spirit of God, those are the children of God.

He uses a strange figure of speech in Greek, as if to say: "Those who are led by the Spirit of God, those only (*osoi...houtoi*) are the children of God." In other words: each time that we allow ourselves to be led by the Spirit of God, we are children of God. Otherwise, we are children of the earth.

When we observe the history of the Church, we discover that all the great spiritual adventures that were born among the children of God were the fruit not of parsimonious observation of the Decalogue, but of enthusiastic obedience—enthusiastic even to the foolishness of the cross!—to the Spirit of Jesus. True son of God, Francis of Assisi when he decided to espouse, as he said, Dame Poverty, for that was not asked of him by the Decalogue, but it was the Spirit of Jesus whom he was following. True daughter of God, Teresa of Avila when she threw herself into the reform of Carmel—an insane venture on the human level—for that was not asked of her by the Decalogue, but it was the Spirit of Jesus whom she was obeying. True son of God, the good Pope John XXIII when he decided with feigned naivete and true guile to convene a Council, for it was no longer the Decalogue that he was following, but the Spirit of Jesus. True children of God are we when we accept the cross that the Lord imposes upon us or the new task that he discloses to us that is well beyond the Decalogue, for it is the Spirit of Jesus who is guiding us. Then we are truly children of God!

Lord, give us the grace of Pentecost. Help us to live as children of God and guide us through your Spirit.

2. The Feast of the Church

The ancient Pentecost was a joyous feast: One rejoiced "in the presence of the Lord" and one presented to him "the offering of the new grain." The first Christian Pentecost was filled with the joy of the Holy Spirit, and the Church offered to Christ the firstfruits of conversions to the Gospel. Pentecost is, in this way, the feast of the Church.

Luke insists complacently on the universality of this Church:

> There were in Jerusalem fervent Jews from all the nations under heaven.
> Acts 2, 5

"From all the nations under heaven": carried away by his enthusiasm, Luke exaggerates a little. But he knows that his affirmation is true on the ideal level. The Church of the first Pentecost represents well all the nations under the sun. Luke then gives a list of nations. Let us count them together: Parthians (1), Medes (2), Elamites (3), residents of Mesopotamia (4),

Judea (5), Cappadocia (6), Pontus (7), Asia (8), Phrygia (9), Pamphlia (10), Egypt (11), and Libya (12). That makes twelve nations, one for each of the twelve apostles. Next come the Romans who end the parade and who undoubtedly go back to Paul.

This list is not exceedingly clear. It is better to suppose that is was added later than to ascribe it to Luke.[7] The list begins with four peoples: Parthians, Medes, Elamites and Mesopotamians—who stretch themselves out as they can from the East to the West. Judea is mentioned almost in the middle of the list undoubtedly because Jerusalem was allegedly the center of the world. One is lost then in the maze of unimportant provinces, like Pamphylia which is situated next to enormous Asia. Greece is forgotten, but not the sands of Libya. Syria is not mentioned; perhaps it is the country of the origin of the list.

We finish with a religious enumeration "Jews and proselytes," then with a recapitulation: "Cretans and Arabs" (or West and East, as we would say today).

But through this medley of nations, the essential is affirmed with power: The Church was born on the day of Pentecost; she was born universal! And it is in all languages that she proclaims "the marvels of God."[8]

A Universal Church

This universalism was inscribed in the Jewish tradition of Pentecost.

It was thought, in fact, that the Law had been transmitted at Sinai not only in Hebrew for the people of the promise, but also in seventy other languages for all the people of the earth.[9] Sinai, the type or prophecy of the Christian Pentecost, was then already a feast of nations.

To understand this feast, other biblical recollections must be considered.

We find at the beginning of the Book of Genesis, just before the call of Abraham, a table of contents of all the peoples of the earth.[10] That list names seventy nations, according to the count of Jewish tradition, which present themselves before the Lord: The diversity of nations is wanted and blessed by the Creator.

When the nations separated after the unfortunate attempt to build the tower of Babel, they separated, according to the tradition of the Targum, into seventy languages.[11]

When the Hebrew bible was translated into Greek—which represents the most fantastic missionary effort between the third and second centuries before the Christian era—tradition says that seventy elders were gathered together. They translated separately, each one on his own in his little room. When their finished translations were compared—then, O marvel! tradition relates—their translations were identical, word for word.[12]

Finally, when Jesus launched the Galilean mission, a type or prophecy of the universal mission to come, he sent seventy disciples to proclaim the Good News of the Kingdom.

In these biblical comparisons there is a formidable lesson that grasps our hearts.

Each people must have its translator, that is, one who transmits and explains the Word of God.

You will say to me: The Bible is already translated into the principal languages of the world. Agreed. However, it is not about a translation printed on paper that I am speaking but about a translation expressed in our lives!

Are you a translator of the Word of God for your brothers and sisters? As a husband, are you a translator of the Word for your wife? As a wife, are you a translator of the Word for your husband? Transforming the question into a prayer: Lord, give us the grace of Pentecost. Make us faithful translators of your Word! Now, the primary quality of a translation is its faithfulness to the text. The primary quality of our life is its faithfulness to the Gospel.

The gospel is the book for Christians. But the life of Christians is the book for pagans. Lord, make the book of our life, through your Holy Spirit, shine brightly with your splendor!

Each people must have its missionary, that is, an envoy who announces Jesus Christ. What can we do, what are we doing to realize that requirement of the gospel? On this Pentecost, on this feast of the Church, let us state the question plainly: Here is a nation—China—that has a billion people. Do I, at least from time to time, pray that the light of the Gospel may rise upon those who do not even know that there is a dawn for which to hope? Do I carry, like a wound in my heart, this pain: the body of Christ is mutilated as long as it lacks even one who is called? Let me state the question even more plainly, transforming it into a prayer: Lord, give us the grace of

Pentecost. Help us to carry, at least to our brothers and sisters who live next to us, your Gospel of peace and joy!

The call of the Lord resounds. Forever it has disturbed my tranquility:

> Whom shall I send?
> Who will be my messenger? Is 6, 8

Let us all answer according to our capabilities, as the Spirit inspires us.

Let us call to mind the evangelical rule: The conversion of pagans begins with the conversion of the missionary. Perhaps there are regions in our hearts that have not yet been fully evangelized...Before leaving for China to convert the Chinese, let us all leave for home and convert our own hearts!

A Church That Sings of the Marvels of God in All Languages

Finally, this Church, formed from all the nations under heaven, gathers together to sing in all languages "the marvels of God."[14]

Often in our days, nations gather together and television is filled with pictures of official handshakes and telegenic smiles. Nations gather together to sing the solidity of their economy, or the stability of their money, or the strength of their armies or even simply to celebrate themselves. We regard all these assemblies with sympathy; we pray for their success. But we know well that they often fail in sadness. Truly, when the nations will gather together to sing "the marvels of God," then they will form an eternal community, cemented in the joy of the Holy Spirit, and their song will resound to Paradise.

On the other hand, it sometimes happens that certain churches do not sing the marvels of God. In that case, they waste away; they become weak and wither as surely as a flower that lacks water. Scripture affirms that "sadness dries up the bones."[15] It also dries up churches and their celebrations. Some communities even think that the more sad and boring their celebration is, the more pious it is. But the Spirit of Jesus is a Spirit of joy and song. Jesus did not say: "Do something boring in memory of me." He said: "Do this in memory of me." And he added, "Let your joy be complete!"[16]

May the day come when we will be able to say: Nations of all languages, come to us, come to sing with us the God of marvels, for in our celebrations there is never any boredom! May the day come when we will be able to say: Peoples of the earth, come dance with us in the joy of the Lord, for in our churches no one is a wallflower; everyone is invited to dance! May the day come when we will be able to say: Friends, you who thirst for love, you who hunger for joy, come eat with us the bread of heaven, the bread of God's tenderness; come drink with us the wine of the joy of the Spirit. And all of you who have a sullen spirit, even you others who have an "evil spirit," as we say, and who are very sad about it, come sing with us in all your languages the marvels of God. For we Christians have a "good spirit," a spirit of joy and praise: truly, we have the Spirit of Jesus!

CONCLUDING PRAYER

Let us now pray to God our Father:
May he send upon the Church and upon each of us
the Spirit of his Son Jesus.

Come to us, O Spirit of the Lord!

On the day of Pentecost,
all were gathered together
with Mary, the mother of Jesus.
Again today, renew your marvels, Lord!
Gather your children, with Mary your mother,
in the unity of a single family
and give us your Spirit.

Come to us, O Spirit of the Lord!

Suddenly a sound rose up like a marvelous wind
that came down from heaven and filled the house.
Again today, renew your marvels, Lord!
Awaken your Church from our lethargy and our fears,
blow upon us the wind of renewal,
and give us your Spirit.

Come to us, O Spirit of the Lord!

All were filled with the Holy Spirit
and each one expressed himself
according to the gift of the Spirit.
Again today, renew your marvels, Lord!
May we all be able to express ourselves in the Church
according to the richness of our language,
and give us your Spirit.

Come to us, O Spirit of the Lord!

Pentecost

There were in Jerusalem believers
from all the nations under heaven.
Again today, renew your marvels, Lord!
Let us all know that we are loved in the Church
for the diversity of the charismata that we bring,
and give us your Spirit.

Come to us, O Spirit of the Lord!

All proclaimed in their tongues
the praises of God.
Again today, renew your marvels, Lord!
May your Church celebrate your praises in a thousand voices
in all the languages of the earth,
and give us your Spirit.

Come to us, O Spirit of the Lord!

Let us pray again for all our personal intentions.

Your Spirit, Lord, renews the face of the earth.
May it also renew the depths of our hearts.
May it transform our old and sometimes boring community
into a young community of joy and praise.
May we all feel valued
for the particular work that we do,
for the unique melody that we sing,
for the personal love with which we love you
in your Son Jesus,
forever and ever. Amen.

NOTES TO PENTECOST SUNDAY

1. Dt 26, 11.
2. See R. Ie Déaut, art. "Pentecôte et la tradition juive" in *Assemblées du Seigneur*, 51 (1963), pp. 22-38.
3. Cf. Ex 19, 16 and 19.
4. C. Ex 20, 18.
5. *Targum d Exode* 19, 2, 8. See R. Ie Déaut, Targum du Pentateuque, 11, SC 256 (1979), pp. 154-155.
6. Dt 16, 11 and Num 28, 26.
7. We know, however, that Luke's geographic knowledge sometimes proves to be a little limited. See L. Deiss, *Synopse* (Paris: Desclée de Brouwer), 1975.
8. Acts 2, 11.
9. See Rengstorf, art. "hepta" in TWNT, vol. 11, p. 631.
10. Gn 10.
11. See R. Ie Déaut, *Targum du Pentateuque*, SC 89 (1978), p. 145.
12. The oldest witness to this legend is found in the *Lettre d' Aristée à Philocrate*. See A. Pelletier, SC 89 (1962), which dates the writing at the beginning of the second century B.C. On the development of the legend, see pp. 78-79. Tradition wavers sometimes between seventy-two translators (six from each tribe) or seventy. The same hesitation is found in Lk 10, 1 (seventy or seventy-two disciples).
13. Cf. Lk 10, 1.
14. Acts 2, 11.
15. Prov 17, 22.
16. Jn 16, 24.

About the Author

Lucien Deiss, C. S. Sp., is a French missionary priest of the Congregation of the Holy Ghost. He was professor of Sacred Scripture at the Seminary of Brazzaville in Africa and taught Sacred Scripture and Dogmatic Theology at the Grand Scholasticate in Chevilly-Larue, Paris.

As an influential member of the Vatican II consilium on the Liturgy, he worked for liturgical reforms. He also assisted in the translation of the International Ecumenical Bible (TOB).

In his desire to create a more biblical church, Father Deiss conducts scriptural and liturgical workshops on every continent. A man of great wit, charm and profound spirituality, he combines his scriptural knowledge and musical talent to help people encounter Christ today.

As an international authority on the exegesis of the New Testament and the Fathers of the Church, Father Deiss has written many books on liturgical, biblical and patristic subjects.

acknowledgments

Alan Hommerding, editor and series director

Laura Adamczyk and Diane Karampas, translators

Patricia Adamik, cover artist

Sr. Cecilia (nuns of New Skete), cover art

Selections from *God's Word Is Our Joy* are available on cassette recording. Please contact World Library Publications' Customer Service department, toll-free: 800 566-6150.